BEYOND $15

BEYOND $15

IMMIGRANT WORKERS, FAITH ACTIVISTS, AND THE REVIVAL OF THE LABOR MOVEMENT

Jonathan Rosenblum

Beacon Press
Boston

Beacon Press
Boston, Massachusetts
www.beacon.org

Beacon Press books
are published under the auspices of
the Unitarian Universalist Association of Congregations.

20 19 18 17   8 7 6 5 4 3 2 1

This book is printed on acid-free paper that meets the uncoated paper
ANSI/NISO specifications for permanence as revised in 1992.

Text design and composition by Kim Arney

Library of Congress CIP data is available for this title.

ISBN 9780807098127 (pbk. : alk. paper) | ISBN 9780807098097 (e-book)

In writing about the present and future of our labor movement, I have drawn heavily from my elders in struggle, whose experience and wisdom have guided me over the years: Tyree Scott, the Reverend James Orange, Will Parry, Irene Hull, and Lonnie Nelson.

CONTENTS

LESSONS IN POWER

A FLEETING INCIDENT MORE THAN three decades ago taught me a harsh lesson about power. The immediate issue at hand was relatively inconsequential, but the lesson stayed with me, pointing me in a life direction that ultimately led to this book.

It was 1984. I was working as a newspaper reporter at the *Ithaca Journal*, an upstate New York daily newspaper owned by the Gannett Company, at the time the largest print media corporation in the country. The thirty of us who belonged to the local branch of the International Typographical Union were overmatched in every possible way. We had an "open shop," meaning union membership was voluntary. We staged a bake sale fund-raiser in downtown Ithaca to cover legal bills. Progress in contract negotiations was glacial. The company attorney would jet in from headquarters to swat away our proposals. Bluntly, he explained, "We're not about to let the inmates run the asylum."

One morning on deadline the copy editor handed me his edits to a story I had written. I objected to the changes, and asked that my byline be removed. He was responsible for approving the copy, but under our union contract, it was my sole prerogative as to whether my name appeared with the story. Indeed, the right to remove our byline was one of the few absolute rights we enjoyed as reporters.

Suddenly, I found myself in the managing editor's office, accompanied by our shop steward. "What do you think you're doing?" asked the editor, his voice rising in anger.

"I didn't agree with the edits," I replied. "So I asked that my byline be removed. I have that right under our union contract." I waved the labor-management agreement at him. A large man, the editor stood up, his face red.

"I don't give a fuck what's in that contract," he yelled, leaning over me, his index finger jabbing in my face. "You do that again, and you're out of here. Got it?"

The contract was a legal document, representing the rules we all agreed to be bound by. Weren't we a nation governed by laws? But it was quite apparent that we weren't in the editor's office having a pleasant chitchat about theories of civil society or the finer points of contract law; my steward and I were being administered a ruthless reminder about how power operated in the real world.

I left the editor's office shaken, newly appreciating that the rights of working people, from trivial to historic, whether in legal workplace contracts or national laws, are only meaningful to the extent we're capable of defending them. Failing that, they're just empty words on paper.

A few months after the editor's smackdown, I quit the *Journal*, stuffed my life's possessions in the back of a rusty pickup, and headed out to be a full-time union organizer—first briefly in Louisiana, then in New England for five years, then as an organizer for the Service Employees International Union (SEIU) traveling around the country, before finally settling in Seattle in 1991.

Once in Seattle, I led the formation of a local Jobs With Justice coalition, staging rallies to support workers organizing and to protect jobs and social benefits. Many Jobs With Justice actions involved civil disobedience. Seniors threatened by Medicare cuts occupied the local Republican political headquarters, and workers took over a corporate banquet held to celebrate the passage of the job-killing North American Free Trade Agreement (NAFTA). After Alaska Airlines fired flight attendants for striking, we led massive street protests, blockaded the company's headquarters, and handbilled passengers at thirty thousand feet. The workers won their jobs back and a new union contract.

Hundreds of community allies blocked patrons from attending a struck theater, forcing management back to the bargaining table, where they reached a settlement with the theater's musicians. When I wasn't planning or mobilizing for the next disruption, I spent a fair amount of time at police headquarters and local jails—sometimes extracting a colleague who had been arrested, more often in handcuffs myself. We were exercising collective power with the tools we had available—and we were winning.

When the World Trade Organization ministers descended on Seattle in late 1999, I was working for the AFL-CIO, directing a multiunion regional organizing project. It was remarkable to witness thousands of union members unite in the streets with even greater numbers of environmental and civic activists, roiling the proceedings inside the WTO meeting. And after the police filled the streets with tear gas and the mayor banned further demonstrations downtown, it was yet more inspiring to witness the new protest alliance defy the mayor, march downtown, and stage an occupation outside the county jail to win the release of more than six hundred arrested protesters. For me the WTO protests represented a grand display of the principle that had first crystallized in my mind after that trivial byline battle at the *Ithaca Journal*—the balance of power is always in play.

Yet even amid these inspiring struggles, the inescapable reality during the decades before and after the turn of the century was that we were, as a union movement, sliding toward the abyss. A Democratic president, Bill Clinton, had forced NAFTA on us, sending jobs overseas, and then had proceeded to slash the already meager social safety net. His Republican successor, George W. Bush, went after public employees relentlessly, attacked pensions, and encouraged companies to offshore jobs. Private employers successfully broke strikes, cut wages, wiped out retirement benefits in every imaginable industry—packinghouses, auto plants, mining, steel mills, trucking, aerospace, and on and on.

When as a young newsroom worker I signed my first union card in the early 1980s, I was joining a labor movement that counted one in every five workers as members—stumbling badly, but at least alive. Just twenty-five years later—a sliver of time in history's arc—when Barack Obama took the presidential oath in 2009, union membership had slid to one in every eight workers. And my newspaper union? Completely gone, along with many others—wiped out by corporate executives who did to entire workforces, communities, and industries what the *Journal*'s editor had done to me and my shop steward many years prior.

IT WAS EASY, of course, to castigate corporate America for this miserable state of affairs. But as I traveled from one campaign to another, becoming acquainted with union members and their leaders in cities around the country, I came to see that corporate America was only half of our problem. The other half was the union movement itself.

In my early years of organizing, my union peers and I would read accounts of how the auto worker sit-down strikes of the 1930s forced the Roosevelt administration to back union rights, or we'd pick up books about militant industrial unions like the United Electrical workers, once three-quarters of a million strong and now reduced to relative insignificance, or we'd talk to an old-timer—likely a communist or socialist of some stripe—about the massive wave of member-led strikes that followed World War II. What was most remarkable about these educational moments was not the savagery of industrialists, or the ruthless efficiency of McCarthy purges, or the cold indifference of political elites who cast aside their proworker pledges as soon as the election was over, but the degree to which unions—and especially the leaders of unions—facilitated their own destruction.

We learned that with the government-enforced industrial peace of World War II, union membership had soared, reaching nearly a third of all workers by the end of the war. In the core of the nation's economy, the manufacturing sector, fully 69 percent of production workers were covered by union agreements in 1946.[1]

But rather than build on that nascent power, most union leaders determined to make peace with political and business elites, believing—incorrectly—that the tripartite domestic détente of World War II was still alive. Even before Senator Joe McCarthy's witch hunts, unions started purging communists and other suspected radicals from their ranks, seeking to demonstrate their loyalty to government and business.[2] The labor federation that emerged in the 1950s, the AFL-CIO, steered away from organizing more workers. Federation president

George Meany famously declared, "I used to worry about the size of the membership. I stopped worrying because to me it doesn't make any difference. The organized fellow is the only fellow that counts."[3] Most union leaders focused on securing economic gains for their members, pledging allegiance to the capitalist economic system in exchange for collective bargaining agreements.

Meany also championed the "business union" model. In place of elected shop-floor union stewards, professional union staff represented members in grievances and at bargaining tables, often without even the presence of the members themselves. Spirited and vigorous membership debates were replaced with staged routines of controlled democracy. Members paid their dues and came to expect to get their money's worth from union staff. Instead of workers seeing themselves as the union, the union came to be viewed as a service. Union stewards were trained to become amateur lawyers who parsed the intricate wording of union contracts rather than organizers who united workers in collective action. For workers not covered by collective bargaining agreements, unions looked increasingly like self-interested organizations, focused on economic gains for an increasingly narrow band of the working class.

By the 1980s business unionism was hardwired into the operating systems of most unions. I'd wince whenever I heard union members complain about the poor service they were receiving from union staff, who didn't return their calls on time or handle their grievances the way they had come to expect. They had become accustomed to seeing the union as a third-party between themselves and their boss, not the collective strength of the workers.

I was quite fortunate to have spent most of my organizing time working with union members and leaders who had higher expectations for their union. The direct-action fights at Jobs With Justice and the WTO protests demonstrated that when workers and allies unite to fight injustice, they can win. After the WTO, I spent most of the following decade working for SEIU's Washington State health-care branch—hospital and clinic workers who carried a rich tradition of exercising their collective power for improved work standards and quality patient care. It was a union steeped in struggle, and it was growing.

But that was not true for the majority of labor. You only had to look at the first years of the Obama administration to recognize how the ossified state of the union movement translated into labor's utter inability to counter the power plays of big business. Wall Street crashed the economy, but while millions of workers lost their jobs and homes, the bankers got bailed out. Labor law reform, the central 2008 union electoral demand, sputtered in Congress and then died, a victim of White House ambivalence and our own inability to create a mass movement demanding legislative action. Health-care reform passed, but instead of purging the profiteers, the new law handed us a Rube Goldberg benefit system that only tightened the chokehold of for-profit companies on our health. Beginning in 2011, Wisconsin governor Scott Walker effectively banned public-worker collective bargaining in the Badger State, survived a recall election, and went on to pass a "right to work" open shop law, emboldening other state legislatures to follow suit. The exponential growth of companies like Uber and the accelerated pace of contracting out and temp work—encouraged and facilitated by Wall Street and elites from both major political parties—created a growing class of tens of millions of precarious workers beyond the legal reach of even the meager protections of existing labor law.

Amid this deepening crisis, in 2011 the leadership of my national union, SEIU, had an organizational epiphany. To stop the slide into irrelevancy, they swung the union's resources into a massive grassroots campaign in 17 cities around the country, deploying 1,500 organizers to reclaim the high ground in the economic debate and to organize workers into unions on a massive scale. In Washington State this path-breaking effort led us to the city of SeaTac, the suburban Seattle community encompassing the region's international airport, where thousands of workers toiled in poverty. I was asked by my union to lead the Sea-Tac Airport campaign.

What evolved in the SeaTac community over the following three years was a bold experiment to build a new kind of union. It was an effort that went far beyond the headlines of $15 minimum wages to challenge corporate power and the assumptions underlying our economy. I was fortunate to have been immersed in this dynamic milieu, to have played a role in its design, and to have witnessed its astonishing peaks and agonizing valleys. After I left SEIU in the summer of 2014, I went back to the workers, community activists, clergy, and organizers whom I had worked closely with, piecing together their observations and conclusions in more than fifty interviews. The insights of these grassroots activists—thoughtful and unpretentious, the sort of reflections that often get overlooked by writers of history—form a backbone of the narrative that follows.

Yet this is more than a story about a group of workers and their lived experiences in a small suburb outside Seattle. It is, ultimately, an examination of power in our society today—how it got so imbalanced, the devastation this imbalance has wreaked, and what working people can and must do to reclaim power and voice in our society.

ONE

AN INTRODUCTION TO POWER INEQUALITY

ABDINASIR MOHAMED TOLD me he'd expected to encounter poverty in America, but what he saw upon landing in New York City in 2008 seemed unreal.

A refugee from war-torn Somalia, Mohamed knew destitution firsthand, and he certainly was aware that America was not all the bling-bling of Hollywood movies. But just two days after arriving in his new country, walking down a sidewalk in Harlem, Mohamed came upon a homeless person—"a white woman with blue eyes just begging there in the street asking, 'Can you spare me a dime?'"

"I was like, 'Are you serious? I just came from Africa. Now I can see people who are begging in one of the biggest cities in the world.'"

We were sitting in my dining room as he recounted his abrupt introduction to poverty in America. Seven years had passed. Mohamed had moved west, to Seattle, and then in 2013 joined the Sea-Tac Airport workers organizing campaign—the first $15/hour wage ballot initiative in the country, a pitched political battle between labor and big business that inspired similar $15 fights around the country.

Mohamed told me he'd given the woman five dollars, and she had told him her story. She had owned a house in the Bronx and held steady employment. But she'd fallen ill and lost her job. Her benefits

1

ran out. The bank foreclosed on her. So here she was on the street, pleading for spare change from other poor people while a few miles to the south the captains of Wall Street tallied their millions.

Beyond the woman's abject poverty, what struck Mohamed was the precariousness of life in this new land. In Africa, at least it was warm. You could build a makeshift house on empty land and count on others to help you out. But here in the iconic American city? You were basically one slender paycheck away from being out on your own on the cold streets. Listening to the woman, Mohamed said he sensed the utter loneliness and destitution of poverty in this new country. As a new immigrant, he was beginning to grasp that for all the hope and opportunity the new land offered, there also was something very sick about America.

And Mohamed, like so many of us who have encountered stark injustice head-on, began to wonder why this was so.

After moving to Seattle, Mohamed got swept up in the 2011 Occupy movement and found himself drawn to an embryonic union-led campaign to improve poverty-wage jobs at the city's airport. Many of the jobs at Sea-Tac Airport were held by fellow Africans—his friends and neighbors. Fluent in multiple African languages, Mohamed was recruited to become a full-time community organizer for the union, tasked with bridging the cultural divide between unions and new immigrant communities.

I was director of the Sea-Tac Airport campaign for the Service Employees International Union (SEIU) and was brought on board at the same time as Mohamed, charged with leading the ambitious effort to organize and win good working conditions for thousands of baggage and cargo handlers, aircraft fuelers, cabin cleaners, passenger service workers, rental car and parking lot assistants, shuttle drivers, hotel and restaurant workers, and others who occupied the bottom rung of the airport economy. The positions were held largely by new immigrants who had flocked to the Pacific Northwest from all corners of the earth, escaping economic privation, wars, famine, and political repression.

From day one it was clear to me that the campaign would require taking on the most powerful corporations in the region: Alaska Airlines, which dominated the airport; the Marriott and other national hotel chains; global airline contracting firms; and the airport concessions companies, all of whom profited richly from the airport's poverty-wage employment scheme. We would have to inspire and mobilize a diverse range of workers from Somalia, Ethiopia, Eritrea, Ukraine, Russia, Mexico, the Philippines, Iran, Iraq, and India whose shared culture was the constant scramble to pay $1,500 monthly apartment rents on minimum-wage paychecks. Mohamed became a close associate of mine as we worked together, along with many others, on this enormous challenge.

As we labored together through the course of the campaign, confronting the stark contrasts of crushing worker poverty and record corporate profits, of clarion spiritual calls for moral justice and a tone-deaf political elite, we came to see that it was not enough simply to point out what was wrong with Sea-Tac, or with America. The facts of poverty at Sea-Tac Airport, just like on the Harlem street, were plain enough. Simply revealing them would not persuade workers and their supporters to join a seemingly quixotic battle against the most powerful businesses in the region. We had to uncover the root causes of economic misery, because only by exposing the causes could we begin to articulate a clear path forward.

In that dining room conversation, Mohamed described to me his 2008 Harlem experience and the question *why* that had lingered with him as he moved across country. That experience and question gained renewed focus in his mind as he immersed himself in the challenge of Sea-Tac, where he saw the injustice of the Harlem sidewalk scene replicated on an industrial scale—workers kicked to the curb by airport executives whose power and profits had soared to dazzling heights.

AS SEA-TAC AIRPORT workers were gathering up their courage to take on corporate power in 2012, another group of workers three thousand miles away decided to make a bold stand. In the week after Thanksgiving 2012, with the holiday season ramping up to full frenzy, two hundred fast-food workers in midtown Manhattan took to the streets one lunch hour for a one-day walkout to demand a $15/hour minimum wage and union recognition. The news coverage, ensured by the prime location of these protests in the world's media capital, transformed the abstract problem of income inequality into the anguished faces and poignant stories of individual workers who had had enough.[1]

As with Sea-Tac, the New York fast-food worker organizing had sprung from SEIU's Fight for a Fair Economy campaign, an ambitious effort to organize low-wage workers in cities around the country behind a demand for populist economic change. The New York protest was the union's first foray into the enormous challenge of uniting fast-food workers against what from all appearances was an invincible industry. Taking on McDonald's, Burger King, KFC, and other international chains seemed brazen, perhaps foolhardy. For Sea-Tac workers—and doubtless for other low-wage workers around the country—the bold call for $15 and union recognition pressed beyond the limits of their imaginations. Union organizers were used to talking about more incremental gains. For $7.25/hour minimum-wage workers, 50-cent raises would be something to celebrate. Fifteen dollars seemed an absurd demand—until the New York workers issued it.

Pamela Waldron was one of those workers who symbolized what was terribly wrong with the economy, a poised spokeswoman for the budding movement. After eight years of ringing up customers at the KFC in New York City's Penn Station, Waldron, paid $7.75/hour, just 50 cents above the federal minimum wage, knew she deserved better. "I'm protesting for better pay," Waldron told the *New York Times.* "I have two kids under six, and I don't earn enough to buy food for them."

She practically ran the store, given her seniority. But, Waldron told CNN, when she asked her manager for a raise, she was told that $7.75/hour was all she could expect—this from a company that cleared $1.6 billion in annual profits. So at lunchtime on November 28, 2012, as customers crowded into her KFC outlet, Pamela Waldron walked out, leaving behind the hot grease and buckets of fried chicken for a crowd of chanting and picketing fast-food workers and union organizers.[2]

While Waldron and her fellow protesters were a minuscule fraction of the fast-food workforce in a city of eight million people, the sight of raucous demonstrations under the smiling logo of Colonel Sanders and the universally familiar golden arches sparked workers' imaginations everywhere. We think of fast-food employees as the most disposable workers in our economy, part time, minimally trained, and easily replaced. The scene of dozens of them walking off their jobs was a powerful statement about their courage and over-flowing frustration. Within months workers and their community allies were staging similar demonstrations in dozens of cities around the country, framed around a fight for $15.[3] In Sea-Tac, workers, for the first time, also began talking about the number 15.

The wage fights owed their genesis to the Occupy movement, which had burst onto the scene the year before, in 2011, energizing a campaign built on a blistering critique of capitalism and the cry of "We are the 99 percent!" By the time New York fast-food workers started walking out, Occupy had peaked and ebbed, the makeshift tents in city parks disassembled, its protesters dispersed to various causes. Unions were eager to snap up many of these activists, and also to channel Occupy's energy into campaigns with goals that were more concrete than doing away with the capitalist system. The fast-food initiative was an obvious next step, as were the growing fights to or-ganize Walmart workers and low-wage airport workers. Soon Black Friday protests at big box stores and worker marches through airport terminals joined fast-food workers on the evening news.

Beyond the facts of low wages, what the faces in these protests revealed to the public was that the nature of work in America was changing. No longer were these minimum-wage jobs temporary step-ping stones for teenagers entering the workforce, ritual way-stations of mistreatment that one passed through on the way to adulthood and stable, satisfying lifelong professions. In particular, fast-food and low-wage retail businesses had become the places where an increas-ing number of parents with children, middle-aged workers, and even senior citizens struggled to eke out a living. And while millions en-dured lousy pay, irregular work hours, and no job security, the CEOs and major shareholders at the big box and fast-food companies were getting astronomically wealthy. By 2010 the Walton family, heirs to the Walmart fortune, had amassed $89.5 billion in personal wealth. Six Waltons held as much wealth as the bottom forty-nine million American families.[4] And that was apparently not enough money. Just four years later, as Walmart workers struggled to buy food, avoid the wrath of the landlord and the payday lender, and endure pov-erty's crushing emotional vise, the net worth of the six Waltons had shot up to $164 billion, a 72 percent growth in wealth in just forty-eight months.[5]

The personal stories of workers moved public opinion even more effectively than the shocking data about skewed income: The Dunkin' Donuts worker who held down three jobs and barely saw her toddler; the seventy-nine-year-old McDonald's janitor and table cleaner who was suspended after he started organizing his coworkers; the middle-aged veteran who lost his good union job in the economic downturn and was forced to drive a Jimmy John's delivery truck for a few cents above minimum wage.[6]

These personal gifts from fast-food and retail workers—putting a face on income inequality—helped to shift the national conversation about the economy. One year after the New York City fast-food workers first took to the streets, President Obama declared that income inequality was "the defining challenge of our time."[7] Pundits noted with alarm that at the largest US corporations, CEO pay had reached 354 times the average worker wage, an eight-fold increase over thirty years.[8] Political consensus solidified around the notion that something had to be done about the problem of income inequality.[9]

For progressive activists like me, this broad public support for raises represented welcome terrain. As campaigns gained steam and we tallied individual wage victories in states and cities, workers and activists grew energized. City councils debated not whether but how much to increase local wages. Companies like McDonald's and Walmart announced pay improvements. Workers were getting raises. Corporations were on the defensive. Change was happening. The *New York Times* reported that a push by congressional Democrats to raise the national minimum wage to $12/hour and index it to inflation "comes at a time of increasing momentum around the country behind changes to the minimum wage." Even historically conservative states like Arkansas and South Dakota, the *Times* pointed out, had raised their wage minimums by referendum.[10] SEIU's Fight for a Fair Economy was changing the political discourse in the nation and winning raises for the lowest-paid workers.

And yet it was all a limiting discourse. Although unions and allied organizations did yeoman work to shine a light on the contrast between the 1 percent and the rest of us, what developed in the streets and TV studios was not, by and large, the sharp critique of capitalism that kindled and drove the Occupy movement, but rather a policy campaign to make America a little less unequal.

By focusing the conversation on wages, the mainstream discussion short-circuited a more fundamental exploration of the forces that produced this level of inequality in the first place. The discussion failed to ask why a newly arrived African refugee could walk down the streets of New York and encounter a woman who had worked hard and lived the American Dream but whose life had fallen into terrifying free fall. The country was talking about the symptoms rather than the disease.

Dig beyond the personal stories of economic travail, beyond the reams and charts of earnings data—beyond the manifestations of income inequality—and you will come face-to-face with the problem of power inequality in our capitalist society. Income distribution is not something that occurs beyond human control, like the orbiting of the planets. "The market" that is talked about so casually on Sunday talk shows and National Public Radio is not some abstract force beyond our reach. It is a particular set of people making and enforcing decisions, acting in their self-interest to accumulate wealth and maintain control. The distribution of income flows from the decisions and actions of those who control the political, economic, and cultural levers of power. These decisions by the powerful ripple out through society, touching every one of us. In economics, nothing just happens on its own. There is always an agent.

For all the lofty rhetoric of fighting for fair pay, the protest demands that flourished in cities around the country beginning in late 2012 were paltry in comparison to the depth of injustice. If President Obama's 2013 minimum wage proposal of $10.10/hour had been adopted across the nation, the Economic Policy Institute estimates, thirty million workers would have received annual raises averaging $1,700/year—a total redistribution of $51 billion to the lowest wage earners in our society.[11] This is an impressive number, until one considers that in just the twenty-four months between 2009 and 2011, the richest 7 percent in the United States saw average wealth gains of $700,000, to reach a net individual worth averaging $3.2 million. In aggregate the gap in wealth between the richest 7 percent of households and the rest of us grew by $6.6 trillion.[12] The president's wage solution, in other words, would have rolled back less than 1 percent of the expansion in wealth imbalance that took place in the twenty-four months following the official end of the Great Recession.[13] Even a $15/hour national minimum wage, lofty as it sounds, would offset just a tiny fraction of the recent growth in wealth disparity.[14] The six Waltons could cut all of their Walmart workers checks to bring them to $15/hour immediately and still live happily ever after on their remaining $150 billion.[15]

Whether introduced by political leaders or street protesters, the solutions being put forward are insufficient because our problem is much bigger than the distribution of income in society. As welcome as the fight against income inequality is, as much as it engages and inspires more people to take civic action, it's an inadequate vision for those invested in building a just society. It treats the fever with aspirin—temporarily knocking down the illness—without going after the underlying disease. It's a fight that fails to ask the simple but vital question of why we have such inequity in our society. By avoiding that question, we won't get to the root causes of our economic ills. We won't understand the problem of power inequality and what we must do about it.

WHAT EXACTLY DO I mean by power inequality? In its most basic essence, power is the ability to do or act, to shape and influence things. We all have some power inherently, though the amount of power we each have is influenced substantially by factors such as class, wealth, race, gender, immigration status, and family. People may have power as individuals, or may need to band together with others to be able to exercise power.

Power manifests itself in modern society in the overlapping arenas of economics, politics, and culture. Economic power resides with those who control the means of production and distribution of goods and services. Political power concerns a society's authority, institutions, and coercive forces—government, laws, police, and armies. Cultural power is about controlling the beliefs and expectations propagated and reinforced by society's media, religious, educational, and civic institutions. Frances Fox Piven and Richard A. Cloward, writing more than forty years ago, noted how these various forms of power are mutually reinforcing: "Since coercive force can be used to gain control of the means of producing wealth, and since control of wealth can be used to gain coercive force, these two sources of power tend over time to be drawn together within one ruling class."[16]

The balance of power between this ruling class—big business and finance elites—and the rest of us is not static. It's continually shifting in the tug and pull of society's opposing forces. The growing divide in the United States is no accident or misfortune. Rather, the leaders of big business and finance have imposed their designs on the rest of us through their disproportionate economic, political, and cultural power.

It's not a new phenomenon, of course. You can go back from colonial history through the Industrial Revolution to contemporary times to examine how power historically has been employed as an instrument to concentrate wealth and opportunity in the hands of the few. Slavery was its most brutal manifestation. When outright owning another person became politically untenable, those with power devised more elegant mechanisms to maintain control: sharecropping in the South, the company towns in coal-rich Appalachia, the indentured Chinese labor system that built the western railroads. Today, it's the debt peonage system for truck drivers and for-hire vehicle operators; the permanent precarious status of freelancers, permatemps, and independent contractors in the "gig" economy; and the second-class status of undocumented immigrant workers in agriculture, day labor, and domestic work. These systems of exploitation all require power to impose and maintain.

There's no shortage of pundits and elites—not just probusiness voices, but also many union leaders, liberal academics, and social change advocates—who conclude that because inequality is inevitable in modern-day capitalist society, political and social justice activists should content themselves with promoting policies that merely cushion the blow for workers and communities. Do not challenge too sharply the underlying power imbalance, they suggest; let's just take some of the hard edges off capitalism. Corporations and the media relentlessly hammer us with the argument that there is no alternative to capitalism, especially after the demise of the Soviet Union. The immense, far-reaching power of global capital drains hope, prompting even passionate activists to restrict their vision to marginal change. So they focus on the symptoms and stop asking why those symptoms exist in the first place.

Campaigns that take on disparities of income, health, housing, education, or persistent institutional racism are vital starting points for challenging injustice. But to fully cure the symptoms you have to go to the source, to trace how power gets concentrated in the hands of those motivated by personal profit, not human need. Only then can you figure out what must be done to reverse it.

THIS BOOK EXAMINES power inequality and describes how working people can organize to resist it and take steps toward building a just society. I've chosen to focus the exploration on one sector of the US economy—commercial air transportation—and on one airport community within that sector: The city of SeaTac, located fifteen miles south of Seattle, Washington, home to the burgeoning Seattle-Tacoma International Airport, or Sea-Tac. I know both intimately; my lens is local but the lessons are universal.

Beginning in 2011, poverty-wage Sea-Tac Airport workers, backed by several key unions and community groups, led an audacious campaign targeting the airport's major economic and political powers. In doing so they challenged the basic assumptions of twenty-first-century life. The organizing campaign peaked in 2013 with the first $15 minimum-wage initiative in the country. But the campaign was about a lot more than just fair wages. It was, at its core, a struggle against the maldistribution of power in society. As director of the Sea-Tac campaign, I became thoroughly acquainted with a largely immigrant workforce that, infused with a deep spiritual call for justice, took on major corporations and their political allies, and against all odds, beat them. I saw community members and faith leaders extend the demand for a $15 minimum wage to a broader call for justice, deftly shifting an economic debate into one about the moral foundation of an economy. And I worked within a coalition that exemplified the best and worst of today's movement—union leaders on the one hand, committing huge resources, political capital, and talent to an untested organizing theory, and on the other hand, churning with internal tension that at the most critical moment nearly exploded and brought the entire enterprise crashing down.

This book tells these stories, not just because they or the characters in them are interesting, but because they offer vital lessons about power in contemporary society, the keen perspectives of working people, and the nature and role of unions and allied organizations. Indeed, I believe that the solutions to the problems facing the 99 percent won't be discovered in liberal think tanks, self-appointed innovation centers, or the academy, but rather by engaging with people involved in day-to-day struggle, and by learning from the ingenuity, creativity, and perseverance that they employ as they struggle with the problem of power inequality at the street, workplace, and societal level. For unions in deep trouble, straining to find a way forward in today's reality of runaway corporate profits and mounting human impoverishment, the Sea-Tac experience points the way toward the great possibilities that exist in a reimagined labor movement.

TWO

POWER SHIFT

IN THE 1970s BEN SMITH led a pretty mainstream life for an airport worker. A United Airlines ramp serviceman at Sea-Tac Airport, he worked on the tarmac loading baggage and cargo onto planes. Thanks to the protection of a good Machinists union contract, the job was steady and pay and benefits were decent. He was active in the union. With Smith's paycheck, his wife, Leila, could afford to stay home. The couple raised three boys in a modest house close to the airport, in a neighborhood that would later become part of the new city of SeaTac. The kids went to public school within earshot of the jet airplanes that their dad climbed in and out of.

On the strength of Smith's blue-collar pay and benefits, their son Adam was able to attend college and then law school, where he caught the political bug. In 1990, while still enrolled at the University of Washington School of Law, Adam ran for the Washington State Senate seat in the district that encompassed the airport, beating a thirteen-year incumbent. At twenty-five he became the youngest state senator in the country. His parents passed away before they could witness his continued ascent: in 1996 at age thirty-one, Adam Smith, the ramp serviceman's son, was elected to the US Congress, a Democrat representing SeaTac and the growing bedroom communities south of Seattle.[1]

In Washington, DC, Adam Smith became known as a quiet, thoughtful, hard-working member, a political moderate who favored working the inside game over the television klieg lights. Members of the labor movement in Seattle viewed him as a mixed bag. On budget matters he was a fiscal hawk, aligning with the Bill Clinton wing of the Democratic Party in the call for cuts to social programming. But on labor issues he didn't forget his working-class roots, frequently reminding his audiences: "Because of the strength of our society, I had opportunity. I had a good public education, access to higher education. My father was a member of a union—so he got decent wages and benefits at his blue collar job. That enabled me to pursue my hopes and dreams, and that's what I want for everyone in society as well."[2]

Smith rose to a senior position on the House Armed Services Committee, and although his district was refashioned to include mostly people of color, Adam Smith, the product of a white working-class family, had no trouble winning reelection every two years.[3]

But as the son of the ramp serviceman gained power and prominence, something very different was happening to the generation of workers who followed in his late father's footsteps. The opportunity that Congressman Smith recognized in his own past and that he spoke about so frequently was slipping away for others. Good Sea-Tac Airport jobs were vanishing as airlines broke unions and contracted out work. The decline in quality jobs at Sea-Tac mirrored what was happening at airports around the country. Jobs that anchored ground services for commercial aviation and used to pay decently—baggage handlers, skycaps, fuelers, wheelchair attendants, aircraft cabin cleaners, security officers—increasingly were becoming minimum-wage, contracted-out positions with no job security. Even mechanics, flight attendants, and pilots were finding that their jobs were becoming more precarious, threatened with contracting out, their pay under constant downward pressure. The Ben Smiths of the airport economy were vanishing. By 2007, within a decade of Adam Smith's election to Congress, Sea-Tac Airport would tally four thousand poverty-wage jobs—employment, much of it part time, which paid minimum wage, offered few if any benefits, and provided no economic security.

Good jobs don't just become bad jobs, as if they were obeying some law of gravity or some natural progression of an inanimate "market." Workers, of course, don't voluntarily give up their paychecks. Good jobs unravel in the push and pull between the competing interests of businesses and workers.

Downgrading good jobs requires conscientious effort by industry executives. But to impose structural changes in employment they first must secure power over industry and government. So while we can look at and criticize the dramatic income shifts of recent years, we have to go deeper to understand and appreciate the signal developments that shifted power in favor of business, and how these developments were the necessary foundation to the vast growth in income inequality that transpired.

Recognizing the causal force behind income inequality matters, because if you develop the wrong diagnosis, then you will come up with an inadequate remedy. A problem that has a power imbalance at its origin won't be fixed by a wage policy solution. You're just dealing with the surface issues, and in time power will undo any policy gain.

Saying that the problem is "income inequality" is akin to looking just at the destruction of a tsunami without recognizing that the wave owes its existence to undersea seismic activity that occurred hundreds or even thousands of miles away from landfall.

As with tsunami formation, economic jolts are episodic, not linear. They happen when a variety of factors—procorporate politics, strength of the economic powers, vulnerability of workers—align to shift power dramatically in favor of business.

To fully appreciate how the US airline industry changed since Ben Smith's heyday, you have to look beyond paychecks and examine the forces that caused the industrial transformation: Waves of corporate takeovers, bankruptcy, consolidation, subcontracting, and union busting have shaken the industry, workers, and communities. The disruptions were strategically executed by corporate executives who saw unnecessary costs and missing profits where others saw good, stable jobs. In order to redistribute wealth in the industry, the redesigners first had to shift power in their favor, and they did so with help from political leaders of both major parties. The first jolt was a set of new laws passed in 1978 that were intended by its authors to disrupt the airline industry and tilt power toward corporations. The second jolt came in how the government and airline businesses used the cover of national crisis in the wake of 9/11 to complete their power grab over airport workers and communities.

Before 1978, when Ben Smith was in his prime years at United Airlines, air travel in the United States was highly regulated. The US government set airline fares, approved routes, and ruled on whether new carriers could enter markets. Competition was limited. For the traveling public, prices were fixed but high; many could not afford to fly. Unable to engage in price wars, airlines competed against one another on amenities and service quality. Airline executives chafed under the strict federal controls, but on balance they appreciated the benefits of a controlled system: the government-established fares virtually guaranteed profits of around 12 percent.[4] There was economic stability for workers because with fixed prices among the airlines there was little incentive for companies to break unions and drive down pay. And there was stability in industrial relations, enforced by transportation labor law that facilitated collective bargaining but made it very difficult for workers to take lawful strike action that could cripple the industry. Airline managements negotiated contracts with unionized employees, knowing that they could petition the government for higher fares based on operational cost increases. The industry was administered essentially as a public utility, with one significant distinction from the utility model: it placed secure profits to executives and shareholders in front of affordable, quality service to the flying public.

Politically this was an unsustainable model, especially as air travel began to expand in the jet age. Ticket prices were too high and the route schedules too inflexible for a world that was moving faster. But rather than fix the problem by putting the public's interest before private corporate profits—the essential mission of a public utility— business and political leaders and economists went in the opposite direction. Beginning in the early 1970s, a broad coalition of probusiness groups began pushing for an end to federal oversight of airline rates and routes. Let the private sector decide based on market demand, they argued. On its face this sounded a lot like the ideology of Milton Friedman and the Chicago school of economists, who articulated their ideal vision of an economy in which business had no governmental restraints and the magic of the marketplace served to regulate the private sector and consumers. There was one major deviation from Friedman ideology, however: the advocates of change wanted the free market for airline competition, but they also wanted the government to continue to subsidize airport construction and operation, pay for rural air service, and protect airlines from creditors and workers who might demand a bigger slice of the pie. They envisioned an industry structure that rewarded business but off-loaded risk onto government and workers.

This idea of government handouts and protections for capitalists was not something that could be lobbied for directly; it needed to be dressed up in more populist robes. Fortunately for the advocates for change, such clothing existed. Consumers were unhappy with the rigid air travel system. Tickets were expensive. Flying often was inconvenient because the routes didn't match up with public need. So corporate and political advocates for change dressed up their disruption scheme in a proconsumer argument: eliminate most government oversight and let the private sector run air passenger service to its liking. You'll get more choices, better service, and lower fares, they said. By the mid-1970s proderegulation forces, leveraging consumer discontent, had gained bipartisan support in Congress. Democratic senator Edward Kennedy, an icon of liberal politics, led hearings on an ambitious package of airline industry changes. When Jimmy Carter entered the White House in 1977, he appointed economist Alfred Kahn to steer the airline deregulation effort, and legislation gained momentum. The existing major airlines themselves were split on the deregulation bill in Congress—some liked the assurance of steady profits under tight regulation, while others pined for greater growth and profit-taking opportunities. An emboldened chamber of commerce lobby, backed by the unusual alliance of economists and consumer advocates, drove the movement for legislative change.

While the deregulation bill was gaining momentum, a second game-changing law took shape in Congress: bankruptcy reform. Prior to 1978 a declaration of bankruptcy was a career death penalty for CEOs and corporate leadership. Upon a company's bankruptcy, a court kicked out its executives and appointed trustees to run the company. The new company leaders could reorganize the company or liquidate it outright. Company executives understandably were loath to head down the bankruptcy path. Bankruptcy took away their control, and it was personally shameful to own the reputation of having led a company into Chapter 11. But the 1978 legislation remade the concept of bankruptcy from a disgrace to be avoided into an opportunity for a new lease on life. Under the new law, Congress allowed management to stay in charge of a bankrupt firm and reorganize the business, shedding old debts and breaking union contracts. Management got a second chance, and when it came to paying off debts, workers had to get in line behind banks and shareholders. Little noticed at the time, the 1978 bankruptcy bill would become a potent business cudgel for bludgeoning workers and remaking the balance of power throughout the economy.

By 1978 the political forces had aligned to bring airline deregulation and the bankruptcy law across the finish line. President Carter had begun his term with a bill to increase tax fairness and a modest effort at labor law reform. Both came under business assault and were rebuffed by an overwhelmingly Democratic, but timid, Congress. Now, facing a chamber of commerce backlash for his reform efforts, Carter tacked away from a liberal agenda to prove his probusiness bona fides. Many Democrats in Congress, elected in swing districts during the post-Watergate wave in 1974 and 1976, also felt vulnerable to attack. Passing probusiness laws in 1978, they reasoned, would help them defend their incumbency. Congress overwhelmingly approved the Airline Deregulation Act (ADA) and the Bankruptcy Act as the election season got under way. Carter inked the new airline law in late October and put his signature to the bankruptcy legislation on the eve of the November midterm elections. But his strategy failed. The Democrats still lost eighteen seats in Congress in a year that saw the ascendance of new Republican faces like Newt Gingrich and Dick Cheney.

The new laws triggered massive changes in the airline industry. The ADA phased out federal fare setting, loosened restrictions on routes, opened up the industry to new entrants, and allowed international carriers to offer domestic routes. New airlines entered the market and intense price competition ensued. In the first years of the ADA's implementation, consumers gained more choices of airlines and on many routes they saw lower prices. But with the stronger competition came disruption. Airlines went bankrupt. Many were restructured or merged; some were outright liquidated. Executives bailed, bemoaning the failures while firmly grasping the cords of their golden parachutes. With each bankruptcy or threatened bankruptcy, workers were called on to sacrifice—through wage cuts, benefit elimination, more arduous work rules, contracting out.

The iconic Trans World Airlines (TWA) struggled under deregulation and was taken over in 1985 by corporate raider Carl Icahn. He sold off the company's most profitable assets and drove it into bankruptcy, forcing massive employee concessions. Icahn left, taking with him $190 million.[5] In 1983 Frank Lorenzo ushered Continental Airlines into bankruptcy, voiding the company's union contracts with the blessing of a bankruptcy court. He fired one-third of the workforce. Pilots struck but eventually returned to work, accepting pay cuts of 30 to 50 percent. At the time, Lorenzo's use of bankruptcy law was vilified by workers and their unions, but hailed by leaders across the political spectrum. "I don't think there is any question that he saved Continental," remarked Kahn.[6] Six years later, Lorenzo, now in charge at Eastern Airlines, filed for bankruptcy when his employees rejected major concession demands. The company eventually was liquidated and thousands of workers lost their jobs. In the decade following airline deregulation, more than three dozen carriers—including majors like Pan Am, Braniff, America West, and Midway—followed the same bankruptcy route, with workers losing their jobs outright or taking major concessions.

And for many travelers, the promise of greater competition under deregulation had proven elusive. By 1987, nine years after Carter signed the law into effect, the business media were noting the return to the pre-ADA monopoly era, with single carriers dominating airports like Dallas, Minneapolis, Saint Louis, and others.[7] Many prices declined, especially those on competitive routes. But service to less-profitable communities suffered, and airline ticketing became an incomprehensible maze of pricing schemes. Airlines stuffed more seats into aircraft by shrinking the size and depth of seats and began charging for meals, movies, first-in-line boarding rights, window seats, and whatever else they could monetize.

Then, two decades into the disruption caused by the changes in regulation and bankruptcy, came the second seismic shock to the airline industry—the terrorist attacks of September 11, 2001. In the days following the attacks—with the nation collectively shocked, commercial planes grounded, the skies eerily silent, with passengers rethinking the safety of air travel, and with airline workers stunned to see their workplaces converted into weapons of mass destruction—airline executives descended on Congress. They warned that "drastic measures are required if we are to avoid becoming the first economic casualty of the war," in the words of Delta chairman and CEO Leo Mullin.[8] The "drastic measures" that Mullin was referring to did not include any reduction in his salary-and-stock-option package—$34 million the year before. Rather, Mullin and his executive peers demanded a multibillion-dollar airline bailout paid for by taxpayers and workers. With planes grounded for three days and customers leery about returning to air travel, airline executives demanded public money to get them through the rough patch. Their political patrons dutifully invoked the threat that airline failure posed to the nation. "If planes don't fly, the whole economy shuts down," asserted Senator Jay Rockefeller, a West Virginia Democrat.[9] Congress dutifully handed airline executives $5 billion in direct grants and another $10 billion in loan guarantees, while making little provision for worker protections. Rodney Ward, a US Air flight attendant, wryly noted, "At the depressed prices of airline stocks, the government could easily have bought a controlling interest in the entire industry for $15 billion. In another place or another time, the airlines might have been nationalized under management by airline workers. But this is far from the reality in Washington, DC, today."[10]

Less than 100 hours after the 9/11 attacks, Continental Airlines announced it would lay off 12,000 workers. Most other airlines followed that path: 13,000 at Delta; 20,000 at United; another 20,000 at American; 11,000 at US Air, including Rodney Ward; and so on. All told more than 140,000 airline workers were furloughed, many never to return to their jobs.[11] *Washington Post* columnist David Montgomery noted that 25 flight attendants died in the 9/11 attacks, and that every flight attendant was bearing the weight of that loss at the same time they were being asked to shoulder primary responsibility for getting air passengers to feel safe in the post-9/11 flying environment. He then asked: "What thanks are flight attendants getting? How does this sound: You're fired."[12]

The mass layoffs were just the beginning. The 9/11 tragedy presented an unprecedented opportunity for executives to refashion the industry with a succession of bankruptcies, contracting out, and worker concessions closely following on the heels of the government bailout.

In the four years following 9/11, most major US airlines declared bankruptcy but continued operations. They used the power provided them in the 1978 law to force concessions from workers, either through bargaining or by court fiat. Executives at US Airways filed for bankruptcy in 2002 and wrested $1 billion in concessions from workers. Less than two years later, they demanded another $800 million in wage and benefit cuts, and when the workers resisted, the executives swiftly took the company back into bankruptcy again. With company executives now freed of their past collective bargaining obligations, they successfully petitioned the bankruptcy court to impose 21 percent pay cuts on the workforce and bailed on their pension obligations—at least those for rank-and-file employees. US Airways CEO David Siegel served only two years at the helm, but he nabbed a $4.5 million severance package on his way out the door.[13]

United Airlines executives declared bankruptcy a year after 9/11, scrapped the pension plan, and squeezed more than $3 billion in pay and benefits cuts out of workers during their three years in Chapter 11. Some 18,000 employees at United, the nation's second-biggest airline, were fired. But the sacrifice was unevenly distributed.[14] In 2006, the airline's first year out of bankruptcy, United's directors rewarded CEO Glenn Tilton with a $39.7 million compensation package.[15] "In Medieval times, people guilty of this kind of greed would have been boiled in oil," said Greg Davidowitch, president of United's flight attendants union.[16]

On September 15, 2005, while United was still in bankruptcy, Delta and Northwest Airlines, the third- and fourth-largest US airlines, went into bankruptcy court within a half hour of one another to double down on concessions for workers. For Delta, $1 billion in pilot concessions the previous year—equivalent to a one-third pay cut—was not enough to diminish the attractiveness of bankruptcy. Armed with the Chapter 11 cudgel, Delta's executives wrested another $280 million in wage and pension concessions from the pilots.[17]

In 2004 Northwest Airlines had secured 15 percent cuts in pilots' pay, but that only whetted the executives' appetites. Showing losses of $458 million in the first quarter of 2005, the company demanded $1.1 billion in concessions from all of its employees, including $176 million in givebacks by 4,400 mechanics.[18] The mechanics balked; they were willing to accept some cuts in pay and even the number of future jobs, but wanted 32 weeks of severance for the terminated workers. Northwest executives said they would cut 2,000 mechanics, almost half the total. The company offered them 26 weeks of severance. The union members struck on August 20. Two weeks later, Northwest increased its demands: $203 million in concessions and 3,100 job cuts, three-quarters of the force. The business press was awash with reports of Northwest's pending bankruptcy. Now desperate for a deal, union negotiators accepted the bigger cuts and the lower severance payout, but it was too late. The company said its previous severance package was off the table.[19] This wasn't real negotiations; the union was bargaining against itself as Northwest ratcheted up the concessions whenever the union acceded to company demands. Northwest replaced all its union mechanics with strikebreakers and supervisors and walked into bankruptcy court.

The airline's take-no-prisoners approach toward the mechanics served executives' additional goal of whipping other employees into line. Eight months after Northwest broke the mechanics union, the airline and the Machinists union reached an agreement on a concessionary contract covering more than 5,000 baggage handlers, stock clerks, and other workers. The contract cost 700 workers their jobs immediately. The remaining employees received an 11.5 percent cut in pay, higher health-care costs, a frozen pension, fewer paid holidays, and reductions in sick pay and vacation. There was no way to put a positive spin on this smackdown. The alternative was to go the way of the mechanics and lose the union completely. "We ain't kidding anybody—this is terrible," said Machinists union leader Bobby DePace. "We're extremely disappointed. It's not right, it's not fair, but that's America today."[20]

Only later did it come out that Northwest's prebankruptcy posturing with its pilots and mechanics had been a stratagem. Bankruptcy was the plan all along; bargaining with employees was merely a ploy to string them along and to raise the bar for concessions. Six months before filing for bankruptcy, Northwest Airlines had quietly directed its lead bankruptcy law firm to develop a Chapter 11 plan and had prepaid the lawyers almost $1 million for bankruptcy expenses. And right after paying the bankruptcy law firm, Northwest's CEO dumped most of his portfolio in the company, netting himself $21.3 million. The fix had been in all along.[21]

In addition to bankruptcy, the other lever the 1978 laws gave airline executives was the tool of contracting out work. Prior to 1978 there was little incentive for airlines to outsource. Employee costs, just like rising fuel prices and the cost of purchasing new planes, could be folded into ticket prices without risk of being undercut by competing airlines because ticket prices, along with virtually guaranteed profit levels, were adjusted by the government. Airlines hired their own employees, like Ben Smith, to load baggage, clean cabins, and staff ticket counters. Many of these workers organized into unions and negotiated contracts with good benefits and decent pay. In the 1970s union density in the air transportation sector was around 50 percent, about twice the US private sector rate.[22] Dealing with unions may not have been their first choice, but to company executives it was a manageable situation. After 1978, however, with prices now subject to competitive pressures, and with the growth of low-cost carriers like Southwest Airlines, executives began looking to slice employee costs. Publicly, airline executives spoke about these cuts as perhaps regrettable, but something they were forced to do as an inevitable outgrowth of "competition" and "the market." Only slightly more privately, to one another, their financial stakeholders, and industry media, they relished the opportunity to realign the distribution of power and pay in the industry. "We outsource everything that we can outsource," boasted Warwick Brady, chief operations officer at easyJet, to the probusiness *Financial Times*. "As long as we can manage it and control it, it gets outsourced."[23] Why should a menial baggage handler make a middle-income wage? Subbing out work could save an airline up to 25 percent, bragged Menzies Aviation in an annual report to shareholders.[24] Contract companies—sometimes created by the airlines themselves—were all too willing to help facilitate the realignment.

In 1995 Delta Airlines launched DAL Global Services, or DGS, to provide a host of contracted ground handling and passenger services at its main hub in Atlanta. As a wholly owned subsidiary of Delta, DGS fell under the complete control of the airline. Yet the contracting sleight of hand allowed executives to reduce compensation for workers because they were no longer officially Delta employees, and thus could not expect to enjoy the benefits that came with employment at a major airline. Delta marketed their new firm to other airlines as an attractive ground-handling alternative to direct hires. Within 15 years, DGS was performing a full range of services, including passenger baggage and cargo handling, passenger services, cabin cleaning, and aircraft and equipment maintenance for 25 airlines at 130 airports in 41 states. DGS employed some 10,000 workers.[25] The company paid most workers close to minimum wage but touted the flight benefits they offered. "If you could fly practically free, would you work anywhere else?" the DGS website boasted, overlooking the reality that the flight benefits were worthless to workers who couldn't afford to take a vacation.[26]

Swissair followed the Delta model and in 1996 established Swissport, a self-serving contract firm that hired staff for passenger and cargo services, fueling, cabin cleaning, and aircraft maintenance. Swissport was set up to serve its parent airline, but like DGS it quickly expanded. In 1999 the new company bought US-based Dynair, then the second-biggest ground-handling contract firm in the United States, to become part of the world's largest ground-handling company. After 9/11 Swissair declared bankruptcy and Swissport was bought out by a private equity firm. Swissport continued to thrive in the decade after 9/11, growing to 265 airports in 45 countries on 5 continents.[27]

The contract company Air Serv was the brainchild of Frank Argenbright Jr., who founded it in 2002 with personal redemption in mind as much as profits. Years before, in 1979, Argenbright had founded a small company that bore his name, Argenbright Security, to provide Delta Airlines with employee shuttle and parking lot security services. Over two decades, the company grew into an international, $1 billion per year airport security firm as airlines looked for contractors to staff security checkpoints. Argenbright Security was the largest US airport security firm, with 40 percent of the market share. But in 2000 things started to go bad for Frank Argenbright. The company was fined $1.5 million for falsifying training and background checks on employees at Philadelphia International Airport. Some, it turned out, had criminal records. Then Frank Argenbright tried to take his company private but was outbid by Securicor in late 2000. The company was no longer under his control, but employee uniforms still bore the Argenbright Security logo on September 11, 2001, when nineteen terrorists armed with box cutters passed through airport security stations and onto airplanes. Two of the four checkpoints used by the hijackers were staffed by Argenbright Security.[28]

Even though he was no longer legally associated with the security outfit, it was Argenbright's creation, with his distinctive name on it. With the Philadelphia scandal still fresh in the public's mind, Frank Argenbright was pilloried in the press, and it stung. In 2002 he decided to stage a comeback—not by going back into airport security, since that work had been taken over by the new federal Department of Homeland Security—but by offering airlines low-cost ticket checkers, cabin cleaners, and cargo handlers. Argenbright's timing was impeccable, coming just as airline executives were looking in the post-9/11 era to slash employee costs. Union cabin cleaners and ticket takers were becoming too expensive for the carriers. Argenbright's new contract company, which he called Air Serv, signed on United Airlines as a customer. Delta soon followed, then FedEx. The company went national, and by 2012 enjoyed annual revenues of more than $325 million. Air Serv was now operating at nincty-six US airports and six in England. Frank Argenbright had bounced back and achieved the personal redemption he had so desperately craved.[29] But he was frustrated with his company's place in the airline industry pecking order. Airlines were constantly pressuring contractors to cut costs. Contracts were always at risk of being underbid by a competitor. "Aviation has too few [airline] customers that can control your destiny and drive down prices," he said.[30] He sold Air Serv to the $4 billion facility management firm ABM and pocketed $67 million from the deal.[31]

In the 1990s the John Menzies Corporation was known in Great Britain as a magazine and newspaper distributor, and also the number one retailer in the United Kingdom of plush hamster-like robotic Furby toys and Nintendo Game Boy consoles. The distribution work led Menzies into the airline cargo business, and by the late 1990s the company had a foothold in the contracted passenger baggage and cargo business at several British airports. In 2000 the company bought out Ogden Aviation Services, a global ground-handling company, and Menzies' focus shifted to the growing airport opportunities. The new Menzies Aviation division spent the next decade buying up other ground-handling companies and expanding its base to 6 continents, 31 countries, and 144 airports. By 2014 Menzies Aviation had twenty thousand employees worldwide. In the United States it was well-anchored at sixteen airports, including major stations like Chicago O'Hare, LAX, Dallas/Fort Worth, and New York's JFK. Menzies Aviation multiplied in fifteen years from a $79 million/year business to almost $1.2 billion.[32]

In the ten years after 9/11, from 2002 through 2012, DGS, Swissport, Air Serv, Menzies, and a host of other contract firms cycled through US airports, gobbling up smaller companies and jockeying one another for market share. The airlines relished the contractor competition. Standard agreements between an airline and a ground-handling firm provided for short-term contract cancellation—as little as thirty days' notice. That left contractors like Frank Argenbright constantly on tenterhooks, wondering if they were going to get underbid by a competitor. It also had the effect—welcome to company executives— of keeping workers in a constant state of instability, not knowing from one month to the next if they would have a job. If a group of contract workers began to create problems, like organize a union, the airline could simply switch to a different contractor and get a new, more compliant workforce. Firing workers for union activity is nominally illegal under federal labor law. But in this case a contractor's workers weren't technically fired in the eyes of the law; they simply were laid off because their employer got dumped by the airline. It was a diabolical way for the airlines to kill unionizing efforts.

Contractors also enforced control by chopping up full-time jobs into part-time and on-call positions. Increasingly, airline contract workers were offered only part-time hours or were placed on an "on-call" list, to be summoned to work only when the contractor needed them.

Executives in other industries also were moving to a "just-in-time" labor model wherever possible, but the airlines were particularly aggressive in putting it into practice. This wreaked scheduling havoc on any worker seeking stability in his or her life to care for a child, to go back to school, or to be able to have a social life. Some contractors even went further, requiring cabin cleaners to clock out between cleaning aircraft. Workers were required to stay at the airport, awaiting the next flight to dock at the gate, but would not be paid for the time they spent waiting. That was illegal, but company managers accurately wagered that permanently precarious workers wouldn't raise a stink.

The realignment of airline jobs wasn't restricted to the grunt work of loading bags and swabbing seats. Following 9/11, airlines began outsourcing aircraft maintenance work, labor that had traditionally been done in-house by trained, unionized mechanics. Between 2003 and 2007, nine of the ten largest airlines—not counting the biggest, American Airlines—expanded their outsourcing of heavy aircraft maintenance from 34 percent of the work to 71 percent. An increasing volume of this work, which included seven-week aircraft teardowns and rebuilds, was being performed abroad.[33] United Airlines began sending planes to China and Hong Kong; Southwest, Jet Blue, and others flew aircraft to El Salvador, where mechanics and helpers were paid the equivalent of $2 to $5/hour in 2011 to rebuild Boeing 737s.[34] In addition to the cost savings for airlines, there was less federal oversight. At bases abroad, mechanics do not have to be licensed and US inspectors are forbidden from making spot checks. A federal report found lax oversight at foreign repair bases.[35] Many of the staff there couldn't even read the repair manuals. But the contracting decision penciled out for the airlines. And in 2012 the lone major holdover, American Airlines, began sending its planes to China for maintenance, costing one thousand Dallas-based mechanics their jobs.[36]

Even entire flights began to get contracted out by airlines, usually to smaller companies that paid workers less. In 2011 Alaska Airlines contracted out several West Coast routes to Utah-based SkyWest Airlines. Passengers would still purchase tickets on the Alaska website, check in at an Alaska ticket counter or kiosk, and board planes bearing the Alaska Airlines livery. But the planes were not staffed by unionized Alaska flight attendants and pilots. Rather, SkyWest

employees, not organized into a union, operated the aircraft at sig-
nificantly reduced wages.[37]

Within a few years of 9/11, the transformation of the US airline
industry was complete. Power had been shifted radically in favor of
the airlines. This shift, once accomplished, allowed executives to skew
income in their direction, away from workers. It was a triumph of the
economists and politicians, who in the 1970s imagined an industry in
which airlines would call the shots, federal regulators would stand
back, and Congress would write laws—and checks—when crises demanded. It was not anything that the Sea-Tac Airport ramp serviceman Ben Smith would have recognized.

IF YOU WANTED to distill the story of airline industry disruption into
a single person, you might come up with Alex Hoopes. I first met
Hoopes in early 2013, when he was working as a baggage handler for
Air Serv, one of the larger airline contractors at Sea-Tac Airport. He
readily became a fixture in the Sea-Tac campaign, attending organizing meetings, recruiting coworkers to join the effort, and spending his
spare hours knocking on the doors of SeaTac homes and businesses.
Unpretentiously friendly, even-tempered even after the beatdown the
airline industry had dealt him, and possessing an uncanny, detailed
memory, Hoopes was eager to tell me his story.

Son of an Air Force medic, Hoopes was born in Turkey in 1962 and
spent his early childhood in idyllic Mediterranean coastal villages. In
1970 the Air Force transferred Hoopes' dad to Washington State. After
high school Hoopes went to technical college where he trained to be
an automotive technician. For about six years in the 1980s, he repaired
cars at Seattle-area dealerships. But the pay and hours were unstable.
In 1989 a friend told him that Alaska Airlines was hiring rampers—
workers to load and unload baggage from airplanes. Hoopes jumped
at the opportunity.

The work was hard but steady. Sea-Tac Airport was the airline's
main base, and there was plenty to do. Baggage handlers scrambled
in and out of the bellies of aircraft to load passenger bags, and raised
"igloos"—the giant trapezoidal freight boxes—on hydraulic lifts to
push them into cargo planes. The work could be dangerous. But life
was looking up for Hoopes. Pay was $8.72/hour—equivalent to $17 in

2016 earning power—augmented by vacation, sick leave, full medical coverage, and virtually free flights. If he could hang onto the job, he could imagine a decent living ahead—a home, car, family and friends, and time off to travel.

One thing about the job gnawed at Hoopes. There was a union, but it was an "open shop." You could join the IAM, the International Association of Machinists, or choose not to join—but either way you got the benefits and protections of the union contract. Hoopes had never been in a union before, but instinctively the open shop didn't seem right to him. If there was going to be a union, Hoopes reasoned, everyone needed to participate and make it strong. He called those who didn't join the IAM "leeches," and as soon as his probation was up, he signed a union card.

Through the 1990s Hoopes participated in picket lines and other protests as the union members battled the company for better terms and a "union shop," a requirement that all workers benefiting from the contract join the union, or at least pay an equivalent representation fee in lieu of dues. Finally in 2000 Hoopes and his coworkers ratified a new contract that included the union shop provision. And three years later, with thirteen years in at the airline, Hoopes hit the top of the pay scale, $21/hour—more than $27 in 2016 dollars. "I was making a comfortable living," he recalled. He had a home in Lakewood, a thirty-mile drive south of the airport but close to his parents and friends. He had an active social life. And thanks to his budding friendship with another Alaska ramp worker, Hoopes was starting to think even bigger.

Bill Boyer Jr. worked the Alaska ramp with Hoopes, and he had an idea about how to improve the air passenger experience. In-flight entertainment was pathetic. You could watch the movie chosen by the airline if you wanted, by craning your neck and viewing one of the small screens that popped down from the ceiling. That was old-fashioned. What if instead passengers were given their own video devices, where they could choose whatever they wanted to watch? Boyer came up with the idea of a handheld media player, with scores of movies and video programming preloaded. In 2003 he contracted with a company to produce a small computer box that he called the digEplayer 5500. It was a bit bulky, but you could prop it up on your airline tray table and watch any movie you wanted, even new releases. It was a huge hit. Alaska Airlines executives loved them and bought one thousand devices. They began renting them out to coach passengers for $10 a flight. Before long, Hoopes was spending his free days in a Tacoma warehouse, getting digEplayers ready to run up to the airport. "We had five hundred players shoved into a big room," he explained. "One guy sat at a computer and he'd punch in all the players and the movies. You'd whip them out and put them in a bag and take them to the airline. I'd bring them to the airport, taking them out on the ramp because we had our badge passes. I'd just go up to each of the planes, like Alaska Airlines, drive up to the Jetway, run up the Jetway with the bags. That's how it was." Customers loved the new amenity. Alaska made millions.

The creative ramp workers also made money on the digEplayers, and they began to invest in other entrepreneurial ideas. When Hoopes wasn't working the ramp and shuttling digEplayers to the airport, he was traveling to Hawaii with Boyer, looking into running an island-hopping airline there. Hoopes was busy—perhaps too busy to notice the shock wave approaching. The wave's proximate cause was the industry's crisis post-9/11, but the coming tsunami's origin could be traced to Jimmy Carter's signatures on the deregulation and bankruptcy laws of 1978. Thus far Alaska employees had escaped the spate of concessions and contracting out that ravaged workforces at other airlines, but the escape wouldn't last.

In the wake of 9/11, Alaska Airlines, with its dominant grip on air travel in the state of Alaska and its strong West Coast route system, struggled less than other legacy airlines burdened with more expansive national markets. Nonetheless, Alaska executives insisted that their employees join the concessions parade. They wanted their workforce of fourteen thousand to give up $112 million.[38] The company demanded cuts from the flight attendants in 2003, and in early 2005 won a federal arbitration that sliced pilot salaries 26 percent. Emboldened by the arbitration decision, Alaska executives presented an ultimatum to the Sea-Tac baggage handlers in February 2005: accept drastic pay and benefit cuts or face contracting out.[39]

Now fifteen years into the job and at the top of the pay scale, Hoopes had a lot to protect. He was willing to give up some of his pay, but Alaska wanted cuts to as low as $12/hour. That was too much. It seemed to him that Alaska management wanted to dictate, not negotiate. In the first week of May, the union rampers rejected management's offer. The union issued a press release denouncing the offer. But indicating readiness to accept some concessions, the union announced it was "prepared to immediately resume bargaining to address the company's competitive needs while preserving our members' jobs."[40] Right after the vote, Hoopes flew to Boyer in Hawaii to look at a business opportunity—running one of the local charter airlines. Sure, there would be hard words between Alaska management and the union, and perhaps a mediator would be called into the bargaining room. In the end, as always, there would be compromise. That had always been the case.

But that's not what happened. Instead, the tsunami came ashore.

It was a little before three o'clock on Friday morning, May 13, when the early day shift baggage handlers arrived to punch in. Alaska managers met to tell them they had been replaced. The union workers were escorted out of the bag well and sent home. Hoopes was still in Hawaii when he got a call from a Sea-Tac skycap: "The ramp's been locked out at Sea-Tac Airport. Everybody's been given pink slips."

Hoopes was shocked. "It was a big stab in the back, definitely. I thought that they probably would come to some agreement and keep it going and work it out over time," he said. After more than fifteen years, Hoopes had built up pride at the company. "I'm a hard-working person. I handled the baggage with pride. It was an honor to work at the airline," he said. Hoopes wasn't closed to making some concessions. "We were willing to work with them. We were willing to come back because we knew the situation that happened in 2001 and with the industry itself." But Alaska was finished with the union rampers. They dismissed 472 union members and hired the global airline contracting firm, Menzies Aviation. Menzies paid baggage handlers $8.75/hour, with no benefits—about one-third of the union workers' compensation package. And, of course, no union. Alaska executives told company shareholders that the move saved $13 million a year.[41]

Alaska's May 13 blow was at the time the single largest airline outsourcing in the United States. It swept away 472 baggage handlers who earned a decent living, supported their families, paid for mortgages, and put wages back into the community. Alex Hoopes, the fifteen-year dedicated employee and proud baggage handler, the purveyor of a breakthrough movie-watching device that reaped Alaska millions, was in the end not an asset to Alaska, just another cost factor to be dealt with in the cold calculus of business.

I WATCHED THE 2005 mass firings of Alaska rampers from a short distance, focused at the time on health-care organizing for SEIU in the Seattle area. This was seven years before Hoopes and I would cross paths, but the airport union busting caught my attention. Alaska's move generated a buzz in the local labor movement, words of outrage for what the company had done, and pledges of solidarity with the workers. But from the Machinists union there was no clarion call for the rest of organized labor to rally to the cause.

That in itself was disturbing; the broader labor movement certainly could have been mobilized. Eight years earlier, in 1997, the 5th Avenue Theatre in downtown Seattle had fired eighteen union musicians who were advocating for contract improvements. At the time I was the Washington State organizer of Jobs With Justice, the labor-community coalition. The musicians asked us for help. In tandem with the local labor council, we mobilized nightly rallies of one thousand people in front of the theater, blocking downtown Seattle streets and preventing the show from opening with replacement performers. The full spectrum of the labor movement turned out to support the musicians: Boeing machinists, longshore workers, city employees, health-care workers, construction workers, tugboat operators, grocery workers, university workers, teachers, and more. Students, peace activists, political radicals, and others turned out. All were energized by the opportunity to defend workers and to send a powerful message about class solidarity not just to the theater management, but to employers throughout the area.

As supporters picketed in the street outside the theater, musicians brought out their instruments and played jazz tunes. Politicians and community members rallied to the cause. King County executive Ron Sims played saxophone with the strikers. The media sympathetically profiled the union musicians and grilled management on the nightly news. A week after the musicians were dismissed, the theater management caved in, took the union workers back, and agreed to a new contract. It was a stunning victory for working people in Seattle, a powerful notice to all employers in the area that the labor cry, "an injury to one is an injury to all," was not an empty slogan.[42]

After the 5th Avenue Theatre fight, no employer in the Seattle area dared to fire workers en masse—until Alaska's move in 2005. I followed the news about the rampers' firings and waited to hear the Machinists' call to the streets. In local labor circles, all you had to do was to say "5th Avenue Theatre" to conjure the memory of powerful labor solidarity and stir people to action. Of course Alaska would be a much tougher employer than the theater, but the company's high profile ensured that unions and their allies would turn out.

The call never came. Instead, the Machinists union leadership fixated on a purely legal strategy, filing a lawsuit in a vain effort to reverse the company's move. It seemed to me that the union leadership was playing by a set of rules that were from a bygone era of labor-management relations—rules that had been wiped out in 1978.

WHEN THE ALASKA firings happened, Alex Hoopes sensed that the Alaska contracting move was about something more than dollars. Yes, the savings mattered to the company's bottom line. But in his estimation, this was more about power and control. Alaska management "didn't like the idea of a closed union shop." Having a stronger union gave the workers significant leverage over the company. If they chose to do so, the rampers could have shut down Alaska's central hub; company executives knew that all too well. Ever since he started at Alaska, Hoopes could look around the Sea-Tac tarmac and see how other airlines were moving to contract out work. The industry was marching toward severing union agreements and cutting labor costs, systematically destroying thousands of good jobs that until 1978 had been shielded from the full force of capitalism. It was only a matter of time before Hoopes and his coworkers would have to confront this disruption at Alaska.

It may seem odd, in hindsight, to observe the naïveté of people at the precipice of disaster: taking note perhaps of warning signs, but utterly failing to add up the signals. One feature of tsunamis is that the approaching wave will often draw back water before striking. A few minutes before the wave makes landfall, the waterline will recede offshore dramatically, revealing exposed seafloor, as if the tide is suddenly rushing out. In these extraordinary moments, people have been known to wander out to gawk at the novelty of exposed seafloor, the fish, the shells, and the suddenly beached boats. When the wall of water appears, rushing shoreward, panic ensues. People run, but it's too late—the water overtakes them.

In the months leading up to the 2005 mass firings, there were plenty of warning signs of the coming catastrophe: the bankruptcies and contracting out at other airlines, the Alaska pilots' concessionary arbitration ruling, and the company's February ultimatum to the rampers. But at the time, the signals that are so clear in hindsight eluded Hoopes and most of his colleagues, rank-and-file workers experienced at doing battle with their employer. They failed to add up the warning signs, wrongly assuming that this was just another tough round of bargaining that would end with compromises and handshakes.

The events of 9/11 and the industry crisis that followed no doubt increased the urgency with which Alaska executives focused on breaking the rampers' power. The 2005 arbitration award that slashed pilot pay certainly strengthened the company's commitment to drive a hard bargain in the ramper negotiations, in two ways. First, the pilot concessions heightened pressure on other employee groups to also give back. And second, having wrested concessions from their most elite, specialized group of employees, the company executives surely felt an urgent need to wring concessions out of the baggage handlers. If the company failed to squeeze them, mere grunts by comparison to the pilots, the pilots would revolt. The company had locked itself into a collision course with the rampers.

So Alaska's threat in the early months of 2005 to contract out baggage handling was not just the usual jawboning that comes with contentious bargaining; it was a real contingency plan. But the union leadership, nationally and locally, and the union members missed the signals. Like haphazard tourists on the beach, gawking at the receding ocean, they didn't want to believe that they were seeing something fundamentally different.

In the weeks leading up to that fateful morning of May 13, Alaska quietly directed Menzies to hire and train workers and to prepare them to take over baggage handling on short notice. When the union members rejected the company's proposal on May 6, the company sprang into action. Publicly, Alaska Airlines blamed the rampers, saying it contracted out the work because after twenty months of bargaining the union rampers refused to accept "a contract approaching the savings available from service providers."[43] The company statement smacked of cruelty, like blaming a drowning man for his own circumstances. But in fact the replacement of the rampers was long in coming, part of the power shift that Alaska executives sought for years. In 2005 the proper conditions had coalesced to allow their aspiration to become reality, and the union's contract rejection merely gave the company the pretext to act. Indeed, the Alaska ramp worker mass firing can be traced back to a force that was unleashed in 1978, gained momentum in the aftermath of 2001, and finally hit shore in 2005 with a devastating blow.

IN HAWAII THAT May 13th, Hoopes thanked his skycap friend for the alert about the bad news, and went to tell Boyer. Instead of returning to Seattle as planned, Hoopes called his parents back in Washington State to say he'd be staying in Hawaii for the time being. Menzies contacted Hoopes and offered him $10/hour, higher than their standard rate because of his experience. But there were no benefits and the drop from his previous salary was too huge. Hoopes said no. For the next few years, he worked as a supervisor at Mokulele Airlines, an island-hopping passenger service, before returning home to family and the Pacific Northwest in 2010.

When Hoopes landed back in Sea-Tac, the same work he'd had there before awaited him, but the terms were different. The airlines weren't hiring, but you could have your pick of jobs with contractors. Hoopes hired on as a baggage handler at Air Serv, the airport contractor that was quickly expanding its Sea-Tac footprint. Hoopes worked as a ramper, loading and unloading bags for United, Continental, and other airlines. The pay was $9.50/hour, well under half his previous wage and even less than what Menzies had offered five years prior. He could no longer afford a car, so he had to take a seventy-minute bus ride to work. Air Serv offered no vacation, no sick time, no retirement. Until Alaska's clean sweep in 2005, Hoopes had been a stable, middle-income employee, the type of person Washington State congressman Adam Smith extolled. He earned a modest paycheck hefting bags and he helped the airline, for which he felt a strong kinship, reap millions through digEplayer rentals. But those days were gone. Now he was just another poverty-wage baggage mule, napping on long bus rides to and from work, grabbing overtime when it was available, and struggling to pay his bills. He was one of thousands of disposable Sea-Tac Airport contract workers, a living embodiment of what corporate executives and their government patrons had imagined back in the 1970s when they set out to remake the industry.

The vicissitudes of airport employment also radiated out into society. The new system created a class of community members who were denied the ability to meaningfully participate in the basic rhythms of civil society because they were continually scrambling for work, juggling family needs, or figuring out how to avoid eviction and hunger. Civic and social activities that so many of us take for granted—the PTA, the church club, neighborhood improvement group, children's sports teams and activities, drinks at the pub, local political activity— all were beyond the reach of most low-wage airport workers.

Perhaps worst of all, though, was the iron trap of poverty employment. Jobs afforded precious little opportunity for upward mobility. No longer could a baggage handler, cabin cleaner, fueler, or passenger service worker imagine owning a home, setting down roots in the community, and sending their kids to college on an airport paycheck. They were economic hostages to precarious employment, always hustling to make enough money to pay the bills, never getting ahead. It was a far cry from the time when it was conceivable to imagine the child of a working-class airport worker growing up to great accomplishment, even election to high political office—just as Adam Smith, the ramp serviceman's son, had done in getting elected to the Washington State Senate and then the US Congress.

Equally unimaginable in years past would have been the notion that an airline CEO could secretly prearrange bankruptcy, make a financial killing by dumping his stock, strong-arm workers into submission, and then—with the blessings and funding of the US government and the backing of a bankruptcy judge—emerge a respected member of the community. By the 2000s, however, it was standard operating procedure; the idea of business failure had been turned on its head. Bankruptcy was no longer the scarlet letter of executive failure, but a potent business strategy to whip workers into line. In 2011, when American Airlines declared bankruptcy, there was no shame in the business or political world. It was simply a smart business decision. "Taking a long-term view, the American [Airlines] bankruptcy is a very positive thing," the head of Boeing's commercial airplane division told financiers.[44] American Airlines declared Chapter 11 and then turned to Mitt Romney's former consulting firm, Bain & Company, for advice—at a cost of $525,000 every month—on how to cut labor expenses and fire workers.[45]

Indeed, the industry changes went far beyond economic redistribution. In the industry makeover, corporate executives had managed to off-load three distinct, intertwined risks—the economic and social hazards of bankruptcy, the risk of employing workers who might organize and demand improved conditions, and the jeopardy of having their business held socially accountable through effective government oversight.

In laissez-faire economic theory, the capitalist puts his capital at risk and therefore is entitled to significant reward. Proponents argue that the capitalist has the right to claim great riches if successful, because he also is risking great loss if he makes bad choices. The government stands aside and lets "the market" pick winners and losers. But in fact the US airline industry had been transformed not into a laissez-faire system but a best-of-all-possible-worlds playground for the captains of industry. On this new playground they could take enormous chances, knowing that they could recoup the cost of bad decisions by slashing worker pay and benefits. And they also knew that the government, rather than standing back, would provide insurance against any business failure—compliant bankruptcy courts, pension bailouts, even direct grants. There was no risk of failure for the CEOs of Delta, United, and their peers. Thanks to the power they now held over their industry, the executives were playing a game they couldn't possibly lose and workers couldn't possibly win.

THREE

GAME CHANGER

Sea-Tac and the Fight for a Fair Economy

FOR THE FORTUNATE ones in Seattle, the twenty-first century opened with boom times. Powered by spectacular growth at Microsoft, Amazon, Starbucks, Washington Mutual Bank, and venture capital and biotech firms, a new class of super-rich emerged in the Seattle area. By mid-decade, Seattle and surrounding King County tallied sixty-eight thousand millionaires, the tenth largest sum of any county in the United States.[1] Housing prices shot through the roof. Construction cranes dotted downtown Seattle, erecting gleaming towers to cater to the new wealth. Wine bars, upscale boutiques, cigar lounges, luxury condominiums, and the other trappings of affluence began to proliferate downtown and in the eastside technology belt.

Just a dozen miles south of the city, a very different picture emerged in the bustling airport community of SeaTac. The airline industry's seismic changes rippled out beyond airport perimeter fences and into the surrounding neighborhoods, shaping not just economic activity but every aspect of people's lives: their housing, schools, food—even how long they could expect to live.

The spate of union busting and contracting out that mushroomed in the first years of the new century, peaking with the 2005 firing of Alex Hoopes and his coworkers, drove down per capita income in SeaTac 14 percent between 2000 and 2010. It was a mirror opposite of the overall income growth in Seattle.[2] That, combined with the continued rise in area housing prices, which did not spare SeaTac, accelerated the churn in the community. People who could get out, did. In just the ten years between 2000 and 2010, SeaTac went from nearly two-thirds white to a majority people of color.[3] Most of SeaTac's new residents were refugees from the economic and political crisis hot spots around the world, especially East Africa. The refugees were willing to take on poverty-wage airport jobs because the work provided an economic handhold, however tenuous.

SeaTac native Mia Su-Ling Gregerson first noticed this shift in 2004 when her daughter came home from fourth grade and began describing African classmates, reciting names her mom found difficult to pronounce. Adopted as an infant from Taiwan, Gregerson grew up in a trim single-family home in SeaTac, much like Adam Smith had a few years earlier. She attended public school in the 1980s, where she noticed the children of Cambodian refugees and a few African American kids, but otherwise—aside from herself, of course—her classmates were white. Most of them enjoyed decent working-class-family lifestyles facilitated by good airport jobs. As a child Gregerson got to travel to Hawaii and Disneyland on flight benefits provided by her best friend's dad, who worked as a unionized baggage handler. After graduating in 1991 from Foster High School just north of the airport, Gregerson trained to become a dental hygienist. With help from her parents, Gregerson bought a modest single-family home in SeaTac—on the same block as her grandparents—and in 1994 her daughter, Alexis, was born. She had a modicum of economic stability, if not wealth.

Her daughter's school experiences prompted Gregerson to begin to see the growing diversity in SeaTac, but it took a few more years before the depth of transformation gained full clarity in her mind. In 2007 a neighbor encouraged Gregerson to run for city council. Gregerson's primary credential was that she enjoyed volunteering. That was a worthy quality, since the part-time elected office only paid a modest stipend. Gregerson ran unopposed in November 2007 and took her seat on the council the following January, a novice to politics and the only person of color out of seven council members on the dais. Now compelled by her elected position to travel more broadly about the community, Gregerson began to meet new clusters of residents—Punjabis, Somalis, Ethiopians, Filipinos, Samoans, and others—and become acquainted with their bleak conditions. The parents scurried to multiple jobs at the car rental companies, hotels, and restaurants around SeaTac, and of course also at the airport; or they drove cabs and limousines for seventy-two hours a week, barely spending time with their children; they crammed multiple families into SeaTac's burgeoning apartment complexes; they sent their children to the same schools that Gregerson had attended, only these children often went on empty stomachs.

As a first-term council member, Gregerson took note of the gulf in civic activity between the largely white residents who came to council meetings and spoke up ardently about city zoning rules, parks, taxes, and services, and the new residents, who had no time to attend regular council meetings and neighborhood action groups. Gregerson's first years on the council challenged her to see her home community differently. She grew a passion for encouraging civic engagement among SeaTac's newest residents and began to see policy questions through, as she put it, "a lens of equity and social justice."

AS GREGERSON WAS settling into what she called "my freshman year" on the council and gaining a new perspective on her hometown, a new minister was taking over at Riverton Park United Methodist Church. Straddling the city line between SeaTac and Tukwila, the church served working-class families from both communities. The Reverend Jan Bolerjack had transferred in 2008 from a Methodist church in Fall City, a small rural community twenty miles east of Seattle. Fall City was a farming community experiencing an influx of new money as tech and venture capitalist wealth seeped from Seattle's suburbs into the exurbs. She had lived in the parsonage ten feet from the picturesque steepled church. The Snoqualmie River meandered nearby. Life was not rushed. Bolerjack had served the Fall City flock for five years, coaxing the congregation to open a food bank to serve the poor residents whom the boom had left behind. By 2007 she was ready to move on, as she put it, "to be where God is at work—with the poor, the broken, the needy." In 2008 she settled into the Riverton Park church, a rectangular block building that sat amid a broad grassy lawn just three miles from Sea-Tac's runways.

A stark contrast to tranquil, overwhelmingly white Fall City, SeaTac was a bustling center of transportation, a diverse mash-up of different languages, foods, and customs, along with alarmingly different driving habits imported from around the world. Bolerjack learned to drive defensively in her new community, never fully confident that other drivers would obey stop signs and travel lanes. It also was a place where the area's new wealth—if only fleetingly—crossed paths with the new poverty. Every day tens of thousands of business and tourism travelers transited through the city of SeaTac to board airplanes cleaned and served by local residents who could only dream of flying away to the destinations that flashed on the airport's digital message boards: New York City. Mazatlán. Beijing. Miami. Paris.

Early on at the church, Bolerjack learned what that meant to her new neighbors. Three days a week the church opened its food bank. Lines of people would form around the church building, many wearing the uniforms of airport companies. Striking up conversations, Bolerjack got acquainted with their precarious lives: multiple jobs with part-time, irregular hours, always scrabbling for food and in danger of getting evicted or having their electricity shut off. Most of the food bank volunteers were Russian Turks, many of whom worked at the airport themselves. Bolerjack recalled one food bank volunteer who worked at the airport and had a son with special needs who frequently required hospital care. One day Bolerjack spotted the worker, not volunteering but in line himself to get food for his family. What happened? she asked. He explained that he worked at an airport company with no sick leave. His wife had fallen ill, and he had to take their son to medical appointments. The company fired him for missing work.

"I was amazed in listening to him, how he just took it in stride," she recalled. "It was just what happens. And I heard these stories over and over, 'Yeah, I was a cabin cleaner, but I got fired.' It used to be that I thought people got fired when they didn't do their job or when they somehow offended the boss. But I found that people just got fired for random causes and there are no second chances."

Bolerjack also became more aware of the effect on SeaTac's children. With parents working irregular hours, late into the night, or on overnight shifts, kids often were left in the care of older cousins or siblings. Teenagers would help the younger ones get dressed and off to school. After school, they'd come by the church. Bolerjack would help them do homework and offer them something to eat. "I might randomly ask a kid, 'What did you have for breakfast?'" she said. "They'd look at me blankly, like, 'Breakfast? What are you talking about?' and I'd realize that these kids don't eat anything until maybe eight o'clock at night."

Sometimes, while parents got help at the church, Bolerjack would play with the smaller children. She recalled showing a Fisher-Price toy house set to some three-year-olds. "This one kid was being particularly fussy, so I got down on the floor with him, and I said, 'OK, let's put these little Fisher-Price people to bed.' I take the little bed out of the house and I put the little Fisher-Price person on it, and I got a Kleenex and put it over him for a blanket, just what you do with little kids. Well, this kid was not engaging, and finally I guess I got distracted. But then I turned around and he had taken these little Fisher-Price people, had laid the Kleenex on the floor—laid it out very neatly—and he had laid them one by the next one very, very close, and put another Kleenex over them. All five of them. Well—duh!— they sleep on the floor and they all sleep together."

What Mia Gregerson and Reverend Bolerjack were discerning was a community in dramatic transition. The human misery they were beginning to comprehend was not an accident or a misfortune, nor was it the result of bad choices by the victims, but rather the logical consequence of vast changes in the economy imagined and imposed by the country's political, business, and financial elite. By the end of the decade—eight years after the wave of attacks on workers that followed 9/11, and nearly five years after the ramp workers' mass firings—Alaska Airlines executives were crowing about growing profits while SeaTac was awash in poverty.

But it would be inadequate to describe the scene as one of income inequality. That would only touch the surface. Gregerson and Bolerjack were observing the fallout from a power shift that had been years in the making. The industry disruption engineered by the airline CEOs required breaking workers' collective power, and once that was completed, the business and finance elite plowed forward with their vision of how to re-arrange the world. The poor health, hungry children, and workers who had no time to participate in the social and political life of the community simply were, as with low wages, by-products of this corporate vision, a vision completely divorced from any sense of morality.

Beyond the individual stories, hard data underscored the depth of change: By 2010 the poverty rate in SeaTac and its adjoining Tukwila was double the rate in surrounding King County. Average household income was 40 percent lower than King County's. About 75 percent of schoolchildren relied on subsidized meals for their daily nutrition—more than double the county rate. Nearly one out of every three adults lacked health insurance, twice the county average. SeaTac and Tukwila moms ranked last in the county in being able to access pre-natal care, and the area also recorded the highest percentage of low-birth-weight babies. Obesity was 50 percent higher than the county average, and teen birth rates were nearly three times higher. The systemic inequities of the airport economy added up to an early death sentence: SeaTac and Tukwila residents experienced higher disease mortality compared to other King County residents, and they died sooner—two years, seven months earlier, on average.[4]

In the world outside SeaTac, the same economic divergence was happening on a much grander scale. As Gregerson was settling into her new role as elected official and Bolerjack was getting acquainted with airport community poverty, the casino known as Wall Street crashed the world economy. Huge investment banks Bear Stearns and Lehman Brothers went bankrupt, insurance giant AIG failed, and the stock market plummeted, casting capitalist economies into crisis. The perpetrators weren't just in lower Manhattan. Seattle-based Washington Mutual Bank, master peddlers of subprime loans and the sixth largest bank in the country, went belly up in late September 2008 and was transferred at a fire-sale price to JPMorgan Chase. From the forty-second floor of Washington Mutual's gleaming head-quarters in downtown Seattle, CEO Kerry Killinger could gaze south toward the airport and Reverend Bolerjack's church. When the bank crashed, Killinger—like Bolerjack's food bank volunteer—was summarily fired. But there was no danger that the executive would end up at the church door begging for food. Killinger nabbed a $15.3 million severance package on his way out the door,[5] a sum sufficient to feed every one of SeaTac's children, up to age ten, for three years running.

Nationally, the economic crisis prompted businesses to fire 8.7 million workers. More than 14 million homeowners were forced into foreclosure and millions more filed personal bankruptcy.[6] It was decimating for workers and their communities. But the Wall Street executives who provoked the crisis bailed along with Killinger in their golden parachutes, aided by the federal government's $700 billion rescue.

For many labor leaders around the country, the concessions, massive layoffs, and misery for workers that followed capital's speculation disaster deepened the already-pressing existential crisis about the future of unions. Owing to the mass firings of workers, within two years of Wall Street's crash, union membership plummeted by more than a million to less than fifteen million members, the lowest level in sixty years. Nearly all of the loss was in private businesses.[7]

The 2008 crisis brought fresh urgency to two fundamental questions within the labor movement. The first was the question of what purpose unions served: Was it their job to accommodate to capitalism and get the best deal possible for their members, or were unions needed to challenge the profit system and fight for the interests of the entire working class? Most observers believed that the question had been settled in 1955 in favor of accommodation. But the depth of the 2008 crisis brought the question back to the surface.

The deeply ingrained, half-century-old business union model contented itself to fight limited workplace battles—largely for its dues-paying members. While on occasion militant unions waged struggles that articulated broader class interests, they remained nationally isolated and unable to challenge the overall prevalence of business unionism. In the new century, the most visible standard-bearer for the dominant business union approach was SEIU president Andy Stern. He modernized the business union model with a call for unions to fight aggressively in the political arena for social change benefiting all—like universal health care. But just as ardently he steered clear of labor militancy, arguing that "class struggle mentality was a vestige of an earlier, rough era." Stern was about making peace with capital, just as AFL-CIO leader George Meany had done in 1955. He wanted unions to partner with employers, focusing on "value added" relationships because "employees and employers need organizations that solve problems, not create them."[8] Under Stern's leadership the union honed the "call center" model as a twenty-first-century model of union innovation and efficiency. It replaced shop-floor union stewards with staffed phone operations that serviced members' needs much like an insurance company, and in doing so effaced any semblance of workplace-based leadership and organization.

Yet this business union model, though gussied up for the twenty-first century with a muscular political veneer, never could fully vanquish the competing call by workers and radical activists for struggle based on class interests. And the economic depression that hit working-class communities beginning in late 2008 exposed the fallacy that workers were better off finding common ground with big business. Many unions had obliged employers in hard times. In return they had been handed pink slips, busted unions, and broken lives. And now, added to the negative balance sheet of the business union model were millions of foreclosures, soaring economic inequality, and ruined cities, while the architects of the financial disaster made off with billions. More people inside and outside unions began to recognize that maybe capitalism was, after all, rotten to the core.

The second fundamental question facing unions was how to rebuild union strength: by investing in major organizing campaigns to recruit new members, or by fighting to "level the playing field" through labor law reform before launching organizing drives? By the beginning of the twenty-first century, most unions had largely abandoned new organizing campaigns, too preoccupied with waging defensive battles for their dues-paying members to have the bandwidth or resources to organize new members. For those unions that nominally cared about organizing, it was a Sisyphean task. Employers, especially those in the private sector, routinely and with near-complete impunity intimidated and fired union activists, delayed and manipulated union representation elections, strung out bargaining until they could decertify the union, and contracted out groups of workers who organized. Labor laws were irretrievably stacked against the workers and unions. Some unions, like SEIU, continued to invest heavily in campaigns, but much of the growth came in organizing public workers, where employer resistance was minimal compared to private businesses. A handful of unions, such as the Teamsters, Communications

Workers, and the hospitality workers union, focused on organizing private sector workers. But given employer resistance, they achieved limited results. Other union leaders argued that before any significant campaigns could be mounted, the labor movement needed to change laws to protect the right of workers to organize. They staked their hopes on winning national labor law reform.

The 2007 Employee Free Choice Act was their vehicle. EFCA bypassed the broken secret ballot election system by obliging employers to recognize and bargain with unions once a majority of workers signed union authorization cards. It increased penalties on employers that violated workers' rights. And it required first-contract arbitration, precluding the possibility that a business could wait out a union by delaying interminably at the bargaining table.

EFCA was introduced in Congress as a rallying point for labor. In 2007 there was no chance it would get through Congress and secure President Bush's signature. But it had a supporter in Senator Barack Obama, and when the Illinois legislator won the White House and Democrats swept to strong congressional majorities in November 2008, hope blossomed that 2009 would be the year unions would win meaningful labor law reform. Many unions had invested significant resources in the 2008 election. SEIU alone spent $32 million supporting Obama.[9] Those hopes were quickly dashed in the first eight months of 2009 by an Obama administration that was more invested in bailing out the financial sector than in expending political capital for workers' rights. Efforts to mount a widespread grassroots demand for EFCA's passage fell short—an SEIU drive to collect one million pro-EFCA postcards to Congress couldn't even muster half that number—and in the absence of a mass grassroots movement, unions lacked the political strength to leverage passage. In the end the failure of EFCA stood as yet another illustration of what happens when unions seek political shortcuts to building power. Like it or not, workers would have to fight for their rights on the uneven playing field.

If EFCA's demise didn't make that point clearly enough, the debate over national health care and the 2010 midterm elections underscored the limitations of labor's power in the absence of grassroots activity independent of the major political parties. Obama began his term pledging to deliver universal health care, including an option for public coverage. Union leaders declared the public option an essential part of any health-care reform. But once in office Obama tacked right, opting to build alliances with the major insurance, medical, and pharmaceutical companies. The president jettisoned the principle of health care as a human right in favor of a bill that expanded coverage by propping up the private for-profit health insurance system. Mandating that individuals purchase health insurance from private companies was a concept that had been championed by Republicans for the previous sixteen years. It strengthened profit's grip over the health-care system. Most labor leaders were so committed to the president's political success that they were unwilling and unable to galvanize meaningful resistance when Obama crumbled on the principles of universal coverage and the public option. As with President Carter in 1978, Obama seemed to believe that compromising with big business would secure bipartisan support, give him political breathing room, and improve his party's electoral chances. As with his predecessor, Obama was dead wrong. The Affordable Care Act barely limped across the finish line in Congress and became a permanent hyperpartisan flashpoint. Democrats lost control of the political narrative to the rising Tea Party and got crushed in the 2010 elections. The post-election tally left the labor movement with a hostile Congress, a million fewer members than when their chosen candidate moved into the White House, one in every six American workers seeking work, and a Tea Party–driven national discourse that placed blame for the economic crisis not on corporate greed but on the federal government, immigrants, and unions.

Within my union, SEIU, another big change happened in 2010: Andy Stern resigned. Ostensibly, he announced he wanted to go out on a high note after securing passage of the new health-care law. But both union insiders and many outside observers also knew that Stern's ongoing internal battles, principally with the large SEIU health-care local in California, had taken their toll. His heir apparent, Secretary-Treasurer Anna Burger, a Democratic Party stalwart, pledged to maintain Stern's focus on political action. Many of us within SEIU were pleased when Vice President Mary Kay Henry challenged Burger. While not a radical, Henry placed greater focus on organizing. Stern swiftly endorsed Burger to replace him, but his coattails proved to be exceedingly short; within two weeks Henry had amassed majority support among SEIU local leaders, and Burger withdrew.

It would be an overstatement to suggest that Henry's election was a repudiation of Stern's go along to get along approach to capitalism and the political establishment. Once in office, Henry was quick to pledge that the union would invest heavily in Democrats in the 2012 elections.[10] But her victory created an opening within the union to restore worker organizing to the forefront of the two-million-member union's mission.

At the start of 2011 the new union administration, forced to confront the ruinous political harvest of 2010, unveiled an organizing proposal that was bold even by the standards of a union prone to declare big plans. Henry and other SEIU leaders concluded that it wasn't sufficient for unions to take on corporations one bargaining or political fight at a time. A much broader fightback for jobs and against cuts was required. And, they argued, it wouldn't be sufficient just to wage a fight for different national policies; unions had to organize new workers into their ranks, not shop by shop, but on a massive scale. SEIU leaders talked about "the 7 percent problem," referring to the percentage of private-sector American workers who belonged to unions. Even with SEIU and other unions continuing to organize on the pace of recent years, they said, labor overall would be unable to reverse the downward trend of union density and power. Part of that danger was reflected in the growing gulf in wages and rights between the overwhelmingly nonunion private sector and the higher union density public sector. Adversaries were beginning to exploit those divisions between workers, putting unionized public sector standards at risk. What was needed was a return to the 1930s "industrial" organizing, in which workers across employers organized together. "It won't be enough to try harder," read one SEIU briefing. "What we need is game-changers."

What emerged was a bold plan, an organizational call to arms. Adopted by the SEIU executive board in January 2011 and called the Fight for a Fair Economy (FFE), the plan had two main thrusts: First, through worker mobilizations that targeted banks and major corporations, change the public debate nationally about who broke the economy and what was needed to get people back to work. And second, launch large-scale private-sector organizing campaigns to "move the union density dial" and rebuild union power.

The FFE plan called on SEIU locals to deploy more than 1,500 full-time organizers in 17 cities in the spring to knock on 3 million doors in neighborhoods where the household income averaged below $35,000. In many of these neighborhoods unemployment was above 40 percent. The immediate goal was to mobilize working-class people to join escalating protests in front of banks, at corporate shareholder meetings, political conventions, and in the streets. In doing so the FFE organizers would identify industries in which the workers were ready to organize unions and launch campaigns inside workplaces. Nationally, the union was committing $60 million/year to the venture and asking local unions to contribute millions more.[11] FFE was envisioned as an all-consuming project.

Just as SEIU leaders embarked on a national tour to unveil their plan, a union crisis erupted in Wisconsin that accentuated the exigency of the moment. Over the protests of tens of thousands of union members and their allies, Governor Scott Walker rammed through a new law that banned collective bargaining and dues deductions for most Wisconsin public workers. It was a declaration of war on workers.

Walker's success was a function of both his own ideological passion and the decades-long atrophy of unions, particularly in the private sector. Nearly half of Wisconsin's public workers belonged to unions, a stark contrast to the private-sector union rate of less than 9 percent. The resulting discrepancy between the workplace rights and benefits of unionized public workers and the largely nonunionized private workers made for easy wedge politics for the new governor.

Wisconsin wasn't an outlier. While a state with a long and proud union tradition, Wisconsin by 2011 had the same public-to-private union ratio as the national scene.[12] That glaring reality underscored the point that the Fight for a Fair Economy program wasn't about derailing some future or isolated threat to working people and unions, but taking on a pressing danger from which there was no safe haven.

By early spring 2011, with the shock waves of Wisconsin rattling the entire union movement, the Fight for a Fair Economy canvasses got under way. In Seattle more than fifty SEIU staffers—some expe-

rienced, many newly hired—along with staff from the local Teamsters union, whose leadership heartily joined the effort, knocked on
more than eighty thousand doors and talked to nearly ten thousand
low-income workers in south Seattle and the surrounding suburbs,
including SeaTac. Locally, the effort was named Working Washington, and while the new organization claimed coalition status, it was
almost entirely a creation of SEIU. The union replicated the effort in
sixteen other cities throughout the United States under a variety of
coalition names.

Around the country canvassers found workers hurting from layoffs
and job cuts, angry because they felt the political establishment cared
more about rescuing banks than their families. They were ready to
take action.

At these first Working Washington protests, unemployed workers,
retirees, and low-wage workers began to come together and see a
glimmer of hope in taking on corporations directly. Early 2011 protests outside of the urban Chase Bank branches and inside the Wey-
erhaeuser shareholders meeting just south of Seattle didn't produce
tangible business concessions. Yet the very act of confronting corporate representatives gave workers confidence that yes, it was possible
to fight back.

While these first actions showed great potential in building a powerful new movement of workers, many of us on local union staffs
were wary about where FFE was headed. We were aware that our
national union leadership had over the years deflected energy away
from genuine worker power building and into glitzy policy fights that
used workers as props in a staged drama rather than as authors and
creators of their own liberation. And we also wondered about how
long the national union would continue to nurture these budding
movements, especially when things got tough. To some outside SEIU,
the union had a "flavor of the month" habit when it came to carrying
out big campaigns.

AS WITH THE FFE canvasses in the other cities, the Working Washington staff tallied unemployment as the top issue they encountered
in conversations at the doors of workers. People were looking for
work, or were stuck involuntarily in part-time jobs, or were on the

verge of giving up hope of ever finding work that paid pre-2008 levels. However, there was one community where the feedback was different: the city of SeaTac. In the neighborhoods surrounding the airport, workers didn't complain about the absence of work opportunities. Rather, they said, they held down multiple jobs—part-time employment with hours that varied every week, or even every day; lousy wages with no benefits; frequent firings; and no hope of advancement. Unlike the rest of the area's economy, the airport hadn't suffered greatly following the 2008 crash; it existed within a bubble, mostly shielded from the economic turbulence outside. Sea-Tac air travel dipped slightly toward the end of the decade but quickly rebounded.[13] Largely new immigrants, the Sea-Tac workers described to union canvassers a company town in which workers cycled endlessly through a merry-go-round of poverty-wage jobs, working on behalf of the giant airlines but employed by a slew of contract firms.

The jobs were poverty traps. Baggage handlers—rampers, like Alex Hoopes—typically made about $9.25/hour, half a dollar more than the 2011 state minimum wage but still well below the area living wage of $14.81/hour for a single adult without kids.[14] At Sea-Tac they were employed by the global firm Menzies or by Air Serv, the domestic company that was about to be gobbled up by the international outfit ABM. Crews hurried to fill the bellies of airplanes with luggage and cargo so that tight departure schedules could be met. For arrivals, Alaska Airlines guaranteed passengers they'd get their bags within twenty minutes; if the rampers missed that window they were penalized. "We used to have crews of five to seven people loading each plane," said Menzies ramper Yahye Jama. "Now it's just four rampers. That could be between one hundred and fifty and three hundred and forty bags to load, each weighing up to fifty pounds. At Menzies, you're nothing. We work outside in the rain and cold, and we get treated with disrespect."[15] Back injuries were commonplace.

Companies like Bags Inc., Air Serv, Huntleigh, and PrimeFlight hired wheelchair attendants at the state minimum of $8.67/hour, and kept employees on ever-shifting part-time schedules. The airlines didn't like to pay the contractors for idle workers, so staffing levels were kept to bare minimums and adjusted daily based on the number of passengers who called in to request wheelchairs. Supervisors would phone attendants to come to the airport, often on an hour's notice. If you refused too many of these calls, you'd be fired. Sometimes the passengers vomited on the wheelchairs when they disembarked the planes. Others soiled themselves. The workers were instructed to take the wheelchairs into airport restrooms and clean them off with paper towels. Protective gloves were in short supply.

Cabin cleaners also were paid minimum wage and worked in lean teams, often made to rush onto planes even as passengers were still getting out of their seats. Delta Global Staffing (DGS), the subsidiary of Delta Airlines, and Air Serv did most of the cabin cleaning at the airport. Workers were given cleaning chemicals that stung their eyes and skin, were directed to clean out toilets and trash chutes with gloves that ripped, and were shuttled from one plane to another in vans whose seat belts and doors didn't work. DGS had eliminated a modest sick leave plan around 2009 and the health benefit package was unaffordable, but the company still provided flight benefits to the workers—$50 to fly anywhere. When DGS cabin cleaner Tatyana Rymabruk and her coworkers needed medical care, they used the flight benefits to fly back home to their family doctors in Ukraine.

Fuelers for Swissport and ASIG—both huge multinational firms—lugged hoses around aircraft, climbing rickety, often broken ladders to connect the fuel nozzle to the underside of an aircraft's wing. It was dirty work, and at the end of the shift their uniforms frequently reeked of jet fuel. ASIG cut its laundry service to save money and required the workers to clean their own uniforms. Some of the trucks—carrying up to ten thousand gallons of Jet-A fuel—had faulty brakes, heaters, and windshield wipers. In one truck, the gear shift was held together with duct tape.

Skycaps held positions of relative prestige at the airport, because they made good money on tips while handling passenger luggage at curbside. But the contractors in charge of skycaps were stingy with allocating work hours, and they played favorites. Hosea Wilcox, a skycap for thirty-one years and a vocal union sympathizer, was reduced to the humbling experience of relying on food stamps after his hours got cut to fifteen a week.[16]

Rental car companies Hertz, Avis, and others contracted out the cleaning and servicing of rental cars to firms that paid $10/hour.

Commercial parking lots up and down Pacific Highway, just outside
the airport, paid their attendants, cashiers, and shuttle drivers close to
the minimum. Several hotels on Pacific Highway were already unionized, but some of the bigger ones, such as the Marriott and Holiday
Inn, were nonunion. They paid housekeeping, dining room, and other
staff near minimum. Most of the restaurant and retail workers inside
the airport were members of UNITE HERE, the hospitality workers' union, or the United Food & Commercial Workers International
Union. Their wages weren't great but, at $12/hour, represented an
improvement over the other low-wage airport workers. And they had
health benefits and better scheduling won through collective struggle
over the years.

Hundreds of Yellow Cab drivers worked out of Sea-Tac Airport,
typically operating their taxis twelve hours a day, six days a week. Unless they owned a cab and license—itself an expensive proposition—
they had to lease a vehicle, at a cost of hundreds of dollars a week.
Add in the cab driver's cost of insurance, gas, maintenance, and dispatch, airport, and county fees, and a typical driver began each workweek $600 in debt. It was a continual race to recoup costs and end
up the week with a net gain—no wonder the cabbies drove so fast.
They also had none of the customary worker rights. Under the law,
they were independent contractors, without workers' compensation
or unemployment benefits, denied protection against retaliation by
the cab dispatch firm, and lacking the legal right to organize a conventional union like private-sector workers.

In talking to the Sea-Tac workers and researching employment records, organizers ascertained that there were more than four thousand of these low-wage jobs in and immediately around the airport.
Sea-Tac seemed to be an optimal testing ground of FFE's ambition to
organize workers by industry: lots of workers employed in jobs that
couldn't easily be eliminated, that collectively were essential to the
operation of the airport, and that couldn't be offshored. In theory the
workers could wield tremendous power—if they united.

In the summer of 2011, I transferred from the health-care branch
of SEIU and joined the Working Washington staff, charged with the
responsibility to figure out how to develop the sort of large-scale organizing campaign that FFE called for. Joining SEIU in the Sea-Tac

venture was the Teamsters union, which had some members at rental car companies and a keen interest in an ambitious campaign.

There were obvious obstacles to traditional union organizing. First, the contract workers within Sea-Tac Airport didn't even have the legal right to petition for a union representation election. Airport workers were covered by the 1926 Railway Labor Act, a law that didn't recognize local bargaining units; unions could only be certified under the law on a nationwide basis. If Sea-Tac's Menzies ramp workers wanted to organize, they had to form a bargaining unit with Menzies workers across the country—people they would never come close to meeting. It was an absurd requirement for the twenty-first century, a throwback to when railroad workers traversed the country and only nominally had a "home base."

The second challenge was the continual turnover of workers at the contractors. More than half of Menzies' ramp workers and DGS's cabin cleaners quit every year, sometimes moving to other airport jobs or leaving the airport entirely. With employee churn like this, building workplace organizing committees that reflected the social makeup of the workforce would be a continual task. The third challenge was the precarious nature of contracted work. If workers at any single contractor organized, or even began to make demands on their employer, the parent company—the airline or rental car company—would dump the contractor and get rid of the troublesome workers. This obstacle alone would discourage most workers from answering a call for action.

It seemed to me, in talking with other SEIU and Teamsters organizers, that a traditional organizing strategy based on existing law and focused on the "on paper" contractor employment relationships was a dead end. Instead, organizers needed to step back and assess who at the airport held power and could give workers the recognition, rights, and improvements that they wanted. Any power analysis led directly to Alaska Airlines, headquartered just a mile from the airport and by far the dominant airline at Sea-Tac.

Started in the 1930s as an intrepid outfit serving small communities in the prestatehood Alaska Territory, the airline had grown over the years to national status, establishing Sea-Tac as a convenient fulcrum point connecting its main geographic service area to the Lower 48.

By 2011 Alaska Airlines accounted for 55 percent of Sea-Tac's flights, serving not just the North Star state but California, Hawaii, the Midwest, and the East Coast. Alaska held business relationships with the largest contractors at the airport, and the airline dictated how it expected contractors to serve Alaska's customers. More than any other business, Alaska shaped the Sea-Tac employment market.

Any observer would recognize that moving Alaska wouldn't be easy. It would require a straight-up power struggle between workers and the company. Given Alaska's history of union busting, that would take a focused and herculean effort on the part of unions and also allies outside the workforce.

It was equally clear that the Port of Seattle, the public entity that ran the airport, would side with Alaska. This reality held a bitter irony: the Port of Seattle was founded in response to corporate greed. By popular vote in 1911, Seattleites kicked out the companies dominating the waterfront—private railroad trusts, the Walmarts and Microsofts of their time—and replaced them with elected commissioners. One of the commissioners' first acts was to declare that since good jobs took priority over profit, all waterfront workers would be union members. But business interests never relinquished their determination to retake control. Over the years, as the Port of Seattle expanded from the waterfront to include the new airport, corporations gained a viselike control by generously funding the election campaigns of probusiness port commission candidates. By the beginning of the twenty-first century, the port routinely offered favorable lease agreements, business marketing, capital expansion subsidies, and other benefits demanded by seaport and airport businesses. Port commissioners turned a blind eye to complaints that airlines and their contractors were treating workers unfairly, claiming that as airport landlord they had no influence over private employment relations.

If Alaska Airlines was the campaign target, then workers and union organizers needed to envision the union much broader than the traditional conception of individual bargaining units at particular employers. That would be too limiting to challenge the airport's leading economic power. To take on and beat Alaska Airlines, the movement needed to be all-embracing, including all those—both inside and outside the airport—who shared a common vision of good airport jobs.

Because workers, especially immigrants and refugees, identified so closely with their own ethnic networks for advice and support, the campaign needed to build a union that respected those relationships and crossed over from the workplace into the neighborhoods. The organizing campaign would need to embrace community and faith leaders every bit as much as workers, a broad community-wide movement to lift up all jobs at the airport. It was a bold concept, just the sort of game changer that the FFE program envisioned. But in 2011 it was a completely untested theory. Would it work?

FOUR

BRIDGING THE TRUST GAP

TALL, CONFIDENT, AND OUTSPOKEN, Muse Abdallah seemed like a natural leader. An immigrant from Somalia, like many of his airport coworkers, Abdallah worked for Menzies Aviation, the baggage-handling contractor for Alaska Airlines. Every shift, Abdallah and his coworkers hefted tens of thousands of pounds of bags into the cargo holds of Alaska Airlines 737s. They were paid just above minimum wage by Menzies, a multibillion-dollar global business based in England. Around the time that the SEIU- and Teamsters-led union effort was commencing in 2011, Menzies supervisors had informed Abdallah and his coworkers that they would no longer be able to use an empty storage room for Muslim prayers, as had been their custom. Abdallah protested. He collected signatures from dozens of workers, demanding a prayer space, and presented the petition to Menzies.

One afternoon Abdallah came into my office at Working Washington, the unions' operational headquarters for the Sea-Tac effort. An Alaska Airlines manager had gotten wind of the petition and had visited him on the tarmac, Abdallah reported. The workers had gotten their prayer space restored. Collective action worked.

Gleefully, Abdallah showed his petition, with all of the signatures on it. "Can you share the list with our organizers, so we can reach out to these workers?" I asked. Abdallah kept a firm grip on the petition. No, he demurred, returning the papers to his pocket. He'd rather wait and see what happened with the union organizing. Abdallah was energized to hear talk about winning good jobs, but didn't quite trust union organizers yet.

Many workers whom the organizers sought out had experience with US unions; they knew that having a union on the job offered job protections and better pay. Still others had experienced unions only through the dues deduction line on their paychecks. But stories also circulated through the community about Somali workers who couldn't get help from the union when they needed it. In 2003 a group of fifteen Somali rental car workers had been suspended for taking a break to pray during Ramadan. They went to their leaders at Seattle's Al-Noor Islamic Center. Sheikh Abduqadir Jama called the workers' Teamsters union representative. "We had at least four or five meetings with the Teamsters," Sheikh Jama recalled to me years later. The representatives said they wanted to help, but from Jama's perspective the union staff were reluctant to take action to enforce the workers' rights. It seemed to Jama that the union representatives wanted to resolve matters by mediating between management and the workers. They didn't want a public fight. But the workers didn't need peace brokers, they needed advocates. Wasn't that what a union was supposed to be? "They were not really helpful. The union did not play the role they were supposed to play," he said.

Frustrated, the workers and Sheikh Jama went to OneAmerica, a fledgling immigrant rights group founded after 9/11. OneAmerica helped the workers file a federal discrimination complaint. The workers won their jobs back—and concluded that justice wouldn't come through the union, but via their mosque and community allies.

The East African community had other brushes with unions as well. Truck drivers at the Port of Seattle's waterfront, who included many from Africa, had an on-again, off-again relationship with the powerful longshore union. Longshore union members empathized with the drivers' poverty working conditions and precarious status as independent owner-operators, which had been the circumstances of longshore work before the West Coast strikes of the 1930s built a powerful union. But in the new century, in the truck drivers' minds, longshore workers reinforced the drivers' relegation to third-class status. At the shipping terminals, truck drivers had to endure the indignity of being forced to stay in their cabs while waiting to pick up the forty-foot containers that the longshore crane operators hoisted off the massive cargo ships. The wait could last hours, and many had to resort to peeing into empty soda bottles inside their cabs, even though there were bathrooms at the terminals, because the longshoremen zealously enforced the port's rule that drivers couldn't leave their vehicles.

By 2011 in Sea-Tac, East Africans constituted more than one-quarter of the low-wage airport workers—the single largest bloc of workers—with the majority being Muslim refugees from war-torn Somalia. So Muse Abdallah's reluctance to joining in with the union cause was a troubling sign. To be successful the budding campaign would have to overcome the mistrust that had taken root over the years between the Muslim community and unions.

During the course of 2011, the East African community and the union organizers seemed to take measure of one another, cautiously at first. Each was interested but wary about how to engage—union organizers probing for motivating issues, the workers intrigued but holding back because of history and unfamiliarity. The key turning point in the relationship was an incident that erupted without warning, an event that no one could have planned. But when it happened, it set in motion a sequence of events that, two years later, proved decisive in winning the $15 ballot initiative.

THE CHALLENGES THAT organizers had to overcome in Sea-Tac were not unique. In order to take effective action together, workers first have to recognize common interests like fair pay, respectful treatment, a voice on the job, the right to vote, the right to a safe environment. But issues are not enough. People move from inertia to action when they feel compelled to take a stand, either because they ardently believe they deserve better or because something they possess is at grave risk. Rising expectations will motivate people. They see others doing better economically and believe that they, too, deserve better. Alternatively, imminent threats, or the feeling that your back is against the wall, also can motivate. Seeing a coworker get grievously injured at work and recognizing one's own vulnerability can spur workers to act. Worker motivation gets supplemented by managers who focus on tight control of the workplace and continual cost cutting. Company executives frequently fail to appreciate the seeds of dissent they plant with their business practices, expressing shock when confronted by worker anger and organizing. But the harvest is of their own making.

This was certainly true at Sea-Tac, where airline contracting out to minimum-wage companies had become an engrained culture by 2011. Invoking "the market," as if some immutable economic law of gravity required wages to plummet, business and political elites simply wrote off poverty pay, irregular work hours, and unstable employment as inevitable by-products of modern air travel.

Union organizers newly on the scene could see how workers seethed under these arrangements. The frustration was made all the more acute by the reality surrounding them every day: the allure of the modern international airport, with its swooping modern architecture and sparkling jet airplanes; high-end duty-free boutiques; crowds of bustling, smartly dressed business travelers; and excited families trundling off to Disney, Hawaii, or some other dreamy vacation site. The workers cleaned, fueled, and loaded the planes but could not afford to fly in them.

And yet the airport organizing in 2011 wasn't gaining momentum in proportion to the frustration. Dissatisfaction, even powerful dissatisfaction, is not enough to produce action. Workers, both old and new to the workforce in the United States, recognize that the act of organizing is invariably regarded by businesses as unwanted, if not downright seditious. Management blowback is predictable and routine—harassment, threats, firings, blacklisting. Labor laws nominally protect the rights of workers to take collective action, but justice is slow and the penalties are mild to nonexistent. For management, breaking a labor law carries a risk akin to driving over the speed limit: You probably won't get caught, and if you do, the fine is a mere nuisance. Pay the ticket and keep driving. And workers know that the law won't save them. Even in soul-crushing circumstances with spiteful employers, people won't take risks if they don't trust their coworkers and allies to accompany them in navigating the hazards of standing up to the boss.

That was the overall state of play at the airport in the summer of 2011. Among the organizers recently hired by the union were young activists from the Somali community, emerging leaders who had been discovered by SEIU during a massive spring canvass of low-income neighborhoods, before I became the airport campaign director. The hirings were a shrewd decision by my union colleagues, an acknowledgment that trust needed to be built. Steeped in the community's culture, the new organizers served as an important bridge between the union and community. In addition to educating the community about the airport campaign, the African organizers also taught other union staff and members about the dos and don'ts of engaging a community that had its own culture when it came to the roles of men and women, the importance of daily prayer, and community leadership structure. Non-African organizers quickly got educated about scheduling meetings to steer clear of daily prayer times. We heard harrowing stories of narrow escapes from war, and tasted the unique flavors of goat and camel meat in community restaurants.

One of the early union hires was Abdinasir Mohamed, the African immigrant who had landed in Harlem in 2008 and had immediately been confronted with the jarring reality of poverty in America. A relative newcomer to Seattle, Mohamed brought his own deep history of human rights organizing. The Somali-born Mohamed grew up in a politically active family in Kenya—his cousin had served in the cabinet of a reform Kenyan government. Mohamed had traveled throughout Africa for Oxfam, campaigning against the child-soldier practices of Ugandan rebels. In 1997 he moved to South Africa and joined up with the African National Congress Youth League, where he found himself advocating for mine workers and lobbying for civil rights throughout the region. The twenty-seven years that Nelson Mandela spent in jail left a deep impression on Mohamed: "He could have just gone into exile like some other leaders and taken care of his own life, but he chose the hard way." For his part, Mohamed spent two months in jail in neighboring Zimbabwe after joining a protest there opposing President Robert Mugabe's crackdown against the media and political rivals. "There was general starvation in Zimbabwe in the streets then, so you can guess when you're in detention, it's much worse. I lost a lot of weight—that was the good part of it!" he recalled.

After two years in New York City, Mohamed arrived in Seattle in 2010, where Bank of America snapped him up to be a teller at the bank's New Holly branch in the heart of Seattle's East African community. In addition to Somali and English, Mohamed also spoke Zulu, Swahili, and Oromo. These were huge assets for a bank trying to make inroads into the New Holly community of southeast Seattle. For Mohamed's multilingual talents, Bank of America paid him $12.90/hour, below the area poverty rate. There were health benefits, too, but they were minimal and too pricey to buy. The bank wouldn't pay for a root canal when Mohamed needed one, forcing him to get a cheaper but more painful tooth extraction instead.

One afternoon Mohamed finished his shift and walked out of the bank into a boisterous protest outside led by Working Washington, the SEIU offshoot. The protest was a follow-up to the neighborhood canvass, one of many public actions that Working Washington was staging in order to draw attention to corporate greed and income inequality. It looked familiar to the ANC veteran, and certainly less risky than confronting the Zimbabwean military. He joined in.

Within weeks, Working Washington hired Mohamed and assigned him to door knock in the neighborhood, a precursor effort to the airport campaign. Working Washington was trying to get people to come out to rallies and public activities in the fight against income inequality, but the message wasn't clicking with immigrant communities. "It was difficult," Mohamed recalled. Many of the people they sought out in the neighborhood had spent years in refugee camps before gaining admission to the United States. "They see themselves as the beneficiaries of the US government. To them, there was no clear line between a corporation and the government. And so for them, going into the street and rallying, they thought that was kind of a betrayal. 'How can I do that against the government?' So doing anything against anyone in the US, to them, was like backstabbing the only country that saved them from a refugee camp or war-torn country."

That was a perspective shared by Mohamed Sheikh Hassan, the director of Masjid al-Karim, more commonly known as the Orcas Mosque because of its location on Seattle's Orcas Street. Hassan was one of the first community leaders that Abdinasir Mohamed and other East African organizers reached out to after they were hired by Working Washington. Hassan noted that for new East African immigrants and refugees coming into the area, "where they come from, nobody ever gave them a chance to express their feelings and their needs and desires. These countries where they come from, the government is telling you what you can do, what you cannot do. There is a saying in our country, 'If you want to live long, stay out of the government's business.'"

Like Working Washington's Mohamed, Hassan had moved past caution and into a life of activism as a result of challenges to state authority. Hassan was in Seattle in September 2001, when the public backlash against immigrants surged after 9/11. Government agents raided Seattle's East African money transfer businesses—vital pipelines for the community's families back at home. And government agents also went after the community's grocery stores, seizing merchandise and cutting them off from the food stamp program, effectively destroying the businesses. The entire community felt cowed, unfairly branded with the terrorist label, and helpless.

Hassan met with other community leaders, several of whom were advocating moving out of the United States. "That's an idea that comes from our culture," he said. "We are a nomadic people. When there's trouble here, we move out of that place, go to a different place. We cross borders."

But Hassan argued to stay. "I said, 'Listen, this is America. No matter where we go, the rules and police are going to be there. But we can stand up collectively and assert ourselves. We are not terrorists to begin with. There are good American people who are progressive and who are going to listen to us.'" Hassan and others met up with a young Indian activist, Pramila Jayapal, who had organized a new human rights group in the wake of 9/11 to defend immigrant communities. Jayapal pledged the support of her new group, Hate Free Zone (it later changed its name to OneAmerica). She assembled civil rights lawyers and activists to organize protests at the raided stores, drawing support from Seattle progressives outside the African community. At the "shop ins," allies from outside the African community came to the stores to buy products and show their support for the owners and regular store patrons.

Hassan recalled being shocked when he showed up at a protest in the spring of 2002 at one of the "shop-in" protests at Seattle's Towfiq Hallal Meat & Deli. As groups of unmistakably non-Africans pored with curiosity over bags of rice, boxes of dates, bananas, and halva, and freezers full of goat and lamb meat, Hassan spotted elected officials, including US congressman Jim McDermott, standing there in solidarity with the African community. "I thought, 'Oh my god, they are going to lose their jobs, they will end up in jail, they will be killed.' Because that's what we knew back in Somalia."

Nobody went to jail that day. Instead, they garnered widespread TV and newspaper coverage. The store won back its food stamp eligibility. Gradually the pressure on the community eased. And Jayapal's words were burnished into Hassan's mind: "Mohamed, you are not alone. We are here with you."

But a decade later, in 2011, the ANC veteran organizer Mohamed and the mosque leader Hassan were struggling to get their community activated. It was hard, even as the Occupy movement burst onto the scene in mid-September, 2011, spreading from New York City's Zuccotti Park to hundreds of cities, including Seattle. The break they got came not from allies or the excitement of Occupy, but from a hostile employer.

On September 30, as activists were preparing to launch Occupy Seattle in downtown Westlake Park, a standoff took place fifteen miles to the south at the Sea-Tac Airport rental car facility. It was a Friday, the most important day of the Muslim week. The day-shift Somali shuttle drivers for Hertz took their customary morning break to pray, something they had done for years. Praying five times a day is obligatory; it's one of the five pillars of Islam. Ritual prayers last but a few minutes, hardly causing a blip in business operations. Hertz management had always accommodated the workers, treating prayer breaks the same as intermittent breaks for workers who smoked: just take it and then come back to work. But on this Friday a manager told the workers to clock out before praying, something they had never had to do before.

Hertz shuttle driver Zainab Aweis recalled her manager, standing with arms extended to block workers trying to get into the prayer room, declaring, "If you guys pray, you go home."

"I said, 'Is that a new rule?' And he said, 'Yes.' I like the job," Aweis said. "But if I can't pray, I don't see the benefit."[1]

For Aweis it was an easy choice: she sidestepped the manager and went to pray, because while money mattered, faith was a fundamental part of her life. As Aweis and her coworkers prayed, Hertz managers "were laughing and clapping their hands, mocking us," said Maryan Muse. On top of the humiliation, Aweis, Muse, and their Muslim coworkers were immediately suspended. All through that weekend, like clockwork, Hertz managers warned and then suspended Muslim workers at each successive prayer time, until by Monday the suspensions stood at thirty-four.

Although the Hertz workers were members of the Teamsters union, it would have been understandable if union leaders took a pass on the fight. After all, they were operating in a post-9/11 environment, cognizant that the vast majority of their union members, not being Muslim, were likely to be quite unsympathetic.

Teamsters union representative Cetris Tucker recalled getting several phone calls that Friday morning from Hertz workers. A former fifteen-year Hertz employee herself, Tucker knew the company and its general disregard for workers' rights. She also knew that this issue had been discussed and resolved in contract negotiations in favor of the workers being allowed to break for prayers without clocking out, just as they took other minibreaks. Tucker left the union office and drove down to the airport rental car facility where she met with shop steward Ileys Omar, along with the group's elder, Hassan Farah. Tucker suggested that the workers could fight back by following the manager's direction under protest and then filing grievances. We can't do that, Farah countered. "Praying for us is not an option, it's an obligation." If the workers conceded to treat prayers differently from other minibreaks, even temporarily, then "we will never get this back," he said. Tucker had come down to the airport assuming she would advocate the union's "work-but-grieve" approach, but Farah had convinced her that it was time to make a stand.

Tucker went back to her union hall and conferred with Teamsters leadership. Everyone recognized that taking on this issue would mean inviting the inevitable blowback from union members and others outside the union who wouldn't understand or sympathize with the Muslim workers. But Tucker recalled that her local union leader, Tracey Thompson, was unequivocal: "This is bullshit. We're not going to stand for this. We're going to take them on. We're going to do everything we can."

The Teamsters announced they would pursue all legal avenues—the union contract grievance procedure, federal unfair labor practice charges, and an antidiscrimination lawsuit—to get the workers back to work. And, notably, the union announced it would mobilize with the community.

A week after the mass suspensions began, more than fifty protesters marched into the Sea-Tac Airport parking garage to the Hertz rental counter with news media in tow. Muslim, Christian, and Jewish leaders, along with union and community activists, prayed for justice at the counter while holding signs that read Respect Me, Respect My Religion, and Hertz Hurts My Faith.

"We had the imams there, the community members, and the unions—people from the Teamsters and other local unions," recounted Mohamed, the Working Washington organizer. "And when they saw that, helping them to have their faith be recognized, that was the first step in getting a united community."

As TV cameras zeroed in on the faith-led protesters, Thompson noted that Hertz workers were typically allowed to take short breaks—for smoking, to get coffee, or to use the bathroom. In this case, however, "they singled out this group of workers when they are engaging in prayer," she said. That made it illegal discrimination. But the violation went further, she said. If Hertz wanted to change its break policy, it had an obligation to negotiate with the union. The company's unilateral action was an affront to all union workers, Thompson declared. Matters of faith and union were joined.

For many East Africans, seeing the multifaith and union support at Hertz, and then hearing about the union's commitment to fight the suspensions, was transformational. To Mohamed Sheikh Hassan it recalled the scene outside the Towfiq market nine years earlier. Seeing a broad community at the Hertz counter that included non-Muslims showed the Africans that "you are not alone"; it gave the Muslim workers a feeling of solidarity and power, the confidence that "you can make a change, that you can stand up, that everything's possible collectively," he said.

Abdinasir Mohamed and the other Working Washington organizers weren't about to let the organizing stop with the rally. They knew that the thirty-four suspended workers prayed at a number of different mosques in the area when they weren't at work. The largest mosque, Abu Bakr Islamic Center, is just north of the airport. A dozen other mosques dot the region around the airport and in Seattle, including Al-Noor in southeast Seattle; Mohamed Sheikh Hassan's Orcas Mosque; the mosque for Oromo speakers; one for Ethiopians; the Gambian Mosque; and a mosque simply known as the Taxi Mosque because it was convenient for downtown cab drivers. The organizers assigned workers to reach out to each of the mosques, to spread the word of what happened at Hertz—and also to tell the story of the community and union support the workers enjoyed. "We sent the workers to their own mosques, and told them, 'Go and share your problem, your issues with your imam,'" Mohamed recalled. Word quickly spread within Seattle's Muslim community.

While the workers were organizing within their own community, Mohamed Sheikh Hassan reached outside. Three days after the rally at Hertz, he went down to Seattle's Westlake Park and told hundreds of Occupy protesters—a decidedly non-Muslim crowd—about what Hertz had done. Emboldened by the community show of support at Hertz, Hassan now flipped the Occupy script: Yes, people should support Occupy by coming down to the park. But the Occupiers also needed to join the airport workers' fight. "We are the 99ers, and together we can fight back."

SHEIKH ABDUQADIR JAMA, the leader at Seattle's Al-Noor Mosque and director of an Islamic school in West Seattle, hadn't been at the Hertz protest. He'd heard about it, but still remembered the 2003 experience with the Teamsters. So when Ahmed Ali, an organizing colleague of Abdinasir Mohamed's at Working Washington, visited Sheikh Jama's school and asked him to get involved, he was hesitant. "I told him I was a little skeptical," Sheikh Jama recalled to me later. "We had a bad experience in 2003. I said, 'Please don't waste my time with the union.'"

Ali empathized. He had his own experience to share with Sheikh Jama. When he first arrived in the United States, having escaped the Somali civil war and endured years in refugee camps and other temporary housing in Kenya, Ali went to work butchering chickens at the huge Tyson Foods plant in Noel, Missouri. The chickens moved down the line quickly, and Ali and his coworkers had two or three seconds to peel the skin off each slippery carcass, again and again, hour after hour, eight hours a day. His fingers grew raw and infected. All of his fingernails fell out. Management wouldn't release workers for bathroom breaks. The pay was miserable, the work mind-numbing. This was the American dream? "There were times I just wanted to cry," Ali recalled. He and other Somali workers knew there was a union contract. They tried to find the union representative, but didn't know where to go. Nobody seemed to have the union's contact information. The lone shop steward was a seventy-year-old white woman who didn't understand them. "The union never appeared on our issues—never. The only thing we saw was the paycheck deduction for dues," Ali recalled.

But now, sitting in the school office in Seattle, Ali told Sheikh Jama, this was different. The union that he saw, and was now a part of, seemed genuinely interested in working with the community.

Ali persuaded Sheikh Jama to attend a follow-up meeting of two dozen imams and other community leaders. We met at the New Holly community center, in the heart of the East African community—union organizers, imams, community leaders, and airport workers and port truck drivers, whose concerns went beyond religious freedom to low wages, intolerable work hours, and mistreatment. The abysmal working conditions were not news to the imams—they heard these stories every day in the mosque—but what Sheikh Jama said was new was that union representatives were asking the community leaders to help out.

The imams agreed to open the mosques up to a series of discussions about working conditions at the airport and seaport. Mosques typically hold "family nights" every month or so, social gatherings after Friday or Saturday prayers to hear from outside speakers or to conduct a community discussion. In these discussions, they reasoned, workers and other community members could hear about the organizing effort and bring their workplace concerns directly to the union organizers. The first mosque to volunteer to host a family night discussion was the one attended by Sheikh Jama. Working Washington organizer Ahmed Ali led the discussion at Al-Noor and recruited several airport workers to the union.

Next up was family night at Abu Bakr Islamic Center. More than one hundred people attended. After a welcome from a mosque leader, an elderly man with a slight build and thick glasses stood up and took the microphone. Samatar Abdullahi was a familiar face at the mosque, having settled in the Seattle area in 1999 with his children and grand-children. Although seventy-six years old, he had no prospect of retir-ing and worked as a cabin cleaner for Delta Global Services (DGS). He labored on Alaska Airlines 737s, wiping down the seats, pulling out the gum and other garbage that passengers left behind in the seatback pockets, cleaning out vomit and feces from the overflowing lavatories, checking for the fake weapons that federal security officers would hide in order to test the workers, and doing his best to make sure the cabin looked spic-and-span for the next flight. Back home, Abdul-lahi had been in the Somali military, rising to the rank of colonel. He was an important man there, sought out for his strategic thinking, respected for his education and multilingual fluency. He commanded an army battalion. But here, he was an elderly man cleaning toilets and being treated rudely by supervisors half his age.

"For nearly nine years, I have worked for the contractor DGS," he told the Abu Bakr crowd. "In three of those years, I was given commendations for exceptional service." But then his daughter had a difficult birth. The doctor told Abdullahi: Your daughter needs you bedside and your grandchild is in intensive care. The newborn likely had a stroke. The doctor gave Abdullahi a note so he could claim fam-ily leave. He brought the note to his supervisor. "She told me, 'You are lying, I don't believe you,'" and denied his leave request.

He didn't give up. While DGS had recently stopped giving work-ers any paid vacation time, Abdullahi, a senior employee, still had a few hours accrued on the books. "I went back to her and asked her, 'Could you please just give me the six vacation hours that I have to attend the hospital today to help my daughter?' And she told me, 'You don't deserve anything. I will cancel from you even these six hours.'"

Besides the sheer cruelty and humiliation was the poverty pay. "When I started working at DGS I was paid $8.25 an hour. After nearly nine years I'm only making $9.89 an hour, and DGS has now reduced my hours. So I make less money than when I started."

As Abdullahi sat down, a baggage handler stood up to speak; then a taxi operator; then others in turn. Many had been reluctant to talk with organizers at the airport, but here they were at their mosque—in their community—speaking out about the abject airport working conditions, gaining confidence as they found their voices, and beginning to ask organizers how they could get involved.

The mosque meetings provided the opening that the campaign needed. As more mosque meetings progressed over the weeks, the organizing became a central discussion point in the East African community. Imams frequently included airport organizing updates in the weekly Friday mosque announcements. And workers warmed up to organizers at the airport, saying, "I heard you were at the mosque," or, "The imam told us about the union."

IN LATE APRIL 2012 more than eight hundred airport workers, family members, and community supporters assembled on a sunny Saturday to celebrate the coming-out rally of the airport workers' campaign. Sikh taxi drivers marched with Somali cabin cleaners, Ethiopian wheelchair attendants, Mexican and white fuelers, and African American skycaps, all carrying signs with a simple message: Make Every Airport Job a Good Job. Immigrant rights groups, ministers, and other unions turned out. An imam gave the rally invocation. Elected officials joined in, including Congressman Adam Smith, who recalled his father's airport career. "My father made more money, and got more benefits being a ramp serviceman in 1985 than the workers at Sea-Tac Airport do right now. And that is the problem," he said.

Waving flags from their native countries and stepping to the beat of drums, the ralliers marched a mile down SeaTac's main boulevard to a park immediately adjacent to the corporate headquarters of Alaska Airlines. This was a buoyant, celebratory march with colorful banners and chants in multiple languages.

And perhaps more significant than the visible sight of a parade of workers, the organizing now had the intangible, missing element it had so badly needed. Unions had begun to build trust with the Muslim community; a trust that seemed so elusive just a few months before and had gained traction only when union leaders reached beyond comfort zones, and community leaders cast aside their doubts and memories of past disappointment with organized labor.

In hindsight, union leaders could have chosen a more pragmatic decision in responding to the Hertz suspensions: file a grievance and pursue a legal path. That would have fulfilled their duty to represent members but not call attention to a fight that would be controversial within the union membership, let alone the general public.

Indeed, the backlash against the Teamsters was as sharp as it was unsurprising. The Hertz story went national with wire service and TV coverage. Messages critical of the union poured in from around the country, many spewing hatred toward the Muslim members. Thompson and her staff had to meet with non-Muslim union members to explain why a Muslim issue was also a union issue. Most of them understood, Teamsters representative Tucker said, but it took a lot of educating.

Instead of weighing the practical pros and cons of waging a public fight, the union leaders had acted on instinct: A principle had been violated, and a strong response was called for. Even if there were negative consequences, it was a just cause.

By inviting leaders of different faiths to rally at the Hertz counter, the Teamsters aligned the issue of religious freedom with the secular union principles of antidiscrimination and due process, elevating the matter from a workplace concern to a community-wide issue of morality, rights, and freedom. The union stepped out of its special-interest role—representing its dues-paying members—and into a role embracing broader values.

Community leaders were forced to stretch as well. They came to see the workers' right to pray at Hertz not as a stand-alone issue for their constituents, but as part of a bigger set of demands for dramatic change at Sea-Tac. Joining up with the union meant folding into a public fight against the region's major economic powers. For an immigrant community that preferred to stay away from the public limelight, particularly after 9/11, this would require stepping outside of comfort zones.

Even after the Hertz protest, Working Washington organizer Ali recalled, trust was beginning to take shape but "it wasn't an easy thing to keep. There was a hesitance on the part of community leaders.

Unions were viewed more as organizations looking out for their self-interests." The director of Abu Bakr Islamic Center, while welcoming the union to family night, was wary about being too closely linked to the union. After all, SEIU and other unions supported things like gay marriage, something not approved of in the Muslim community. Ali responded that this wasn't about blending in with another organization, but rather recognizing and acting upon the common cause shared by two distinct groups. As the single largest group of low-wage workers at the airport, East Africans had a duty to lead, he asserted. And, he told the director, this wasn't just about the right to pray: "This is about all workers' freedom."

Another abiding lesson was that trust was not something you simply conjure up or will into being because working conditions are so oppressive. Trusting relationships get built in motion, over time. You have to get people to commit to work collectively on mutual interests, taking risks together and learning step-by-step. It needn't be as dramatic as a televised interfaith confrontation against management. It can be a coffee klatch in a workers' apartment, a private delegation to political leaders, a meeting with allies, a press conference, a worker petition to management. As people toil together they learn one another's habits, communication styles, aspirations, and interests. They overcome past suspicion. They come to realize that no matter how significant their cultural, social, or educational differences might be, they are more tightly bonded by the hopes and dreams they hold in common for themselves, their families, and their community.

Trust solidifies into unity. Worker unity projected into collective action—demonstrations, pickets, media events, outreach activities, strikes—yields power. And sustained over time through repeated actions, that power is what achieves progress for workers and their communities.

Even once obtained, however, trust is not static; it is a fragile thing. Trust needs to be nurtured and sustained through continued activities that underscore the necessity for workers to stand together, or else past doubts begin to seep back in. Trust is always vulnerable to being undermined by hostile management action that aims to divide workers or by narrow, short-sighted thinking by movement leaders. The fault lines within the working class are many—gender, education level, race, language, age, ethnicity, sexual orientation and identity, citizenship status—and employers over the years have skillfully exploited divisions among workers to break insurgent organizing. Over time the most potent employer tool has been manipulating race and ethnic differences—a product of the nation's legacy of slavery and history of exploiting each new wave of arriving immigrants. Mine operators imported black strikebreakers as far back as the nineteenth century. One hundred years ago, East Coast textile owners set one group of European immigrants against another, and more recently the big agricultural employers sought to pit Cesar Chavez's farmworkers union of Mexican workers against white Teamsters. The nineteenth-century railroad magnate Jay Gould reportedly once boasted, "I can hire one half of the working class to kill the other half."[2] Gould's contemporaries have honed the skill of capitalizing on the suspicions and cracks that develop between different groups of workers, successfully stalling organizing campaigns even when wages and working conditions are abysmal.

Indeed, Sea-Tac in 2011 was poised to be another chapter in the history of failed organizing campaigns. For years, the major actors had been playing their familiar and customary roles: the East African community was defending its interests in the manner it knew, without connecting them to broader working-class issues, and the labor movement was making pragmatic choices, avoiding big risks that would incite divisions in the ranks. Those approaches yielded unsatisfactory results for everyone. It was only when the actors decided to take risks and go outside their accustomed scripts that things began to move forward.

It took more than a year for the Teamsters to reach a resolution with Hertz over prayer rights. In the meantime, many workers moved on to other jobs; others returned to work, their rights belatedly restored. But more important, Zainab Aweis, Maryan Muse, and the other Hertz workers had given us all a gift with their courageous stand: their suspensions had obliged the people in their community and their union to reach across the broad cultural divide and join hands. And on that embryonic foundation of trust, a powerful movement began to take shape.

FIVE

A MORAL MOVEMENT

TO THE SEA-TAC TRAVELERS lined up at the skycap stands, it must have been a remarkable sight. A diminutive and quite obviously pregnant woman, barely five feet tall and dressed in black with a white clerical collar, was absorbed in conversation with a burly police officer and a Port of Seattle manager. It was early on the morning of September 11, 2012, rush hour for travelers disembarking from taxis and friends' cars for the curbside check-in counters at Sea-Tac. What they saw as they stood in line was not an exchange of sidewalk small talk, but an earnest discussion about whether the Reverend Lauren Cannon was prepared to go to jail that morning.

Cannon had been handing out flyers to travelers about poverty-wage jobs at the airport, acting in direct violation of the port's rules, which barred leafleting on the sidewalk outside the terminal. The Port of Seattle, a municipal government, had established rules to maintain order; she was in obvious breach. Was she going to follow the law?

She was not.

"I understood this was part of my constitutional right to offer basic information," Cannon told Sergeant Mark Tanga and the airport duty manager, Ruth Shumeye. Her voice was pleasant but resolute.

"You don't have permission to be out here," Shumeye responded.

Cannon held her ground. "So if we continue to give information, what would happen?"

Shumeye didn't reply. Instead, she and Sergeant Tanga turned and retreated to consult with other port officials, warily eyeing the proceedings from behind the glass terminal doors. And as skycaps and other baggage handlers looked on with delight, Reverend Cannon resumed her outreach to passengers, welcoming them to Sea-Tac Airport with her information about poverty jobs. The port's rules were trumped, at least for that morning.

The standoff between Cannon and the port authorities was a small taste of the brewing conflict between the Port of Seattle, which operates the airport, and union organizers working with the airport's low-wage baggage and cargo handlers, cabin cleaners, fuelers, rental car and food and retail workers, and wheelchair attendants.

For months union staff had been circulating through the airport, huddling with workers at all hours to discuss organizing plans, circulate petitions, and plot out actions. Our breakthrough in relations with the Muslim community meant that East African workers were now getting involved in the organizing. Other workers, sensing momentum, also began to engage as 2012 progressed. Under the watchful eye of port and airline authorities, workers were beginning to meet in larger numbers at baggage claim carousels, in the smoking area, at terminal coffee shops, and by the security doors they used to go to work. And they were beginning to take visible action, too, showing up at airline offices with community supporters to demand fair pay, and handbilling travelers with startling information about filthy and unsafe working conditions. For the airlines, trouble was brewing as 2012 progressed.

If there was a single image that embodied the growing worker courage, it was the face of Hosea Wilcox. A skycap, Wilcox had been involved in organizing for most of the thirty-one years he worked the airport curb, employed by a series of minimum-wage airline contractors. Over the years Wilcox had been featured on TV segments about low airport wages, and he was a familiar face to business travelers. Beginning in the spring of 2012, Wilcox had starred in airport digital ads that Working Washington had purchased, taking advantage of the port's lenient ad content policies. Every day tens of thousands of travelers awaiting their luggage at each of the airport's sixteen baggage claim carousels could look up and see the visage of Wilcox and his call for better pay. Doubtless airline and port executives regarded the ads as subversive intrusions into their domain.

When Delta decided to change skycap contractors, the new firm declined to hire Wilcox and two other union activists. In response, a group of thirty-five workers and allies took over the Delta Airlines ticket counter one morning, refusing to leave until a manager reconsidered hiring Wilcox and the others. A week after the Delta sit-in, activists dressed up fifty large suitcases with oversized signs denouncing Delta Airlines, rented wheeled luggage carts, and paraded the suitcases through the terminal at a leisurely pace.

Port officials looked on askance. Traditional picketing and sign carrying were strictly forbidden within the terminal, but in this case protesters were doing what thousands of air passengers did every day at Sea-Tac: rent luggage carts and haul them through the airport. Delta managers complained bitterly to port officials as the single-file picket line of carts cruised slowly past their waiting passengers.

It was my job, as the campaign director, to field the increasingly insistent demands from port representatives that organizers stop breaking their rules. Under established court precedent, bolstered by the specter of 9/11, US airports have wide latitude to restrict the time, place, and manner of First Amendment activities. As organizing activity ramped up, port officials clamped down. Their attorneys sent us threatening letters: We weren't supposed to gather large numbers of people, except in designated places. We weren't allowed to handbill the public without the port's permission. We weren't allowed to picket anywhere on the airport property. And we certainly weren't allowed to occupy ticket counters and disrupt business. Though the port was a public agency with elected commissioners nominally accountable to the greater community, its leaders were frank in telling us that their main customers—the primary constituency they cared about—were the airlines and major airport concession companies. These business customers were unhappy with the organizing activity and were pressing the port, as the landlord, to take action.

Following the Delta ticket counter sit-in, an annoyed port CEO, Tay Yoshitani, e-mailed Port of Seattle commissioners: "I'm afraid this will all happen once again. But know that Delta is upset with the port for not being more aggressive in enforcement of existing rules.

We can't allow our customers/passengers to be subjected to aggressive demonstrations. Wish I had better news for you."[1] Yoshitani directed his legal team to develop a counterattack.

We had a different view about what legal restrictions could be imposed on our organizing activities, and knew that we'd only secure our rights if we asserted them. We also knew that eventually things would reach a crisis with the port.

In late July workers and their allies staged another action inside the airport. Cabin cleaners, fed up with abuse from supervisors, broken equipment, and constant demands to hurry up, confronted Alaska Airlines management and demanded that the airline crack down on its contractor. A vacuum cleaner had caught on fire; workers were ordered to keep using it. The vans used to shuttle workers between planes lacked seat belts and working doors. The contractor ran out of gloves and told workers to make do without. Managers yelled at the cleaners to hurry up. So one morning workers surrounded the Alaska station manager in the middle of the terminal and downloaded their frustration as travelers navigated their way around the crowd. Port officials looked on, visibly disgruntled.

A month later, on the eve of Labor Day weekend, the port struck back, announcing it was instituting new rules limiting organizing activities. The new rules required the port's advance permission for leafleting and for gathering groups, barred delegations to airlines and other businesses, required that organizations submit to the port the names, addresses, and phone numbers of all participants in group activities, and imposed new penalties for violators that included banishment from the airport. As for sorting out the innocent from the guilty, port staff would serve as police, prosecutor, judge, and jury. Port officials knew they held the upper hand in a legal fight. We might kick up a political protest but couldn't expect the general public to rally to the defense of organizing rights within the airport. We could challenge the new rules in court, but we'd be stuck there for a long time, with uncertain results. In the meantime the airport organizing, which relied upon meeting with workers at the airport, would wither.

To overcome the new restrictions, we had to take the fight beyond the political and legal terrain. We had to turn the right to organize at the airport into a moral question.

REVEREND CANNON WAS well suited to play a leading role in this unfolding drama. When port officials confronted her on the morning of
September 11, they may have believed that, armed with their new arsenal of restrictions, a few pointed words would back her down. They
had no basis to know that they were confronting an activist whose
commitment to justice work had been cultivated in terrain much
harsher than the curbside of an international airport. Years prior,
after the first US-Iraq war, Cannon had joined peace delegations to
Basra, Iraq, openly flouting the federal embargo and prison threats.
She studied civil disobedience with Jesuit activist Phil Berrigan and
had spent thirty days in a Massachusetts maximum-security state
prison after blockading a Raytheon cruise missile manufacturing site.
Living among hungry Iraqi children and then carrying pictures of
the kids into the cruise missile plant were transformative experiences
for the young activist. "We are sourced in a liberating god," she realized. "A god who has a preferential eye for those who are struggling.
This is not just talk—for many of us, taking serious risks ourselves is
part of trying to follow in the way of Jesus." Cannon's path through
Basra, Raytheon, and prison led her to seminary school in Chicago,
and eventually to the pulpit of Keystone United Church of Christ in
Seattle, where she encouraged congregation members to engage in
acts of social liberation.

Earlier in 2012 Cannon had been approached by organizers from
Puget Sound Sage, a community group that had joined with the
unions and Working Washington on the airport campaign. The Sage
organizers were building a coalition of faith leaders and activists to
support the organizing, and wanted her to meet some of the workers.
Keystone's members didn't work at the airport—they were a smattering of professionals, academics, and retirees. But social justice had
been a long-time mission of the church. Cannon readily agreed to
meet with airport workers, and in the ensuing months came to see
their struggles as a core part of her ministry.

What Cannon understood—more than the port officials did that
September morning—was the power of the moral voice in overcoming legal threats. "All the rules and regulations that the airport

authorities were trying to hang things on couldn't hold a candle to the spirit of truth," she recounted later. "My history of nonviolence comes into step in these moments. There was a true spirit as we engaged with the airport travelers, where you just know that you're speaking from and representing a truth that needs to get out."

Reverend Cannon kept handing out leaflets that morning, openly defying the port authorities because to her there was a higher law. And, being an experienced activist, she also knew that the port leadership was smart enough to avoid the public relations mess of handcuffing a gentle, diminutive minister who was in her third trimester of pregnancy.

THE CAMPAIGN LEADERSHIP recognized that it would be difficult to tackle head-on the airport's political and economic powers. Alaska Airlines was a multibillion-dollar company with a sparkling public reputation for reliable service, good customer relations, and the down-home feeling of a local company. Port leadership felt largely immune from popular pressure. True, they were elected by King County voters, but in elections that saw the major shipping lines, retail companies, and airlines contribute hundreds of thousands of dollars to hand select their chosen representatives. Nominally a democratic institution, the port commission was a government captive to corporate interests.

To win the economic and political fight, we had to alter the terrain of the struggle. We also recognized that many workers, even those who don't explicitly identify as religious, would be emboldened to overcome their own fears and get involved as they saw and heard from respected members of faith communities. For workers, the presence of faith leadership shifted the fight from workplace issues—demands for higher pay or benefits, more work hours, and so on—to a struggle based on values: a morally based call for human dignity at the airport.

Too often union organizing campaigns focus exclusively on the economic and political dimensions of the fight, bringing in faith leaders to play accessory roles only once things are well under way. The term that organizers casually use is "rent-a-collar." Religious leaders are asked to help campaigns, often with little notice and when the campaign trajectory is already established; perhaps in a crisis.

Virtually everyone involved in these tactics—from the organizers to the recruited faith leaders—recognizes tacitly the limited nature of the relationship. Everyone plays their roles. The campaign needs a validating faith voice, but is not seeking strategic guidance from these outsiders. Faith leaders are asked to stand up and justify on moral terms an economic struggle that they did not initiate or plan. The cameras roll, the ministers recite their lines ably, and afterward the organizers thank them. The campaign moves on, and the corporate target can brush off the transitory discomfort.

It's quite different to ask faith leaders to help at the beginning to build a morally grounded campaign. A movement that is defined around values and principles is more apt to weather the ups and downs of organizing. Opponents can take the air out of an issues-based campaign by co-opting the issue or meeting demands halfway. Unilateral pay raises, replacing an unpopular supervisor, improving staffing levels temporarily—these sorts of accommodations defuse protest energy and ensure that the company retains a firm grip on power. In a morally grounded campaign, what develops is still a fight that—outwardly—is about workplace or community issues. But a morally grounded campaign is more durable in confronting economic and political power because it derives from values, which can't be co-opted.

On their own, most union organizers lack the credibility to lead a fight based on values. Workers see unions as issue-based organizations. They see organizers as the experts who can propose and implement strategies to achieve concrete goals: a wage increase, safety and job protections, and so on. Values go deeper. A partnership with faith leaders, initiated at the beginning of a campaign, is essential to build an authentic values foundation.

The first opportunity to test this approach came four months before Reverend Cannon's sidewalk standoff, inside the May 15, 2012, shareholders meeting of Alaska Airlines. A delegation of thirty-seven Christian and Muslim leaders, workers, organizers, community allies, and a local elected official had gained admission to the auditorium. We were a combination of allies who had purchased single shares of stock or who held proxies authorized to represent other shareholders, like union pension funds. We filed into the auditorium and dispersed through the crowd of two hundred other shareholders, executives, and members of Alaska's board of directors. Our aim was to force the company to meet directly with community leaders and workers.

This shareholders gathering was to be a coronation, a handing off of the CEO baton from Bill Ayer to longtime Alaska executive Brad Tilden. It also would celebrate yet another year of record profits. A northwest native, Tilden had grown up three miles from Sea-Tac Airport, earned business degrees at local universities, and risen through the ranks at Alaska over the course of two decades. Genial and unassuming, he was an exemplary choice to lead the Sea-Tac-based airline in its next stage of expansion and battle against larger multinational carriers.

Now, barely fifty years old and standing on the stage at Seattle's Museum of Flight, Tilden graciously accepted a handshake from Ayer and told the shareholders that one of Ayer's enduring lessons to him was always to try to "do the right thing." Tilden then deftly moved the gathered shareholders and board members through an impressive PowerPoint presentation of the company's profits and expansion plans. The shareholders applauded. Tilden opened the floor for questions. He was aware of the presence of several airport workers and their allies, but probably didn't foresee what was about to unfold. And, truthfully, neither did we.

First up at the mic was the Reverend Josh Liljenstople, a retired minister: "You mentioned that, Mr. Ayer, you can count on him to always do the right thing," Liljenstople said. His tone was inquiring and civil. "My question is, was it right to create this situation with critical employees, turning them over to subcontractors who are not paying an adequate wage, in view of the fact that the disparity of income in our country is tearing our society apart?"[2]

Standing alone on the stage, Tilden deflected from the critique of Alaska in an effort to find common ground on the bigger economic picture. "One of the things our country needs more than anything right now is good-paying jobs," he began. "I totally agree there is more disparity to many income levels, and that's what America needs to get our country moving again, so I totally agree with that.

"We think that if we run a good business we will be able to be a good employer and we will grow good jobs and grow good high-quality jobs, and that will help get our economy moving, it will help get people employed in these jobs. So that is our view of the best way to approach this, but I do respect that other folks would come to this from a different position."

Tilden may have wanted to conciliate with Northwest niceness, but his words only incited the gathering dissent.

Alex Popescu, an airport fueler, shot out of his seat. "I served twelve years in the military, honorable discharge, combat tours in Kosovo, Afghanistan, three times in Iraq. I have to choose between putting gas in my car or food on my family's table, because I work for one of your substandard paying subcontractors. I am the face of it," he said.

Tilden shuffled uncertainly on the stage.

"Oh, put your feet to the fire, huh? At a loss for words," Popescu challenged him.

"If it's time for me to respond, I will," said Tilden. "The first thing I would do is thank you for your service to our country."

Popescu cut him off. "By paying me a better wage!"

Tilden turned to the other side of the room, where a second mic stood. Perhaps this questioner would be less acerbic.

"I want to thank the executives," began Mark Glover. "Obviously you guys have done a great job. Over the last couple of years we've made a quarter billion dollars profit each year. Not bad at all. We know we've got a lot of power in the room."

Tilden relaxed, blind to the setup.

"Your presentation was kind of the direction I was going in, about doing the right thing, taking care of your stakeholders," continued Glover, a hospital nurse and union activist. Then turning to face the crowd of shareholders, he said, "Just show of hands, maybe even applause, I think a lot of people have the same idea. We're looking for fair wages for your frontline employees, and the ones we're talking about are the contract employees. And maybe it's just time for Alaska Airlines to pay fair wages, what do you think?"

The room echoed with applause as the meeting slipped from the CEO's grasp.

Truth be told, campaign organizers hadn't imagined such a wide operating latitude. Corporate shareholder meetings are tightly orchestrated events. Opposing voices are given limited time to speak, if

any. Troublemakers are quickly removed by hired security staff. Organizers had trained the thirty-seven workers and allies to expect to have
fifteen to thirty seconds at the most to speak. Prior to the meeting we
had people practice, over and over, the three or four sentences that we
thought they would be limited to. We reminded people to breathe,
to not be nervous when speaking up, and to speak loudly because we
probably would be denied access to microphones. We rehearsed what
to do if we were evicted by security.

What we discovered in the actual confrontation was that the best-
laid plans and meticulous training became superfluous as the opening
salvos—Reverend Liljenstople's gentle grace and Popescu's venting
rage—unlocked the floodgates. A psychological barrier had been collectively shattered. The CEO wasn't invincible after all. Fear melted
away and the prepared statements we had spent hours rehearsing
were cast aside in favor of stories, passion, and argumentation that
tumbled forth while speakers lifted the fight from economic terrain
to a moral plateau.

Anita Manuel, a chaplain, stood to speak. "I watched your presentation, when it got to targeted outsourcing, I said, 'I really think there
is a problem here.' What I think of it as is pulling a Walmart. And I
know something about Walmart because my mother knew Sam and
Helen Walton before that company lost its ethical compass. And I'm
concerned about this company losing its ethical compass," she said.

"So the question that I have is what are you and the other officers
going to do to be honest about the effects of your actions, and to accept your responsibility as Sea-Tac's major air carrier and one that sets
the standard for healthy conditions, not only for your own employees
but also for all of the workers that provide services for you at Sea-Tac?"

"Thank you for your question," Tilden said. "I'm trying to listen,
and trying to not be defensive."

Michael Douglas, a Sufi minister, stood up and introduced himself
as an Alaska shareholder. "By and large I'm very proud of our ethical
and moral record as a company," he said. "I'd just like to point out
that outsourcing jobs does not give us moral insulation, even though
it gives us legal and economic insulation."

Laura Davenport, a University of Washington clerical worker and
union activist who lived just north of Sea-Tac's runways, talked about

meeting her neighbors who work at the airport. "I got a lot of really interesting feedback from people about how they can't make ends meet, how multiple families are living in one home because of poverty wages," she said.

"I live right across the street from my child's elementary school," Davenport continued, "where a lot of these other kids go to school. And I watched my kid bundle up, get him out the door in one of his many coats, because he's always losing them, right? And I watched other kids walking the neighborhood not wearing coats. Their families—and I recognized these kids as the children of contract airport workers—their families cannot afford coats. I listened to the school principal put out an appeal begging families that could donate reasonable coats to do so, so that all the children in my child's school could go to school with a coat on. This is wrong.

"This company is profitable, this company will continue to be profitable, and I will continue to be a proud shareholder of this company," Davenport said. "I want this company to step up, lead the way, and model the ethical behavior that it's founded on."

There wasn't much that Tilden could say about children lacking winter coats. He looked at the clock. "Okay, just in the interest of time, I think we're approaching three thirty, maybe one final question and then we'll break for the afternoon." The barrage had been going on nonstop for nearly forty-five minutes. Three thirty couldn't come soon enough for the new CEO.

The Reverend John Helmiere stood to speak, thanked Tilden for listening to everyone, and issued a challenge. "Are you willing, within the first sixty days of your tenure as CEO, to meet with the actual folks who are doing this work and to listen? Listen as compassionately and openly as you've been listening to us, and maybe that might inspire change."

Yes, said Tilden, he would meet.

With the CEO's concession in hand, we could declare victory on our goal for the day. The emboldened thirty-seven participants left the auditorium excited, having experienced the power of confronting our adversary directly in his home turf. That taste of success boosted the confidence of workers and organizers as we headed back into the airport to spread the good news that Alaska's CEO had agreed to talk.

BEYOND THE POLITICAL WIN, many of us leaving the meeting were coming to appreciate the formation of a different organizing framework. On our side, we had righteous indignation due to poverty-wage jobs and limitless corporate greed. Tilden was comfortable engaging in that arena. He had the data and industry history to support Alaska's decision to contract out work to low-wage companies. He was confident in his analysis and Alaska's business plan. And he knew that a significant sector of the general public, especially editorialists, pundits, and the political establishment, would accept the trickle-down economics argument that a successful Alaska Airlines would grow jobs and income. But Tilden had no answer to the assertion that the company's practices lacked moral insulation, or to the question of why the children of airport workers had to go begging for coats.

This was powerful stuff. But the challenge for those of us in union leadership was to avoid the tendency to look at faith allies in a utilitarian role, as credible voices subordinate to a political agenda. Moreover, faith leaders would instinctively shy away from activities that seemed to exploit religion for political advancement. It seems cheap, even coarse to employ scripture or deeply held beliefs as tools to advance a material cause.

The subtle but crucial distinction that some of us were beginning to grasp was the power, not of the moral argument in service to political demands, but instead political demands made on the basis of a moral foundation. To Reverend Helmiere and his colleagues, public speaking by clergy "is indeed a plea for justice and social change, but the roots of it aren't an economic agenda or political agenda." Rather, he said, the economic or political agenda is an outgrowth of faith and spirituality.

At the 2012 shareholders meeting, Reverend Helmiere, Michael Douglas, Laura Davenport, and others were shifting the terrain from dollars and cents to values and justice, challenging the company not with math problems contained in corporate balance sheets, but with moral questions of how executives ought to be treating their fellow human beings.

This also proved to be a learning moment for us on the role of theology and scripture in the campaign. Most faith leaders seemed reluctant to openly raise scripture or theological teachings in the rallies, press conferences, and other public events we staged.

But in more private gatherings, in mosques, churches, and community meeting halls, faith leaders spoke passionately about the common thread woven between scripture and the modern-day struggle, and the power of story to motivate and sustain themselves and their congregants. To the Orcas Mosque's Mohamed Sheikh Hassan, the Battle of Badr, where Muhammad and his ragtag band overcame an army ten times their size, served as an instructive lesson for Muslim Sea-Tac workers, he told me. "The Prophet understood that 'Yes, they are more than us, but we are on the right track. If what we have is true faith, then we will overcome,'" he said. Reverend Cannon quoted Jesus in the Book of Matthew, who said, "What you do for the least of these you do for me," as a way to explain the moral imperative that placed her in confrontation with port authorities. For Reverend Jan Bolerjack, the newly arrived Sea-Tac minister, the airport campaign broke convention and rebelled against entrenched economic truths— like poverty wages—much as Jesus broke custom when he spoke to a Samaritan woman at the well.

These clergy were among those who formed the nucleus of our multifaith community meetings, where I often found myself invoking the Bible's Exodus story, a common framework for the varied traditions and cultures of white mainline Protestants, Orthodox Christians from Ethiopia and Eritrea, and Muslims from throughout East Africa. The tale of a people fleeing slavery to freedom, a story shared by all three Abrahamic faiths, stood as a fitting parable for the importance of fusing faith with human action to overcome obstacles. We knew we had to cross obstructions together, sometimes against all odds, just as the Children of Israel had crossed the Red Sea.

We didn't have to wait long after the shareholders meeting to encounter one of those difficult moments. Tilden had agreed to meet with us, but as we approached the sixty-day deadline, no meeting was scheduled. The CEO's staff had questions for us, but no dates. The sixty-day mark came and went in July, and still nothing was set.

Faith leaders came together and agreed that further earnest appeals to meet would be ineffective; as with the Hebrew slaves, they needed to escalate the pressure. In early September more than a dozen faith leaders marched at the front of a parade of five hundred people—airport workers, community allies, and home-care workers attending a nearby union convention—down the main boulevard in SeaTac to the headquarters of Alaska Airlines. In their hands the ministers and imams carried a letter signed by more than sixty area clergy and lay activists, calling on Tilden to fulfill his May promise.

The Reverend John Helmiere was one of the ministers at the front of the march, having been deputized by his colleagues to deliver the letter to Tilden. But as Helmiere marched he was feeling uneasy in the leadership role. A young, newly minted minister out of Yale Divinity School, Helmiere had arrived in Seattle two years prior with the goal of building a progressive spiritual congregation from the ground up. He had grown up in Tampa, Florida, where in church they encouraged you to feed the homeless but never discussed why there were homeless people in the first place.

So walking at the front of the march, surrounded by ministers and imams who each could count many years of pulpit time and flocks in the hundreds, Helmiere felt ill-equipped to the task of leading this delegation. They turned into Alaska's corporate parking lot, and there he encountered another obstacle. A lone security officer waved Helmiere down and told him the group wouldn't be allowed onto the private property. "I remember thinking, 'Oh, I guess we can't go on,'" Helmiere told me later. "I'd always operated in the world where there are rules and structures and laws and that's just how everything works."

Go on, I urged Helmiere, and then it occurred to the young minister that perhaps he didn't have to follow the established rules. "There's five hundred of us and there's one security officer. Seeing the force of human organization was exciting." Helmiere stepped forward. The crowd followed, surging around the security officer and to Alaska's front door.

Flanked by airport workers, Helmiere knocked on the glass door. An Alaska manager came out, carefully shut the door behind him, and announced—no surprise—that CEO Brad Tilden was unavailable. But, he continued, Alaska's director of public relations was eager to talk with a small number of clergy—inside, apart from the crowd. Did a delegation want to come in? Helmiere recalled scripture for his response. "It was like the temptation of Christ in the moment, like, 'Oh, you can come in and have special access and be treated different.' I said, 'No, we go together or we don't go in. You're not going to split us off.' It was a really insightful experience for me. It revealed a lot to me about how they saw us and the power of being together."

Helmiere and the workers delivered the clergy letter to the manager outside, shook his hand, turned around, and left. The new minister, whose leadership at the shareholders meeting had shown union organizers the power of moral argument, had just gleaned an important union lesson about the power of collective action. A synergy was developing between the union organizers and faith leaders. And before September was over, we had a date scheduled with Brad Tilden.

TRADITIONALLY, WHEN UNIONS gain a direct audience with corporate leadership, they will send top union officials, and usually not even workers: the business union approach. But this time we wanted to let Tilden know he had to deal with the broader community, not just a labor union. The delegation that met Tilden in an airport conference room consisted of five faith leaders and three airport workers, plus one union staff, whose sole function inside the meeting was to translate. "So right up front, Brad Tilden and his folks know this—there is a moral side to the picture," recalled the Reverend Paul Benz, a Lutheran minister and delegation member.

Workers took advantage of the opportunity to confront the CEO directly. Leon Sams, an aircraft fueler, told the Alaska executives about broken ladders, fuel nozzles, and carts. Samatar Abdullahi, the seventy-six-year-old cabin cleaner, recounted to Tilden the abuse his supervisor heaped on him when he tried to take time off to visit his hospitalized daughter. Baggage handler Tyler Steele told the executives about how managers on the tarmac constantly talked down to the workers and how he still lived with his parents because an apartment was financially out of reach.

Tilden and his executives were happy to engage on matters of safety and fair treatment. The CEO sympathetically allowed that Abdullahi's treatment was "probably illegal." And he admitted that the company could do better in sharing profits with contracted workers, though significant raises were out of the question. The company valued the work of these contractors, Tilden said. Perhaps, he mused, Alaska should sponsor job fairs and interview workshops to help workers move up to better jobs.

But the platitudes and commitments to address safety concerns dodged the main issues that centered on power: the delegation's demand that Alaska respect workers' right to form a union and bargain for living wages and benefits. On those topics, Tilden was blunt, recalled Sheikh Abduqadir Jama, the Al-Noor Mosque leader and one of the delegation members. "He said, 'I am here defending the rights of the shareholders. My responsibility is to make profits for them. The people you're advocating for are not directly employed by Alaska.'"

"The workers are not shareholders, but they are stakeholders," Sheikh Jama rejoined. "They are the people who contribute to your company's safety, cleanliness, success. You're hired an intermediary company—but you're the only ones who have the leverage to go to the intermediary and fix things."

Sheikh Jama, Reverend Benz, and the other clergy knew that Tilden was not going to give ground in this first meeting. But they also recognized that they had forced a direct dialogue with a reluctant target, largely because of the moral voice that Tilden knew he would be unwise to ignore. The very occurrence of the meeting was proof that we were on the right track.

At the airport and in the community, reports of the meeting gave hope. Sheikh Jama told people at the mosque and his Islamic school about the encounter. They were thrilled. "They were saying, for the first time, their concerns were taken from their mouths, directly to the head of Alaska." For a group of largely immigrant workers, to be able to reach the CEO of a major company was an accomplishment.

The meeting ended with handshakes and pleasantries, a commitment to keep talking. At moments like these, when the employer is willing to engage but not ready to concede, campaigners have an important decision to make. Should they hold off on protests to give the employer the opportunity to make a positive move, or ratchet up the pressure? There was strong agreement: the meeting with Tilden showed that we had his attention, but were far from getting his agreement to our demands. A few days later, as if to demonstrate the accuracy of this assessment, Menzies announced a 25-cent raise for Alaska baggage handlers—a recognition perhaps of the growing pressure, but a paltry sum given record airline profits. Workers fumed at the trivial bribe. It was time to escalate.

Reverend Helmiere, along with Reverend Bolerjack and other faith leaders, chose December 10, International Human Rights Day, for their next demonstration.

In the early afternoon of December 10, Bolerjack, joined by more than twenty clergy, many of them decked out in colorful stoles draped over their shoulders, walked into the airport with more than one hundred airport workers, community supporters, and organizers. Parading around the inside of the terminal, they carried colorful posters calling for respect for the human rights of airport workers.

The march emboldened workers, both those participating and those on the clock who watched as the parade traveled by. Wheelchair attendant Saba Belachew, who helped kick off the march with a call for workers' rights, said the faith leaders gave workers the confidence to join in. "We let them go first," Belachew, an Ethiopian immigrant, later recalled, referring to the clergy. When Alaska Airlines management and Sea-Tac travelers saw the crowd, "they saw the religious people first, and then they would see us." For Belachew and other workers, this wasn't about hiding behind the clergy, but rather presenting the faces of the moral argument ahead of the economic one.

The group gathered beside one of the baggage claim carousels for an opening prayer from the Reverend Dick Gillett, an Episcopal minister who recently had moved to Seattle after years of social activism in Los Angeles.

"We affirm that all human rights derive from the hand of the divine creator, who created all of us in God's image," Gillett began, comfortably shedding any reservations about introducing theology in mixed company. "Today, out of that faith, we underline the words of the United Nations Declaration, that 'everyone who works has the right to just and favorable remuneration, ensuring for himself or herself, and his or her family, an existence worthy of human dignity.'"

Port officials and police officers looked on but didn't try to intervene. Thus far the faith-led crowd had broken the port's rule against staging rallies and parading and picketing with signs inside the terminal. Now, headed for the Alaska Airlines ticket counter, we were about to break a few more rules. The Alaska ticket counters were built as kiosks in the middle of the floor, not against a wall. You could walk entirely around them, and that's precisely what the demonstrators did, forming a picket line and launching into the church song, adapted for the moment: "Solid as a rock, rooted as a tree, we are here, standing strong, for airport workers." Passengers turned their heads to see what the singing was about as the parade circled the ticket counters again and again.

For Reverend Gillett, a veteran of Southern California labor protests, the parade around the ticket counter recalled spring marches into Beverly Hills on behalf of hotel workers, where the ministers handed out Easter lilies to supportive employers and bitter herbs to the problematic ones. The ministers learned that their vestments and symbols helped them get into places and do things that would otherwise be off limits. Now circling the Alaska ticket counter, Gillett felt that power once again. Religious symbolism and faith leadership could break through barriers that economic and political protest could not.

I was standing a few feet from Reverend Gillett and the circling parade when a port police officer approached me. I expected the usual threats and orders to leave. But instead, he simply had a message. He had spoken to Alaska management, he told me. They were OK with us circling the ticket counter one more time, but asked—pleaded— that we stop after that.

It was an extraordinary request. Just three months prior, we had been threatened with eviction from the airport. We had been stymied in our demand to meet with the Alaska CEO. With clergy in the lead, we had escalated actions, we had broken the rules at the airport and at Alaska's headquarters. We now had the company's attention, had begun to see tangible concessions offered to workers, and had beaten back the port's rules and secured our right to organize and protest at the airport. And now, with clergy leading the tuneful parade, we found ourselves in the new and amusing position of being asked nicely by Alaska and the port to please give them a break.

We circled the ticket counter two more times, and then broke off for a spirited victory celebration.

SIX

IF YOU WANT BIG CHANGE,
YOU NEED A BIG IDEA

WORKERS ALL OVER THE airport were jazzed as they heard about the clergy-led picket around Alaska's ticket counter. But Samatar Abdullahi, the elderly cabin cleaner, was disconcerted. He ran into me after his shift ended on the day of the clergy-led march in December 2012. "We need union," he said. "No more actions, we need union." Well, we were organizing the union, weren't we? I thought. And collective actions were part of building the union. What's missing? "We need union," Abdullahi repeated, waving his hands. Abdullahi's English was limited, and my Somali was nonexistent, so we stood there on the concourse in awkward animated conversation, unable to bridge the language divide.

The next day Ahmed Ali, the Somali organizer for Working Washington, called me. "Samatar wants to meet with you." The three of us gathered a few days later at a local McDonald's. Through Ali's translation, Abdullahi explained his thinking to me. A former military officer in Somalia, he knew a few things about having a clear strategy. And he wanted to tell me that, from his perspective, our campaign didn't have one. "Whenever you start a campaign, you should have the end goal in mind," he began. "You have to know what the fight is. You have to know the obstacles that you face on the way, because this is a long journey."

Abdullahi recognized that we had taken a lot of actions in 2012. He had led a worker delegation to his cabin-cleaning employer, DGS. He had joined the parade of luggage carts bearing proworker, anti-Delta signs through the airport. Menzies baggage handlers had signed a mass petition demanding improved treatment, and the company had responded with 25-cent raises. More than fifty airline contract workers had filed health and safety complaints against their contractors and the airlines, prompting state regulators to launch a series of investigations. Those were important activities, Abdullahi allowed. The active involvement of Muslim faith leaders and other clergy also was vital, he said, because it gave confidence to his co-workers. But he had little faith that more symbolic actions alone were going to yield justice. We needed to take the next step—formally organize unions and demand bargaining with the employers, he said.

For Abdullahi, it was perplexing that we hadn't moved in that direction. In Somalia, he said, companies had labor-management committees, and workers backed up economic demands with strikes. Established labor-management relations were common in other parts of the world, he observed. But not here. Work relationships in the United States seemed more archaic than those in less-advanced economies. But, he insisted, that needed to be the next big step. We needed to form unions and demand negotiations with the employers.

To an outsider, that may seem like a fairly straightforward proposition. Why not get workers to join the union and demand negotiations? Ironically, the resistance to this strategy came from the unlikeliest of places—the union headquarters leadership.

In the headquarters of the Service Employees International Union, airport campaigns came under the aegis of the Property Services Division, which included commercial building janitors, security officers, and a range of service and industrial jobs. Two decades earlier, this branch of SEIU had led the dramatic Justice for Janitors campaign. Militant janitor rallies and strikes beginning in Denver and then Los Angeles spread around the country, rebuilding the union's power in the cleaning industry. Scenes of Latino immigrant janitors marching in the streets—and in the case of Los Angeles, getting beaten up by the police—galvanized public sympathy.

Drawing inspiration and ideas from the organizing work of Cesar Chavez's farmworkers union, Justice for Janitors organizers built pressure campaigns against commercial real-estate owners and the cleaning companies they hired with rallies, strikes, vigils, blockades, and other direct worker and community actions. Their goal was to force the building owners to order their contractors to reach agreements with the union. Justice for Janitors campaigns sought out political and financial channels for pressuring real-estate owners to dump hostile cleaning contractors in favor of ones that would work with the union. The large real-estate owners found themselves badgered by tenants, local government officials, and even worker-sympathetic building investors, like union pension funds. Any opportunity to drive a wedge into the property owner's business plans and relationships was fair game: a business debt coming due, pending owner-tenant lease negotiations, an owner's petition to the city for building permits, third-party lawsuits. A successful Justice for Janitors campaign besieged the owners from every possible angle.

No single union tactic was decisive, but in combination the assaults created an untenable environment for real-estate owners. What began as a minor nuisance morphed into a major headache harming their bottom lines. Most of the larger real-estate owners lacked powerful antiunion ideology; they were businessmen who simply wanted to maximize revenue on their investments. Cleaning contractors were a small part of the cost of doing business. They preferred to keep cleaning costs down, but when the cost of resisting the union exceeded the cost of settling, they made a practical decision to deal with the union. Once a contractor agreed to talk, the union would negotiate a voluntary union recognition agreement, skipping the drawn-out and contentious election process.

The Justice for Janitors model of organizing replaced the traditional approach of having workers sign union cards and petition for an election overseen by the federal government. That traditional approach had turned into a dead end for the union; with a federally supervised union election, contractors fought back and workers could expect a protracted litigious process even to get to a ballot. During the interval between filing for an election and a vote—several months, in many cases—contractors typically threatened and even fired union supporters, knowing that federal labor law was impotent to stop them. And if the workers even got to a union vote, the building owner could switch contractors on short notice, effectively firing the employees and dispensing with the union problem.

Under federal labor law, an explicit call for union recognition could trigger the election process, which janitor campaign organizers wanted to avoid. So the organizers developed an intricate strategic dance that involved pressuring real-estate owners but assiduously avoided any call for union recognition until the parties were sitting down. Outwardly, the worker actions and the leverage exerted through tenants, government officials, and building investors only sought better pay, fair treatment, safer working conditions, and the like, but everyone knew the unstated price of settlement. Twenty years into the Justice for Janitors organizing model, SEIU Property Services Division strategists and lawyers had refined leverage tactics to an art form, sometimes consigning worker actions to secondary importance, mere street theater.

To SEIU Property Services Division leaders, public airports seemed to offer similar opportunities: create enough pressure, whether on the airlines or on airport authorities, to force the airline contractors to recognize the union. Union headquarters staff were particularly averse to any straightforward demand for union recognition at airports. As bad as labor law was for commercial building janitors, it was worse for airport workers. Workers in the transportation industry—including airport workers—come under the federal Railway Labor Act (RLA), a labor law that prohibits virtually all union-related strikes and disruptive activity. An airport worker demand for union recognition, headquarters staff reasoned, could trigger an employer to seek a federal RLA injunction prohibiting not just strikes but a wide range of other worker demonstrations. By keeping picketing, rallying, and other collective actions focused on safety issues, unfair treatment, or other workplace concerns, the headquarters staff believed, they could escape the RLA injunction trap.

Furthermore, the law only permitted airport workers to call for union elections on a national basis. Workers like Samatar Abdullahi were not allowed to petition for an RLA-sanctioned union election covering his 200 DGS colleagues at Sea-Tac. To organize an election under the federal law, he would have to collect signatures from a majority of 30,000 DGS employees scattered around more than 130 airports in the United States. That was an absurd proposition.

However, federal law allowed voluntary recognition agreements between unions and contractors that covered single-airport groups of workers. Indeed, over the years, SEIU, the Teamsters, and other unions had secured voluntary recognition for groups of contract workers at a number of other airports, largely on the East Coast and in California. Headquarters staff believed that pursuing voluntary recognition at individual airports was the most viable path forward. The logical course to take, in their view, was to create enough pressure until the contractors called the union seeking a peace deal: the same strategic dance that had worked so effectively in the commercial cleaning industry. The headquarters staff believed that supportive public airport authorities could put decisive pressure on the air carriers and their contractors.

The problem with this organizing theory, as I was coming to see, was twofold. First, it underestimated the resistance of airlines and their contractors. By 2012 the airlines had implemented decades of wrenching change to refashion the industry, through deregulation, union busting, and contracting out. At no small effort, they had recaptured power in the industry. The idea of airlines now tolerating unions at their contractors was not the same as commercial real-estate owners making a practical cost-benefit decision to abide a janitors' union. Airline executives had come this far and were not inclined to slide backward.

The second problem with SEIU's Property Services Division organizing theory was that it relied heavily on the union's ability to get airport authorities to leverage airlines and contractors. But airport authorities, while nominally public entities with commissioners appointed by government leaders or even elected by voters, offered weak leverage to influence big business. Airlines provide significant revenue to airports through taxes and landing fees. Most airport authorities have come to view the airlines as constituencies to placate, not agitate. This was especially true at Sea-Tac Airport, where port staff regularly referred to Alaska, Delta, and the other airlines as "our customers."

Two months before my conversation with Samatar Abdullahi, other Sea-Tac workers had tested the limits of the Property Services Division's approach. Aircraft fuelers employed by ASIG, the major fueling contractor at Sea-Tac, had grown tired of working around unsafe equipment. When fueler Alex Popescu—the veteran who had challenged Alaska CEO Brad Tilden at the shareholders meeting—was suspended after speaking out about poor working conditions at an airport commission meeting, his coworkers voted to go on a one-day strike. With the Reverend Lauren Cannon and other Working Washington activists beside them, the fuelers had marched into the ASIG management office to announce their intent to strike.

Airplanes have to be fueled with precision and timeliness to maintain flight schedules. A delayed flight at one airport can trigger a cascade of multiple interruptions throughout an airline's network. Fuelers aren't easily replaced; it takes training and security clearances to load jet fuel into a $100 million aircraft. A walkout by Sea-Tac fuelers could have crippled air traffic in the region and beyond. The workers had power, and the company knew it.

ASIG, aided by Alaska Airlines and the Port of Seattle, rushed into federal court and quickly secured a broad RLA injunction barring not just strikes by fuelers, but virtually any type of collective job action that the company could allege was slowing down fueling operations. Working Washington's attorneys protested, noting that because the strike wasn't motivated by union organizing, it could not be banned under the RLA. The federal judge disregarded our legal arguments. To him it looked like a union activity, and he enjoined actions by the workers, Working Washington, and anyone who might want to help them. It didn't matter to the federal judge that the fuelers had expressly said their strike was not about union recognition. They just wanted to have safe equipment. But it was no matter to the court.*

The object lesson at ASIG was that we had gained no tactical benefit by dancing around the word "union." And now, sitting with me and Ahmed Ali at McDonald's, Samatar Abdullahi was insisting that rather

---

*Some two and a half years later, an appeals court threw out the injunction and restored the legal right of the fuelers to strike, but for all practical purposes, the damage to ASIG workers' rights at Sea-Tac had been done.

than run away from the word, we had to embrace it. Abdullahi was not alone in expressing frustration about the campaign's long-term focus. Other workers had been raising questions to organizers, with increasing frequency, about where we were headed.

I left McDonald's feeling a tug between the simple clarity of Abdullahi's challenge and the admonitions of the strategists and lawyers back in headquarters who counseled threading a tricky path in hostile legal terrain. Surely we had momentum at Sea-Tac. But we still lacked the big, transformative idea that would build worker power and dramatically improve work conditions. Yet simply demanding union recognition was an incomplete strategy, because we knew that the airlines and contractors likely would refuse negotiations. Then what? The ASIG experience taught us the practical limits of airport workers taking industrial action under the Railway Labor Act. We had to have a powerful follow-up to the likely refusal.

As I began raising with other organizers this idea of demanding union recognition, the puzzle pieces began to fit together. SEIU and Teamsters campaign strategists had been exploring a voter initiative strategy to improve airport working conditions. Traditionally, unionized private sector workers bargain pay and benefits with individual employers. But bargaining required workers first to persuade an employer to recognize their union, an increasingly challenging legal hurdle. The initiative could be an end-around employer resistance to unions.

An initiative was a novel idea, but as a stand-alone strategy it wouldn't build worker power. Plenty of local living wage initiatives around the country have succeeded in raising pay without building a strong worker organization to enforce the gains and build for greater fights.

But in tandem with Abdullahi's proposal, the initiative path began to make a lot more sense. Workers would form unions and demand negotiations. If the employers said no, as anticipated, workers and their community allies could pursue a bold ballot measure to improve working conditions. The Washington State constitution provides for the right of voters to adopt local initiatives. Voters couldn't require employers to recognize unions and negotiate with workers—such a local requirement would be preempted by federal law. But voters could establish minimum-wage and benefit levels. This popular right hadn't been attempted in tandem with a union organizing campaign; the city of SeaTac provided an apt testing ground.

Under this strategy, the campaign's message to Alaska Airlines and the contractors became: "We ask you to recognize the union and negotiate improvements in working conditions. But if you refuse, we will have the voters impose the improvements on you." On paper that was a powerful idea, an elegant way around the RLA obstacle.

Workers galvanized enthusiastically around the strategy. In early February 2013 workers from the major contractors ratified the plan and began an around-the-clock push, along with organizers, to get a majority of contracted airport workers to sign union authorization cards—legal affirmations to join the union. Our goal was to get a majority of workers at the major airport contractors to join the union by the spring. Back at SEIU headquarters, the Property Services Division staff were skeptical. It didn't fit their airport organizing model. They thought it was too risky to make a frontal assault on Alaska Airlines. But they didn't try to block the plan.

We also began to engage local politicians in the strategy. Their support would be vital in the court of public opinion, and we'd especially need the SeaTac City Council to prevent any shenanigans aimed at blocking a voter initiative. I met with Mia Gregerson, the SeaTac native and unlikely politician. She readily took on the role of persuading her city council colleagues, recognizing that even her prounion colleagues would be nervous about such a bold labor-led initiative against the major airport powers. For Gregerson this vision provided the equity lens she was so keen to employ, a way to connect the dots between the hunger of schoolchildren, the overworked families living in crowded apartments, the lack of access to health care, and the community's economic engine. Gregerson also recognized the downside of exercising political leadership on such a bold plan: she would be inviting the enmity of businesses and their political allies.

WITHIN THE AIRPORT WORKFORCE, racing to majority union membership required campaign staff to train and work closely with worker leaders at each of the contractors. Union organizers met with workers before and after their shifts, during breaks, at area restaurants, in people's living rooms. Workers came in to the airport on their days off to recruit colleagues to the union.

Just because airport working conditions were miserable didn't make union sign up automatic. Saba Belachew, the wheelchair attendant who had marched with faith leaders around the Alaska ticket counter, encountered resistance at first from her fellow workers. They liked the idea of forming a union and demanding negotiations, but were skeptical that they could win. It was completely outside their experience to fight corporate power. It seemed futile to take on Alaska Airlines and the ever-changing collection of contractors. And would it make a difference in the end, even if they were successful in forcing negotiations? How could a bunch of minimum-wage wheelchair pushers arm-twist a company as dominant as Alaska?

Belachew knew firsthand what a difference having a union could mean. In her second job she served food at the airport's Wolfgang Puck café, where she was covered by the hospitality workers union contract. At the café, in contrast to her wheelchair job, wages were better, she had health benefits, and she couldn't be fired if the supervisor didn't like her. Her wheelchair coworkers knew that, but even so, Belachew had to spend a lot of time talking with them before they would join the union. It's true, Belachew acknowledged, that joining the union wouldn't guarantee success; but on the other hand, she said, not taking a stand guaranteed poverty into the future. She pressed her coworkers to imagine the power they had collectively. Every day ninety thousand people and their luggage transited swiftly through the terminals thanks in part due to the daily exertions of thousands of minimum-wage workers. "The Port of Seattle, without the employees, it's nothing. Imagine if all the wheelchair agents were out one day, imagine the mess that would happen in the airport!" Belachew recalled telling them.

Yasmin Aden practically lived at the airport in the winter of 2013. Aden was a new union staffer and one of more than a dozen organizers assigned to the airport. A slight, thin woman, she played an outsized role, recruiting her fellow Somalis, as well as others, in all occupations throughout the airport. Language posed no barrier for Aden but cultural differences were an impediment. Like her fellow Somalis, Aden was a refugee of her homeland's ongoing civil war. But unlike most of her compatriots, Aden shunned the customs of Muslim life: she didn't attend prayers in the mosque, she smoked, she wore jeans, and she didn't cover her hair modestly with the traditional hijab.

In the Somali refugee community surrounding the airport, hewing to Muslim tradition was an act of cultural solidarity, a vital link to heritage when so much else had been uprooted. "People gave me a hard time for not covering up," Aden recalled. Meeting with one of the leaders of the Somali wheelchair attendants, "I wanted to talk about the union, but she said, 'Let me talk to you about this other thing first— you need to cover yourself.'" Over time the Somali airport workers came to recognize that they weren't going to change Aden. They also realized that the stubborn boldness that made her a community outlier also served her well in challenging airport authorities as well as workers who shied from involvement. She would go back repeatedly to workers anxious about rocking the boat, simultaneously reassuring them of the union and community backing they had, while challenging them to expect better for themselves and their community.

Aden took a longer view of things than just the immediate working conditions. In her mind, she and her compatriots hadn't escaped war and traveled halfway around the world only to get abused by airport employers. They deserved better. A dozen years earlier, Aden had arrived in Seattle. She was young, single, homeless, her family scattered around the world or dead. Her father, a civil servant, had been a victim of the Somali civil war, first jailed and then executed by the military dictator Siad Barre. She had barely known him. Aden's mother, a farmer in northern Somalia, raised goats and sold sugar, but her earnings were not enough to sustain the family. She sent Aden, a child, to live with an older sister in the capital city of Mogadishu. Then war broke out in the city. Aden and her sister escaped to Kenya and a UN refugee camp. At first they thought the camp would provide temporary respite until the war blew over; then they could go back to family. But over time the war escalated and reality settled in: Yasmin Aden was not going home. She was a teenager, ripped from her parents and homeland by violence. After a few years in the UN camp, she secured passage to America.

Aden landed in the United States in 2000 and wound up traveling with a friend to Seattle, working at a newspaper clipping service but unable to afford an apartment because landlords wouldn't lease to someone who had no rental or credit history. Social service aides at the local YWCA placed her in one of their tiny studio apartments until she was able to save enough money to stake out her own rental. In addition to the clipping service, Aden got hired on as a janitor for Metropolitan Building Maintenance. She'd work days at the clipping service, then rush to her janitor job at five thirty and clean buildings until two in the morning. It was a brutal, unrelenting schedule. She slept about four hours a night, plus whatever precious nap time she could grab during lunch breaks.

Aden's union introduction came not from an organizer but from management. One day she was checking her janitorial pay stub when she noticed a strange deduction. She went to her Metropolitan manager, Laurie. "Who's taking this money?" she demanded to know. It's the union; they represent you, Laurie replied. "I was like, 'I never said they're supposed to take my money. I never met them. So I want to stop the deduction. I need that money,'" Aden recalled. Sorry, Laurie said. Paying dues was a condition of employment.

Far too many workers, especially immigrant workers, have been introduced to the US labor movement in this way. It's an alienating slap, one more reason why unions are seen by newcomers as an exclusive club for people who don't look like them. Aden was unhappy about this unchosen arrangement with an organization that snatched her precious dollars without even bothering to reach out. But when she got into trouble with the owner of the building she cleaned, she decided to test her manager's claim about the union representing the workers. To Aden's pleasant surprise, the union representatives responded. They helped her secure a transfer to the Seattle Municipal Tower. The good news was she escaped a hostile building owner. The bad news was now she was responsible for vacuuming and emptying garbage and recycling on twenty-four floors in downtown Seattle every night. Every minute counted. Aden hustled through lunches to get the work done so she could rush home and grab a little sleep before rising for her day job.

Four years into Aden's routine at the municipal tower, Metropolitan starting cutting the janitors' work hours—but not their workload. Then they started cutting people, beginning with an elderly Asian man who had put twenty years into the building. By now Aden was a union shop steward, elected by her peers. She called the union office. They want to transfer Phillip, the long-time janitor, she said. The union representative urged her to circulate a petition, but cautioned her that ultimately the company had the authority to move Phillip. Aden collected signatures from the other twenty-two janitors in the building and presented her petition to Laurie, the Metropolitan manager. "This doesn't mean anything," Laurie replied dismissively. "I'm transferring him to another building."

"Phillip was here a long time. If this can happen to him, it can happen to me, too," Aden thought. "So I went and asked the other workers, 'Are we going to support this guy?'" Yes, they said. The next afternoon Aden gathered her colleagues outside the building. It was after five o'clock, but Aden proposed that no janitors go in—not without Phillip. They waited outside as Metropolitan managers grew frantic. An uncleaned building could cost the janitorial firm its contract.

The walkout violated the no-strike clause of the collective bargaining agreement between Metropolitan and the union. Workers refusing to clock in were subject to being disciplined and even fired. But no matter; janitors were flexing their collective muscle behind the steely leadership of their Somali shop steward who cared less about the written word of labor-management agreements and more about the principle of fair treatment. After half an hour, Laurie called Aden. What do you want? the manager asked the shop steward. Put Phillip back to work, Aden replied tersely. "OK, he can stay," the manager conceded, and the janitors marched into the building with Phillip, victorious in their thirty-minute strike.

Aden's audacity caught the attention of the union's leadership, and a couple years later she was nominated to run for the number two officer position in the union. She defeated a long-time incumbent to become, in 2011, the secretary-treasurer of SEIU Local 6. The formerly homeless refugee who a decade earlier wasn't allowed to rent an apartment was now responsible for leading four thousand union members and overseeing a million-dollar treasury. Besides the full-time union staff position came the responsibility to organize, something she had great instinct for but no formal training. Aden was dispatched to Sea-Tac to hone her skills.

Aden was a year into organizing at the airport in 2013 when the union membership drive got under way. Her main technique for grabbing workers' interest, as she patrolled through the main terminal, was to show workers a simple chart comparing wages and benefits at Sea-Tac with those at Los Angeles, San Francisco, and other West Coast airports. The workers at those airports, performing the same jobs for the same airlines and contractors, were paid $5/hour more. And they had health insurance, paid time off, and basic job protections—all things that the Sea-Tac workers lacked. Do you know what the difference between them and you is? Aden would ask the Sea-Tac workers. Those other airport workers have a union—and you can, too, she said.

Mohammed Kadhim was another worker flung to Sea-Tac from the catapult of distant war. Actually, two wars. Kadhim grew up in Baghdad, Iraq. His parents were skilled artists and they enjoyed relatively comfortable lives in the city, until the United States invaded the country in 2003 and shells started falling. At first Kadhim's neighborhood was relatively safe, but by 2006, with US forces suppressing insurrections elsewhere, paramilitary factions were competing intensely for control of his streets. Kadhim's family had never been politically aligned, and they were not particularly devout. They weren't taking sides in the civil war brewing around them. But there was no room for neutrals in this new world, and after family members were shot at, the parents decided to get out. They escaped to a safe city: Damascus, Syria. Two years later, Kadhim's parents secured visas to go to England, but their son wasn't allowed to follow. The parents left, hoping he'd be able to come later. In 2010, as war crept in on Damascus, Mohammed Kadhim got permission to leave. He asked to go to England and reunite with his parents. You can't go there, the authorities said. So he opted for his second choice—Washington State, where he had an older brother.

Kadhim moved in with cousins in a SeaTac apartment and worked a few odd jobs before hiring on at Air Serv as a baggage handler for Delta Airlines. The work was hard: loading hundreds of bags on each flight, working in the rain much of the year without proper protective gear. All that for $9.50/hour and no benefits. And while they were given full work schedules, frequently they would get called off—told not to come in—on short notice. Kadhim chafed under the ever-changing schedule and the lousy wages. In Damascus he had earned a two-year degree in information technology, and he wanted to continue his computer schooling in the United States. But he couldn't afford to attend community college on the airport wages, and even if he had the money, the contractor's frequent schedule changes would have wreaked havoc on school.

Two years into slinging bags at Sea-Tac, Kadhim met up with Yasmin Aden, introduced by a cousin who worked with him at Air Serv. The Somali organizer showed him the wage comparison chart. Kadhim was shocked. If Air Serv could pay its LAX workers $15/hour and benefits, why not here? They were serving the same customers, loading the same bags, working for the same airline. Kadhim and other airport workers had long been told that these were poverty-wage jobs because that's just the way things were in the United States. But now he saw, starkly, that this was not so. Kadhim decided to get involved in the organizing, and along with his cousin they persuaded the other Iraqi workers at Air Serv to sign union cards.

Kadhim's coworker, long-time ramper Alex Hoopes, relished the idea of forming a union of contracted airport workers. For him, it would represent redemption, or perhaps revenge: an opportunity to undo the injury Alaska Airlines had inflicted on him and his coworkers in 2005. Hoopes would greet workers when they arrived at work. "You see that sheet there?" Hoopes would ask them, pointing to Air Serv's timesheet. "You clock in and you write your name next to that number. You have a name of course, but you're just another number to fill the shift." He'd tick off the facts: minimum wages, no sick leave, abusive treatment. And then he'd hand them a union card to sign.

One day Aden was sitting in the terminal across from the US Airways ticket counter when a wheelchair attendant, a middle-aged man with a shock of white hair, sat down next to her. "Are you waiting for someone?" he asked her. No, I'm with the union, Aden replied. They struck up a conversation, and later that day, the wheelchair attendant, an Iranian named Assadollah Valibeigi, began recruiting coworkers to meet Aden and the other union organizers.

Valibeigi was one of the many airport workers who held multiple jobs and were continually hustling for more hours to pay the bills.

When he moved to SeaTac in 2006, Valibeigi hired on at Huntleigh, escorting wheelchair passengers to and from their flights for minimum wage and an occasional tip. Huntleigh serviced several airlines, including Alaska. A couple years after Valibeigi began work, Alaska fired Huntleigh and brought on a Florida company, Bags Inc., to run the wheelchair operation. Bags hired Valibeigi but didn't give him enough hours. So he also continued working for Huntleigh, which still had the wheelchair contracts for several of the smaller Sea-Tac airlines. It was a constant scramble to get enough hours from the two companies so he could pay the rent every month.

A Tehran merchant and taxi driver, Valibeigi had been studiously apolitical in his home country. It was a survival instinct. But after hearing Aden talk about the union, he was captivated. He agreed to recruit coworkers to the union effort, often employing metaphors and hand gestures to overcome language barriers within the workforce. "One hand doesn't have a voice, but with two hands—you can make a noise," he would say, raising his hands to clap.

Some workers, Valibeigi said, wanted to see what happened to the first ones who joined the union before they would step out. "Some people think, 'Let him go fight. If he die, he die. If somebody punch him, somebody punch him, not me. But if he wins—I have fifteen dollars!'"

To that Valibeigi would respond, "If everybody thinks this way, the airlines will have the power to do whatever they want."

More than fifty workers, including Belachew, Kadhim, Valibeigi, and Hoopes, backed up by union staff like Aden, recruited coworkers to join the union. After seven weeks of intensive recruiting, the organizers had built majority union membership at five of Sea-Tac Airport's largest contractors. The next step was to present this news to management.

On the morning of March 26, 2013, some eighty airport workers, clergy, community supporters, and union staff boarded chartered buses at the airport and began a tour of management offices, scattered short distances from the terminal. It was an impressive delegation—Somali, Latino, Ethiopian, Asian, and white workers and community members, coming together for the singular purpose of demonstrating collective power to the leading airport businesses.

First stop was the Delta-owned cabin-cleaning contractor DGS, Abdullahi's employer. Management got word that the delegation was coming, and locked the door. Aden and several workers knocked anyway, to no avail, as managers hid in their office, refusing to answer. The workers slipped their letter demanding union recognition under the door. Next up was Menzies, the multinational baggage-handling company. Union staff held open the Menzies management door while workers crowded into the office. The manager hid in a back office and refused to come out. Flanked by Reverend Bolerjack and Menzies coworkers, baggage handler Spencer Havens led a call-and-response chant that echoed through the building: "Respect. Union. Menzies. We need—better pay." Workers left the recognition demand letter on the counter.

The delegation climbed aboard the buses and headed to the third contractor, GCA, the car-cleaning and shuttle-driving contractor for Avis and Hertz Rent-a-Car. Four GCA workers, Somali women, paraded through the rental car offices with a huge banner bearing the simple word "Union" on it. Leading the delegation, they approached the manager's office. A burly manager behind the door tried to shut it. Teamsters representative Cetris Tucker stuck her foot in the door and forced it ajar. But she could do no better than jam the door partway open while managers pushed back on the other side. Workers tossed the recognition demand letter inside. At the fourth stop, Bags Inc., management had the decency to accept the workers' petition, and at Air Serv, the general manager came out of his office, accepted the letter from Alex Hoopes, and bantered a bit. It wasn't his decision how to respond, he said, but he would pass the letter on to his superiors.

The delegation had one more stop—Alaska Airlines headquarters—to deliver a letter calling on the airline to get its contractors to respect the workers' decision. While Alaska did not employ any of the workers who had organized, it had decisive power as the company that hired the contractors.

We were still a short bus ride away from Alaska headquarters when my phone lit up with a number from Alaska Airlines. It was Megan Lawrence, the airline's government and community relations director. She and I had talked a number of times before—arranging the meeting with Alaska executives and discussing our presence at the company's shareholders meeting. Our relationship had remained cordial even as the conflict had unfolded. But this time she called not for dialogue but to deliver a message.

"Jonathan, you can't come here. We're not going to let you guys on the property," she said.

We're only coming to present a letter, I told her; then the delegation would leave.

"You can't. We won't let you," the Alaska director insisted.

We're coming, I told her.

The buses dropped the delegation off at a nearby park and we walked up the sidewalk toward Alaska's headquarters, familiar conflict ground. A row of bushes blocked our view of the property. Given Lawrence's ultimatum, I didn't know what to expect. Perhaps a wall of private security guards? A phalanx of SWAT officers blocking our way? We were likely headed into a confrontation. In my experience a firm declaration by management was to be taken seriously. We may choose to challenge it, but we at least had to recognize what we were up against.

Led by the Reverend John Helmiere, the young minister who had led the earlier delegation to Alaska headquarters, the group now swung around the corner and entered the corporate property via the main driveway. I was astonished by what I saw. Some two hundred feet of open parking lot lay between us and the headquarters building. No police were there to stop us. There in the intervening space was a solitary private security officer, imploring us to not pass.

The Alaska executive had been bluffing.

This time Helmiere harbored no reservations about disregarding orders. He and the rest of the delegation blew past the officer and crowded around the headquarters door. An executive came out and informed us that—once again—CEO Brad Tilden was not available. This was getting to be routine. Helmiere and baggage handler Socrates Bravo handed the executive a letter from the workers and community leaders, calling on the airline to direct its contractors to recognize the union. Then the diverse delegation turned around and left, chanting, "We are union—we are one," as we once again passed by the lone security officer.

No one was surprised when in the succeeding days each employer rejected the call for union recognition. Menzies management posted a terse message at work. DGS sent the union office a ten-page exposition, complete with footnotes and legal citations, explaining why under the Railway Labor Act they had no obligation to respect the Sea-Tac workers' request. Alaska Airlines issued a letter asserting that its only duty was to comply with the Railway Labor Act—in other words, no.

Inside the airport the action upset the social order. Word spread about the delegations and management's response. The prevalent term that workers came to use in talking about what happened was "fear." For the first time, they had seen their managers shrink at the sight of workers coming together: hiding behind doors, refusing to come out of their offices, sending factotums out to declare their unavailability. Since the beginning of their employment at the airport, workers had been conditioned to accept the routine abuse and capricious edicts of their managers. Suspensions or firings for no good reason, supervisors yelling at workers, last-minute schedule changes, humiliating lectures in front of passengers—all that and more had been customary, on top of the low pay and lousy working conditions. Typically this maltreatment had the added racial dimension of a white manager lording over an immigrant person of color.

But now the script had been flipped. Workers were standing up. Delegation members who confronted management were pumped up. "It felt great just to stand there and say, 'We're giving you this petition because of what is not right. We're not going to lay down. We're going to stand up and fight,'" Hoopes recalled.

Hoopes and his coworkers returned to their regular work shifts to find their supervisors more cautious, more restrained in directing the workers. The workers had confronted their managers, they had lived to tell about it, and now they saw fear in the eyes of their superiors. The confidence was infectious. It revealed the emerging power of airport workers, and in doing so opened a window into the future possibility of a more dignified existence.

We had taken the union-forming step that Samatar Abdullahi had insisted upon, and had gotten the expected response from the companies. The next step in our big idea was to go to the voters.

SEVEN

SPEAKING TRUTH IN
THE HALLS OF POWER

IN WASHINGTON STATE you can place an initiative on the local ballot by getting 15 percent of registered voters to sign a petition. In a
large city this is a high hurdle, but in a small community like SeaTac,
which had only eleven thousand registered voters, it was relatively
manageable.

Unconstrained by the compromises inherent in a labor-management
negotiating process, we assembled a ballot initiative that was ambitious but would not overreach the sensibilities of SeaTac voters. In addition to consulting with key workplace leaders, I worked closely with
campaign strategists from SEIU and our partner unions—the Teamsters; the United Food and Commercial Workers International Union;
UNITE HERE—along with Puget Sound Sage, the community group,
to assemble the elements of the initiative, which SEIU lawyers drafted
into legal form. We started with the New York fast-food workers' call
for $15/hour minimum wage and built from there, adding elements
to address particular issues that airport workers faced.

The SeaTac Good Jobs Initiative set the immediate wage floor for
workers in and around the airport at $15/hour and added paid sick
leave for all workers. We included low-wage workers both inside
the airport property, and also outside the airport if their jobs were

substantially airport dependent: parking lot attendants, hotel workers, and rental car workers.

To address the problem of rampant part-time employment, the initiative required employers to offer additional work hours to existing part-time staff before bringing on new hires. The full-time-hours provision solved two problems. First, it gave workers opportunities to work at one job only, without having to cobble together several part-time jobs. And second, without even mentioning the words "health care," the provision netted health benefits for workers. The newly passed Affordable Care Act, Obamacare, required employers to provide health benefits to workers employed thirty hours a week or more. Many airport contractors purposely kept employee hours just below that threshold to escape the benefit requirement. The initiative would ban that practice. If a part-time worker wanted benefits and more work hours were available, she would be able to get the hours and the health care that came with them. It was an elegant solution.

To deal with the problem of workers losing their jobs when airlines changed contractors, we included a "worker retention" provision, which required that contractors newly brought on by the airlines hire existing workers first. This would solve the problem of precarious airline contract work and deny airlines the ability to break unions by swapping contractors.

We also included tip protection in the initiative. Nonunion hotel managements, especially, routinely kept part of the service charges and tips that customers paid. The initiative required that 100 percent of service charges and tips go to the workers providing the service.

Then there was the question of workers enforcing their rights under the initiative. Other cities that had adopted wage floors or paid sick leave typically created an administrative enforcement mechanism. If you thought you weren't being paid properly, you could file a complaint with a city bureaucrat, who would have little power to investigate much less compel an employer to conform to the law, and who likely would be swamped with other responsibilities. These administrative enforcement provisions developed out of negotiation among unions, employers, and government officials. They were compromises, watered-down enforcement tools.

For the SeaTac initiative, we took a starkly different approach. We included the right of individual workers or unions to sue noncompliant employers in court. This private-right-of-action provision was a powerful hammer: an employer could be dragged before a judge, forced to turn over documents, testify, and even under some circumstances pay damages to workers. With a powerful enforcement tool, we could expect much greater employer respect for the initiative's economic and workplace rights provisions. Of all the elements of the initiative, this was one that many businesses came to rail against the most.

Finally, there was the question of collective bargaining. No local initiative could require employers to recognize and bargain with a union—those rights, limited as they may be, are covered by federal law. Local governments are preempted from adopting regulations that conflict with federal law. But there was another way to nudge employers into a bargaining relationship. The SeaTac Good Jobs Initiative provided that employers who recognized a democratically formed union were free to negotiate exceptions to the initiative's provisions with the union. For instance, union members and their employer could negotiate lower starting wages in exchange for improved health benefits, or an enforcement mechanism less onerous than private right of action. Of course, no group of workers would in their right minds negotiate less than the total compensation and benefits provided under the initiative. But the collective bargaining option gave workers bargaining power and offered employers—at least forward-looking ones—the reward of potential flexibility if they respected workers' rights.

By early May union organizers, community supporters, and workers were knocking on the doors of SeaTac voters, collecting signatures to qualify the SeaTac Good Jobs Initiative for the November 2013 ballot. Within three weeks the campaign had collected enough signatures to qualify for the ballot. But before turning in the petitions to city hall, we wanted to exercise our power directly to see if there was any possibility that Alaska Airlines might change course and decide to negotiate.

The 2012 Alaska shareholders meeting had marked the first direct confrontation between the company and the airport workers and allies. Speaker after speaker had challenged new Alaska CEO Brad

Tilden. They had been direct, but polite and within the rules of the meeting. We decided in 2013 to double down on pressure inside the meeting. In the months leading up to the 2013 shareholders meeting, groups of faith leaders, workers, and other community supporters bought individual shares of Alaska Airlines stock and met extensively to plan a series of disruptions inside the shareholders meeting. As long as Alaska executives denied workers their rights, we would not abide business as usual. We intended to occupy the company's meeting, take it over. To accomplish that we needed to break the rules.

When Alaska Airlines shareholders began filing into the auditorium at the Port of Seattle's waterfront conference center on May 21, 80 of the 220 people in the room were workers or allies—company shareholders or proxies committed to bring righteous chaos into the meeting. There were even workers and organizers from LAX, another major Alaska Airlines airport.

The auditorium was full by 1:55 p.m., five minutes before the start of the meeting, when Reverend Helmiere rose out of his seat and led a group of twelve clergy to the front of the room. They stood in a row in front of the shareholders, holding hands. "I've been asked by some shareholders to say a prayer," Helmiere began, over the murmurs of the crowd. At six feet seven inches tall, Helmiere, wearing a starched white clerical collar and black suit, commanded attention. Heads bowed in silence. People clasped their hands in prayerful pose. A hush fell over the auditorium. Off on the side of the room, an Alaska executive admonished a shareholder to quiet down. "Shh— they're doing the prayer now," he said, oblivious to the imminent act of corporate apostasy.

Reverend Helmiere had practiced his prayer over and over again, memorizing it. His prayer was an idea cooked up by the faith leaders in our delegation, a daring assault on the conventions of the meeting. The words would be a clarion call to justice, spoken by an irreproachable messenger. Helmiere felt electric. But now, standing in front of the silent auditorium, his memory suddenly failed him. The prayer was written down just in case words eluded him, and the paper was in his shirt pocket. But he was holding hands with the other clergy. He dared not break the symbolic bonds and read from a piece of paper. That would seem crass.

"I closed my eyes," Helmiere later recalled to me. "My first prayer was silent, and it was, 'Oh God, please help me. I don't know what I'm supposed to say and everyone's waiting for me to say something.' So I just started, I opened my mouth, and I felt like the Spirit prayed through me."

"God of Mercy, God of Justice, God who transforms our hearts," he began. "We give thanks for the privileges and powers that we have been given." Drawn in, the crowd now was respectfully silent as Helmiere veered the prayer sharply: "God, we ask that you give our leaders the wisdom to do right by their workers, do right by their community, to make our company a business beacon and an ethical beacon as well. Guard us from the gravity of greed, save us from the snares of selfishness. And help us to live your eternal truth: that we belong to you, and to one another."

The ministers returned to their seats and sat down. Corporate executives sat stunned for a moment, perhaps still not quite comprehending how their meeting, the annual showcase of the company's finesse and success, had just been hijacked, and in the most unexpected of ways. This was not a rough group of uncouth workers and organizers—something they expected—but a delegation of clergy come to challenge their moral bearings.

And it was just an introduction to their troubles. A few minutes into the meeting, the company's executives introduced each of the nominees for the board of directors. Eleven nominees for eleven positions. It was entirely pro forma. The meeting chair, General Counsel Keith Loveless, called for people to mark their paper ballots.

"Mr. Chair!" shouted a shareholder, rising out of his seat. "I rise to urge my fellow shareholders to support all of these directors." The speaker was plainly out of order. Yet Loveless let him continue; why should he silence this friendly voice?

But the speaker wasn't a shill for the company—he was Will Layng, an SEIU organizer from Portland, Oregon. "These shareholders have done a great job of keeping profits and share value high," Layng continued, "by keeping worker wages down. I say we support them!"

A smattering of boos rose from the crowd at Layng's last words—not even all of our allies realized he was playing a role. Kaeley Pruitt-Hamm, a Quaker activist, rose to challenge our straw man. "I disagree!" she shouted. "We should be treating our workers fairly—respect them and their right to form unions." Applause broke out.

"I love our workers!" she cried, and at that cue, eighty people in the room stood up, held up large pink hearts, and chanted, "We love workers, yes we do! We love workers, how about you?" And at the last word, eighty index fingers pointed directly at CEO Brad Tilden, seated in the front row.

Then, just as quickly as the disturbance had erupted, everyone sat down and handed the meeting back to Loveless. As with the opening prayer, the pink hearts and pointed fingers action grew out of the creativity of community supporters, who had determined to confront corporate greed with expressions of love. The tone of protest must have been surprising to Alaska executives, as was its scale.

Next up was the advisory vote on executive compensation, another pro forma item given who controlled the shares. As Loveless read the resolution, a worker stood up and shouted, "We need a union!"

Before Loveless could react, the worker sat down, and another worker in a different part of the room popped up and shouted "Better pay!"

"Health benefits!" yelled a third.

"Safety at LAX!" roared another.

Alex Hoopes jumped up: "Brad, if they can give you a raise, why not us?"

A dozen workers, scattered throughout the auditorium, took their turns in this pop-up action, with the final one leading a chant that everyone joined in on: "What do we want?" "Union!" "When do we want it?" "Now!"

Then everyone sat down, silent.

Loveless had one more business item—a shareholder-introduced resolution limiting executive golden parachutes—before he could hand the meeting over to CEO Brad Tilden, something he must have been quite eager to do by this point. But as Loveless recited the resolution, Carol Harris stood up for another intervention.

Harris was a hospital worker, a local union vice president, and a passionate and devoted leader in her evangelical African American church. She had immersed herself in the airport campaign a year prior after meeting with workers and learning about their mistreatment and unsafe conditions. "First I had to get over the shock that this was really happening, because being on the outside looking in, you think that the airport workers are being treated real well," she recalled. Harris had grown up outside New Orleans, in a segregated town on the west bank of the Mississippi. Her mom cleaned the houses of white folks and Harris grew up thinking it was normal for black people to enter houses through the back door. The idea of flying in airplanes seemed as fantastical as walking into a white person's house through the front door. "We could never afford to fly in an airplane," she said. Airports held a distant and romantic aura of splendor and adventure. "Anyone who worked there—oh my god, they've got to be doing really well," she thought. So when Harris started hearing about the poverty conditions of Sea-Tac workers, "it was just like, 'Really? Are you serious?'" She thought, "We've got to do something. And when I realized other faith leaders were helping, and knowing there's power in numbers, then I decided I want my number to be counted. I want to be there."

Harris was asked by a community organizer if she would sing at the shareholders meeting. It would take complete self-assurance to stand up in an auditorium full of shareholders and belt out a tune. At first she demurred—singing wasn't her strong suit, even though she sang plenty in church. But as she reflected on the airport workers she had met and the risks they had taken, Harris concluded that singing at the meeting was to be her contribution to the struggle. As Loveless recited the last resolution, Harris stood up, her sense of righteousness sweeping aside any trepidation. "Solid as a rock!" she belted out in her most boisterous church voice, and eighty people responded, "Solid as a rock!"

"Rooted as a tree!" Harris sang, and the rest of us repeated her words. "We are here, standing tall, for airport workers!" she sang, her voice reverberating through the auditorium.

On the repeat verse, the other faith leaders began clapping. Harris waved her arms in the air to put a flourish on each righteous line. Alaska executives sat in their chairs, stone faced. Loveless gripped the sides of the podium, helpless. This was no longer a corporate business meeting, but a revival service.

Harris finished leading the insurrectionary chorale and sat down. We were flush with success.

"If there's another disruption," Lawless announced, "we'll end the meeting early." I doubted that. The company would be hard-pressed to shut down their own CEO, who was up next. In any event, we were done launching our surprise actions. And to my surprise, the company was making no move to evict us. Perhaps they calculated that there were too many of us, and it was easier to endure the discomfort of our presence than to restore meeting order through a show of force.

Brad Tilden took the stage. His voice quavered a bit as he welcomed the shareholders. Was he going to face more upheaval? It would be natural for him to assume that we would interrupt him during this part of the meeting, the presentation on spectacular profits, growth plans, and shareholder value. But this was an afternoon of surprises for the company, and the last surprise in our arsenal was letting Tilden run through his presentation uninterrupted. We wanted to listen for any hints of compromise.

Tilden gave an upbeat report on the company's prosperity—a record $306 million in annual profits. And he announced several strategic route expansions, tempered by warnings of growing competition from Southwest and Delta Airlines. Regarding the airline's contractors, he maintained, Alaska recognized there were problems but had no influence over contractor labor relations. As for the initiative, he noted that Washington State already had the highest minimum wage in the country. Raising it to $15/hour in the airport would represent a 63 percent increase, jeopardizing company profits, he asserted.

And the CEO warned: "I've watched the movie of airline after airline after airline not honor the requirement to make a profit, and what they do is they file for bankruptcy. And hundreds of thousands of people lose jobs, pensions get cut. So one of the things we believe in our core is we have to run this business successfully. We absolutely have to do that—the market matters."[1]

In essence Tilden was asserting that fair pay and union rights were not issues to be judged by fairness and morality. Rather, they should be determined within the ebb and flow of the capitalist marketplace: "The fares we charge our customers—if Southwest can offer a low fare, we've got to be prepared to offer a low fare. In terms of when we compete for labor in the market, we need to be somewhere close to market. When we buy airplanes from Boeing, we need to be close to market. When we buy fuel from Arco or whomever, we need to be close to the market. You can have strategies to nudge you a little bit on some of those things, but if your goal is to provide market returns to your investors, you can't get too far out of whack on those things. So the market does matter," he said.

We had gone into the shareholders meeting with the goal of fusing a moral call for justice to a confrontational demonstration of our power—combining the two core strengths of the campaign. Without a doubt we had shaken company executives. But the question was whether we had disturbed them enough. Tilden's ringing defense of the company and the iron laws of the market gave us the answer. There would be no settlement, no avoiding the initiative battle.

Workers, clergy, and other supporters filed out of the auditorium feeling a mixture of pride and frustration. "It's like they hear you but they don't listen," recalled Alex Hoopes. And yet, he thought, "Things like this, you have to keep doing it."

From purely an economic perspective, Tilden's rejection of negotiations was illogical. His decision to resist union recognition and to invite the initiative battle ended up costing the company more money in the long run. Why didn't he agree to negotiate?

The answer is that debates around money, profitability, income inequality, and "the market" were merely proxy terms for the real issue at stake: power. By yielding to the union's demand for recognition and negotiations, Tilden would be ceding power to workers and their organizations. The company would have to negotiate with workers; it would no longer be able to unilaterally impose whatever it wanted. It would be a throwback to before 2005. Alaska and the other airlines—fierce competitors for customers but loyal compatriots when it came to class interests—had toiled mightily for decades realigning the balance of power in the industry. They had wrenched power from workers through deregulation and bankruptcy maneuvers, tough bargaining, and contracting out. And Alaska was not about to begin backpedaling now, even when the alternative was a costly voter initiative.

Money was secondary. For $10 million—just 3 percent of the company's net profit of $306 million—Tilden could have paid all of his contract workers $15/hour.[2] Ostensibly, the campaign in the ensuing months would be about $15/hour wages, paid sick leave, and workplace rights, but in truth these issues merely were surrogates for the fight over the balance of power at Sea-Tac.

Two weeks after the shareholders meeting, with colorful balloons and media cameras in tow, airport workers and community supporters paraded into SeaTac City Hall and delivered boxes of signed petitions for the SeaTac Good Jobs Initiative. A marching brass band escorted the delegation; wheelchair attendant Assadollah Valibeigi kept time on a drum as the parade circled city hall and then ducked inside to present the petitions to the city clerk.

We were headed to the ballot and an epic battle for power in the twenty-first-century economy.

IF BRAD TILDEN was surprised at the rapid pace of events in the spring of 2013, he was hardly alone. As the ballot idea emerged, community members moved from initial disbelief, to skepticism, to a firm embrace of the bold vision.

When Omar Mumin first heard a rumor in early 2013 that Sea-Tac Airport workers were launching an ambitious ballot campaign to win $15/hour wages, his reaction was, "It must be a myth." A 63 percent wage jump wrested from the multinational corporations that ruled the airport? Not possible.

A Somali who grew up in Kenya, Mumin arrived in Seattle in 1997 and went to work at Hertz Rent-a-Car as a car shuttler. Along with other shuttle workers, Mumin would board a van that took them to a holding lot, where they would get in rental cars and drive the vehicles a mile to awaiting customers inside the airport terminal. The Hertz supervisor didn't trust Mumin and the other African workers to drive the company's shuttle van, even though they were perfectly qualified to do so, forcing them to be chaperoned around work like children by nonimmigrant workers.

Shortly after 9/11, Mumin picked up work as an aircraft fueler for ASIG, the main fueling company at the airport. He wore a long beard at the time, a symbol of his Muslim dignity. Other workers—non-Muslims—joked with him, saying that his beard drew suspicion. "It was a joke but I didn't take it as a joke," Mumin recalled. Then, three months into the job, his supervisor ordered him to shave the beard off, saying, "You resemble some people who are very suspicious." Mumin quit.

By the time Mumin began hearing about the SeaTac initiative, he was a decade gone from working those airport jobs. He had returned to college for a business degree and led a nonprofit group that sent donations to Kenya to fund well digging and food banks. To make ends meet for his wife and six children, he drove a limousine and served as a medical and court interpreter. When he first heard about the $15 initiative, his reaction was, "If we couldn't change the small things back then, how would we be able to get to fifteen dollars an hour now?"

Mumin and I were sitting in a south Seattle mosque a year after the initiative when he described to me why he was initially incredulous about the airport campaign, and how he came to believe in the possibility of great change.

As an interpreter, a charity worker, and a devout Muslim, Mumin circulated widely throughout the community. Mumin explained that as he talked to more people in the mosques and other community gathering places in the spring of 2013, he came to see that, beyond the $15 minimum wage, the campaign was a bold community bid to tilt power away from the corporations and political elites who controlled the airport, and back toward the community and workers. As Mumin explored further, he saw immigrants and refugees uniting with American-born citizens who also chafed under lousy airport working conditions. And standing with all of them was a broad array of religious and community supporters and other workers. It was not something he had witnessed before in America.

"I saw how this social movement was being organized," Mumin recalled. "We're being helped, being given a lot of support. That really changed my mind. And I stopped thinking that this was a myth."

MUMIN ALREADY HAD been connected to campaign organizers. In 2011, a mutual friend had introduced him to Abdinasir Mohamed in a local restaurant. Both Swahili speakers, they hit it off. The Occupy movement was in full swing. Mohamed invited Mumin to join a bank protest organized by Working Washington. Through the Working

Washington protests he met union organizer Ahmed Ali, and Ali introduced him to me. Mumin began volunteering on the campaign, putting his extensive community contacts to work. When the initiative drive took shape in 2013, I hired Mumin as a community organizer.

Mumin was energized by what he saw, but in his first forays into the SeaTac community, he encountered the same skepticism that he had himself once harbored. One day he knocked on the door of an elderly Somali woman. Excitedly, he told her about the budding social movement in SeaTac that would deliver $15 wages to airport workers. "It's not going to happen," the woman replied, shaking his confidence. She was well aware of the poverty conditions—she had a daughter who took care of her and also worked at the airport. But the idea of wresting such money from Alaska Airlines and the major businesses—through the voters, no less—seemed implausible, even absurd.

Mumin rallied. We live in a democracy, he replied. If voters approved the new wage, it would become law, and businesses would have to follow it. Finally, after a long talk, Mumin was able to persuade the woman to join the cause, but as he continued door knocking he found these conversations typical. "It took a long time for us to convince a lot of immigrants, our people, that this can be a reality," Mumin said.

Union organizer Yasmin Aden ran into similar skepticism. One day while knocking on doors in the Crystal Manor apartments, a low-rise cluster of buildings just up the street from the airport, Aden ran into a friend, Sarah Mohamoud. They already were acquainted through the Somali social network. "What are you doing here?" Mohamoud asked.

Registering voters and educating them about the $15 initiative, Aden replied.

Mohamoud didn't work at the airport, but she had more incentive than most to back the campaign. For her, living wages at the airport could reunite her family.

Her husband, William, used to work for Menzies Aviation as a baggage handler. In 2007 their first child was born, a son. Paid close to minimum wage, William had to work double and even triple shifts to get enough income. He was barely home. Even so, the family was late on rent most months. Then, she said, the company cut vacation time and other benefits. William came home one day and announced "I'm done. I just can't do it." A friend told him about the good pay other Africans were getting for fishing in Alaska, and took him to a waterfront hiring office. William got hired on the spot, and two days later left for Alaska. He worked on a ship in the Gulf of Alaska nine months out of the year, a world away from Sarah, his son, and a daughter just born.

Given Mohamoud's family situation, which Aden knew, the union organizer figured it would be a cinch to win her support. Not so. Mohamoud resisted the idea even of registering to vote, let alone getting involved in the initiative. Diving into a political campaign in their new home was not something that many Somali immigrants were inclined to do. Along with her family, Mohamoud had been lucky to escape the everyday bombings and gunshots in Mogadishu that dominated the first years of her life. She was smuggled out of Somalia at age seven, hidden in the bed of a truck that lumbered across the Kenyan border only after the driver managed to bribe multiple warlords stalking the road out of Somalia. Mohamoud and her family spent four years in a Kenyan slum before securing passage to the United States. She felt lucky to be alive and grateful to be in the United States. Rocking the boat by taking on big business at the airport seemed an unwise step, Mohamoud told Aden. She wanted to keep a low profile.

"Your son Abdul doesn't see his dad," Aden reminded her.

You're right, Mohamoud acknowledged. What drove William to Alaska was the lousy airport pay. "I'm literally a single mom. If he had good benefits and a good-paying job at Menzies, he would've been there for the kids and been more involved with the family." She registered to vote, and then agreed to introduce Aden to her neighbors at Crystal Manor.

Mohamoud spent the rest of the day knocking on doors with Aden. Being a sociable person, Mohamoud knew all of her neighbors—what country they hailed from, which ones worked at the airport, and what companies they worked for. They went door-to-door, registering new citizens to vote and dealing with skeptical questions. Yes, SeaTac voters had the right to mandate a $15/hour wage. No, getting a higher wage wouldn't increase their rent. And Mohamoud told her neighbors she wanted the initiative passed so she could get her husband back from Alaska.

By the end of the day, the pair had registered several voters, won new commitments for support, and dispelled misunderstandings about the initiative. Mohamoud was excited. Getting out there and telling her family story had gotten her over the hurdle of passivity. She told Aden, Let's do this again tomorrow. They did, and the wife of a reluctant Alaskan fisherman became a fixture on the campaign trail, motivated by the hope of giving her children a full-time father.

Part of the challenge that Mumin, Aden, Mohamoud, and the other staff organizers and volunteers faced was the twofold skepticism they continually confronted: First were the doubts of workers and neighbors about the idea of legislating a huge raise through popular vote. The idea was far beyond their experience or understanding of US democracy; at first glance it seemed downright bizarre. And second were the organizers' own lingering hesitations about promoting a strategy that had no analogue or precedent. None of us could say, "They did this over there, so we can do the same thing here." Organizers had to apply a measure of faith—a belief within themselves and in their conversations with others based not on proof or precedent—in cajoling people to take a step into uncharted territory.

Alex Hoopes, the baggage handler who worked for Alaska Airlines until the mass firings of 2005, also knocked on SeaTac doors, concentrating on the modest single-family ranch homes of the city's older working-class neighborhoods. Hoopes used a personal narrative to connect with fellow white working-class voters. "I told them how back in 2005 I was making a very comfortable living. Being paid that, you can give back to your community. I'd describe the businesses around the area I'd gone to—this business and this restaurant here, and other businesses up and down Pacific Highway."

Hoopes also went out with staff organizers to local businesses around the airport—teriyaki restaurants, used car lots, convenience stores, even bars. They'd go into the store and ask for the manager. Their message was eminently practical. Because airport workers didn't have spending money, local businesses were missing customers, he told them. More than two dozen business owners and managers publicly endorsed the initiative, a modest but notable counterpoint to the chamber of commerce, Alaska Airlines, and other big businesses.

The Iranian wheelchair attendant Assadollah Valibeigi went door knocking as well. He, along with one hundred other workers, community allies, and staff organizers spilled out of the Reverend Jan Bolerjack's Riverton Park United Methodist Church after a canvass training and motivational speeches. They were psyched up, ready to make history, brimming with confidence. Their cause was eminently just. Valibeigi was paired up with union organizer Sisay Wagnew, an Ethiopian. They came to their first house and knocked. A white man opened the door. Valibeigi began to tell his story about poverty airport wages in his broken English. Oh, really? the man replied. Then quit. If things are bad, then you should go find another job, he told the Iranian.

It was a rude jolt, but Valibeigi didn't give up easily. "To you, maybe it's easy. But for some people, it's not easy to find a job." And even if you don't care about the workers, Valibeigi continued, consider the traveling public. "Who is going to push your mama, your papa in the wheelchair? Who is going to clean the toilet in the airport that you are using? Somebody has to do the job."

The man was unaffected; Valibeigi and Wagnew moved on, beginning to appreciate that just because the matter of justice was obvious to them didn't mean that voters, even working-class voters, would immediately rise to the occasion. They had better luck at the remaining doors that day, but many voters still required persuasion.

AIRPORT WORKERS AND ORGANIZERS eyed a pivotal date on the initiative calendar—July 23, when the SeaTac City Council would officially place the SeaTac Good Jobs Initiative on the November ballot. The vote was a formality; under the law, the council was required to put an initiative with enough signatures on the ballot. But with the media flocking to SeaTac, the July hearing was a key opportunity to put our best arguments before the cameras and show the breadth of support for the initiative. The opposition would mobilize as well. They had been preparing since we had announced the initiative.

The day before the start of signature gathering, the general manager of SeaTac's Holiday Inn warned his SeaTac hospitality industry peers of the initiative's "catastrophic effect on the travel and tourism industry in our city"—unemployment, business failure, a freeze on future economic development. He implored city council members "to soundly and unanimously reject this proposed ordinance."[3] We knew that the Holiday Inn manager's salvo was just a hint of the gathering storm we would face from SeaTac employers—the airlines, airport concessions companies, area hotels, restaurants, rental car companies, and parking lot operators.

We also knew that a second prong of opposition would emerge from the older, conservative elements of SeaTac's working class. This was in some ways the more dangerous of the two, because it had a genuine grassroots foundation and capacity to mobilize voters. By 2013, what had been a majority-white community a generation earlier was now 61 percent people of color—mostly new immigrants from Africa and Asia. For the old-timers, the semirural community of modest single-family homes that they knew was rapidly getting supplanted by traffic jams, large apartment complexes, and a population that didn't look, speak, or act like them. But even though they were now the minority, whites constituted 62 percent of the voting population; many of the new residents were not yet citizens.[4] Several of the more conservative old-timers were active in local politics. Three had been elected to city council. SeaTac was a picture of America's future, but it voted clinging to the past: in 2012, while surrounding communities were voting two to one for marriage equality in a statewide referendum, SeaTac voters were evenly split.[5]

The conservative activists formed the nucleus of a Tea Party chapter that faithfully attended city council meetings to berate the four council members whom they considered to be out of step. They fulminated in the blogosphere against the latest liberal conspiracy in their small community: city zoning decisions, council member travel expenses, fireworks permits, and alleged ethical breaches—any issue, no matter how petty, that in their minds proved how local government was angling to trample on citizens' constitutional rights. Many of the council votes were four to three, tallied only after prolonged council debate and scathing speeches from the audience and the conservative council members. The activists reserved their harshest words for Mia Su-Ling Gregerson, the only person of color on the council. Born in Taiwan, Gregerson reflected the emerging face of SeaTac. In a sharply fought contest for reelection, she had beaten one of their Tea Party members in 2011 by a slim 31 votes out of 4,500 cast, a decisive race that flipped the council to majority non–Tea Party. They were not about to forgive her.

The SeaTac initiative provided a huge, welcome target for the conservatives: a law in which government would confer on a group of mostly immigrant workers a sudden, bountiful handout—money, sick leave, workplace rights normally only seen in union contracts—played right into their revulsion of liberal politics. To them, you got ahead in America through hard work and respect for business, not through welfare and government intervention. This was Obamacare on steroids, imposed on their community by outside unions, benefitting people who were new to SeaTac and had not paid their dues. Indeed, SeaTac Tea Party activists themselves could not have dreamed up a better political issue with which to galvanize their base.

More than two hundred initiative supporters and a couple dozen opponents filtered into SeaTac City Council chambers on July 23, and when people kept coming, city staff opened up an adjoining room for the overflow crowd. Still, once all the seats were occupied, dozens more gathered around the perimeter of the room, leaning against the walls. Many held signs: Good Jobs, Healthy Communities; More Home Ownership; Hope for Our Children; Support Small Businesses. The room churned with energy as conservative activists took their customary seats in the audience only to be hemmed in by an animated, mostly immigrant crowd that had never before occupied the council room. In the hallway a Tea Party member shouted that one of our supporters was threatening him. Police intervened before the confrontation turned physical.

Mayor Tony Anderson brought the meeting to order and invited speakers in turn—first ours, then theirs.[6] We wanted to elevate the debate beyond the specifics of the initiative to community values, people, and families. We knew the other side would attack the details as they assailed the notion of social engineering in a capitalist society.

Reverend Bolerjack was first up, telling the council and crowd about being introduced to the airport economy through the church's food bank. "It didn't surprise me when this campaign for good jobs at the airport came up, because I had been seeing the workers—the workers in their Menzies jackets or other airport uniforms—coming to the food pantry," she said.

"I saw the fatigue and stress on their faces with only a few hours to catch some sleep before they would go back to the tarmac or the car rental agency—but rather than sleep they had to come and wait to get food.

"My hope," she continued, "is that with a livable wage our communities could be stabilized. Families could be under less stress. Parents would have time and the emotional availability to sit with their children, read to them, play with them, even attend school events with them—those things are missing in times of stress."

Luis Escamilla, a local high school teacher, noted that more than 70 percent of his students qualified for reduced-price lunches. And he went on: "We have a below seventy-five percent on-time graduation rate, which speaks to a lot of factors. Economics play a huge role. Tons of our older students have to work near full-time hours because their families can't make ends meet.

"It's time to acknowledge," Escamilla continued with a nod toward the opponents, "that we have a group of people, many newer residents, who don't have the same types of opportunities that others had back in the fifties and sixties."

Wheelchair attendant Evelyn Olano described wage theft at the airport: "I work eight hours but I'm told to put down for seven because if there are no flights, we have to stay clocked out at 'lunch' until the next flight."

And she told about how jobs were chopped up to keep workers below thresholds for benefits, such as health care: "I used to make minimum wage for thirty-two hours, but under the new manager I only work three days. We trained new people—the manager said we need to share. So now I'm paid minimum wage for twenty-one hours. So I have a second job at the airport, also minimum wage, for Olympic Security Incorporated. Neither job has to give us benefits. I don't have paid sick leave. If I have an emergency I have to take unpaid time off. If I take too much time off I'll get fired."

Then it was the other side's turn, and the speeches turned to scolding. "I would like everyone to know that I am not antiunion," began Vicki Lockwood, an older white woman. She was raised in a union family, and had been a Teamsters shop steward, she explained. "I'm not antiunion—but I'm antigiveaway. People need to acquire education and skills to make themselves worth more money," she insisted. There were grumbles in the crowd.

"The truth is this law will hurt business and residents alike," Lockwood continued. "Businesses will have to pay more for people. Then they will have to raise their prices. People—which includes, by the way, people like us not making fifteen dollars an hour—will pay more for services. There will be fewer jobs. So taxpayers will shoulder the burden of those newly unemployed. The downward spiral seems pretty simple to me."

Lockwood's boosters applauded. She yielded the mic to Kathleen Brave, who faced the council members but intended her words for the ears of audience members behind her.

Brave recounted moving with her husband from South Dakota to SeaTac more than forty years earlier. Her husband had worked as a warehouse mechanic and picked up second jobs to keep the family afloat. But they still struggled; they had four children. She went to work in a hardware store at minimum wage. "I was really good at what I did, and I got constant raises because I did a really good job. I had a decent education. I don't think at any point did either my husband or I say, 'Huh, I don't think I'm getting paid enough, I need to ask for more money.' It never would have worked anyway. They would have laughed at us and shown us the door.

"I still struggle on Social Security and a small pension," Brave continued. "I would love to make fifteen an hour. I'm not getting close to that, OK? And I never have. I'm seventy-two years old and still struggling. Many seniors on a fixed income are struggling. Unfortunately, we can't tell Social Security, 'Gee, I'm not making enough money, I'd like to have a little bit more so I can live a little bit better.'"

For Brave, the initiative ran directly counter to the ethics that guided her life: you struggled, you worked hard, you didn't ask anyone to help you, and you accepted your lot. Giving some workers a leg up but not others was inherently discriminatory. It was undeserved.

Brave continued: "Now we have many—and not all, I'm not talking about all of you, but many—unskilled, uneducated people and many who obviously weren't born in this country who think they deserve more."

Loud boos filled the room. Brave turned to the audience. "You *weren't*," she reminded them.

"Please respect her right to speak," Mayor Anderson interjected.

Brave continued: "Many who weren't born in this country who are uneducated and unskilled who think they deserve more than I do, or my neighbors do. My dad's family came on the *Mayflower*, and no one helped them. My mom's family came from Switzerland with no help. My mother-in-law raised five children with no help whatsoever, no food stamps. She worked two jobs."

The initiative, Brave concluded, "goes way too far and in the long run you're going to be disappointed when you lose your jobs because all this is going to do is line the pockets of union workers."

Scott Ostrander, general manager of SeaTac's Cedarbrook Lodge, called the initiative "well intended but very misinformed." His boutique hotel, he said, had 117 employees. He treated his staff well: "I do not pay any one of them minimum wage. They all get two meals a day, complimentary. They've got great benefits."

And, he went on, the initiative would be devastating for his staff, because with higher pay requirements he inevitably would reduce the number of people on his payroll. "I'm shaking here tonight because I'm going to be forced to lay people off for something that is not their fault. Something that they have no control over. I'm going to take away their livelihood. God that hurts. That really, really hurts."

Ostrander choked up. "This initiative," he concluded, "will destroy this community."

Prior to the hearing, we had told the airport workers and their supporters to expect sharp dissent, xenophobia, and racist attitudes. But it's one thing for workers to be told about what to expect to hear, quite another thing to experience the unmasking of brute ignorance, venom, and condescension. Sitting in the audience, Sarah Mohamoud, the fisherman's wife, was hardly alone in being shocked by the opposition's words. "The language they were using, and the demeanor—they were looking at these immigrants like pieces of shit. Like nothing," she told me later. The blunt directness of the Tea Party speakers was a rude awakening. "Just the language, like, 'They want everything handed to them; they don't want to work.' I know they think about it, but just to hear them say it was painful," she recalled.

It would be easy, too, for union campaigners to dismiss, even laugh off, the overblown rhetoric from the other side: Lockwood's and Brave's "uneducated" characterization of the immigrant airport workers, many of whom spoke multiple languages and held degrees and professions in their homelands; Brave's whimsical recitation of the *Mayflower* settlers toughing it out on their own, erasing any memory of the aid native people provided to the European immigrants to help them survive those first winters in America; Ostrander's overwrought warnings about SeaTac's impending demise and his unqualified assertion that he would somehow be forced to fire workers if the initiative passed—to say nothing of his ironic admission that Cedarbrook staff depended on free food handouts from management.

But we would discount the rhetoric at our peril, because the economic and social mythology being recounted by our opponents was in fact deeply rooted in society, and more specifically within a significant portion of the SeaTac electorate. To win we'd have to confront and overcome these arguments.

We knew that there was a part of the white working-class population in SeaTac that, while not attached to the same myths, was at least susceptible to believing that there was a grain of truth in them. They, too, had accepted the economic legend that in America you worked hard, lifted yourself up by your own bootstraps, and didn't ask for outside help. They, too, lived in a community in rapid transition. They didn't have to accept the full-blown racism and xenophobia of the Tea Party adherents to doubt the wisdom of a law that directed employers how much to pay workers and how to treat them.

I watched Lockwood, Brave, and the others carry on in the packed, stifling hearing room, earnest and passionate in their convictions, and wondered what signal events or influences had marked their life journeys. They were solidly members of the working class, as far from CEOs and chamber executives as anyone else in the room. They had known hard work and tough times. Lockwood and Brave were paid poverty wages. But rather than be drawn by their experiences to find common cause with people in the same economic circumstances, they had reached the exact opposite conclusion: you're on your own—

defiantly, proudly so. For them, Alaska Airlines and its record profits were not an issue. They had bought the full gamut of capitalist myths: the impersonal "market" that governs all, the immutable correlation between higher wages and higher unemployment, the inherent role of profit in driving the economy forward, and the principle that you should work hard and not complain. They would have applauded Alaska CEO Brad Tilden's defense of capitalism at the shareholders meeting earlier that spring.

No doubt their values had been drawn from a national political culture that unremittingly attacked any policy initiative that tilted, however modestly, toward a social good—national health insurance, progressive taxation, gun violence prevention, or antidiscrimination and worker protection laws. And certainly their political views had been sharpened on the ever-spinning grindstones of Fox News and reactionary talk radio shows. It all played on their fears of change, a drifting away from the mythical time in America of white picket fences and boundless opportunity through hard work. Racism and xenophobia doubled down on the fears.

But as I watched them, it also occurred to me that it wasn't just the presence of reactionary media that shaped them, but also the absence in their lives of any countervailing working-class ideology that put people's needs before profits, that preached class solidarity and mutual aid. We would be wrong to label Lockwood, Brave, and their peers as outliers, to belittle them for their conclusions; they represented a point of view that resonated with many workers. Lockwood and Brave had entered the workforce after World War II, after the vast majority of the union movement had abandoned any semblance of social mission backed by militant action. These members of the working class grew up understanding that unions were special-interest organizations. Unions served their dues payers in a business-union model, delivering higher wages and better benefits to their members, unconcerned that over time as the gap widened between union workers and the rest of the workforce, their very success was helping to reinforce divisions within the working class. And now on full display before us in SeaTac City Hall were the fruits of that narrow union approach. Lockwood and Brave represented not just the triumph of capitalist ideology, but equally the failure of the labor movement in the past seventy years to articulate and build unity around a working-class vision of society. In a political vacuum, the antiunion ideology flourished. Union supporters couldn't blame Fox News for that.

And where was Alaska Airlines? Company executives skipped the hearing. They had nothing to gain by drawing attention to themselves in city hall. Better to let low-wage members of the working class fight one another—to let, as nineteenth-century railroad magnate Jay Gould put it, one half of the working class fight the other half. Of course the company planned to generously fund the Vote No campaign, but for the public hearing, company executives took a pass, doubtless happy to see Vicki Lockwood, Kathleen Brave, and their cohorts do the company's bidding.

After two hours of debate, Mayor Anderson closed public comments. The council voted to place the SeaTac Good Jobs Initiative before the voters in November, designating it SeaTac Proposition 1. Over the next 105 days, the national and international media would descend on the small suburb and establish it as ground zero for the national debate on income inequality. But first the historic initiative had to confront a shocking court development and an internal union drama that nearly shredded the campaign before the citizens of SeaTac even got to vote.

EIGHT

UNION TROUBLES, COMMUNITY WIN

ALASKA AIRLINES HAD contested the initiative in court since its filing with the City of SeaTac. The company hired attorneys to review each individual signature and raise any challenge, no matter how dubious: penmanship that did not quite match the signature on file, missing dates, smudged addresses, and the entries of voters who mistakenly signed two different petitions. Alaska's goal was to knock 1,000 of the 2,500 submitted signatures out, placing the initiative petition below the required threshold for ballot status. It was a long-shot strategy, as court precedent and state laws both tilted toward counting petition signatures that had minor defects.

But in late August 2013, the improbable happened. Alaska persuaded a lower court judge to invalidate all of the signatures of people who had signed more than one petition—not just their second signatures, but their first ones as well. King County superior court justice Andrea Darvas also accepted hundreds of other signature challenges that, in aggregate, put the petition below the legal threshold. On the afternoon of August 26, a week before Labor Day, Judge Darvas issued her ruling: SeaTac Proposition 1 must be removed from the November ballot.

It was a stunning decision. The lawyers scrambled to appeal, but just as urgently we had to deal with the shock that reverberated throughout the airport, the community, and the team of campaign staff and allied organizations. We might not have a vote on the $15 minimum wage after all. Inside the airport and in the community, supporters were livid with Alaska Airlines. Some wanted to take to the streets against the company and the other SeaTac businesses that had sided with the airline. Others began to wonder if we hadn't taken on an invincible corporate foe. It resurfaced nagging doubts that we had aimed too high.

The legal approach was fairly clear: File a series of emergency appeals to restore Proposition 1 to the ballot. The organizing approach was more complicated. Staff and volunteers, in angst about the latest turn of events, found themselves in wrenching conversations with distraught workers and community supporters. But we had work to do: continue community outreach work with the expectation that we would get back on the ballot, collect more initiative signatures in case the court would accept them, and prepare airport workers and allies to mobilize for the possibility of an emergency appeals court hearing.

Our first full campaign staff meeting in this new, disturbing territory convened the day after Labor Day. The SEIU conference room was full—thirty-five organizers from various unions and community groups. People were quiet, perhaps emotionally drained. Our lawyers had exhausted emergency motions with Judge Darvas, who was resolute in her original decision. They had just filed an urgent appeal with the state court of appeals. We had less than four days to reverse the lower court decision, because that Friday afternoon, county election officials would send November election ballots to the printer—without Proposition 1 on them, unless we secured a legal reversal.

As the campaign's director, I was responsible for rallying the team. But I, too, was distressed, and not just for the obvious reason. Another problem occupying my mind had to do with an internal union conflict that was threatening to unravel the work of the previous two years, jeopardizing both the organizing and the ballot campaign. It was an issue that most on our team were blissfully unaware of, and one that I would have to deal with urgently outside the staff meeting room.

I convened the meeting and acknowledged the extraordinarily difficult moment we all faced. I recounted the tremendous, transformative work that workers, community members, and staff organizers had engaged in together, taking risks and venturing into uncharted territory. None of these actions came without risk of failure, I said. And the bigger and bolder our idea, the more forceful a reaction we could expect from Alaska Airlines and its business allies. This was, after all, a struggle about power, and Alaska had no price limit on defending its power over workers. We shouldn't be surprised that our big idea for the working class had encountered capitalism's full-throated response.

I reminded them that part of what has to drive each of us forward is faith, whether grounded in a particular religious belief, humanistic spirituality, or moral conviction. It's the same faith, I said, that sustained Reverend Helmiere as he stood in front of the Alaska shareholders meeting, defiantly leading a prayer for fair worker treatment; or Carol Harris, who in the same meeting stood up and belted out her song for justice at Alaska Airlines; or the workers who interrupted the CEO to demand union recognition and fair pay. They were driven forward in those moments by a powerful belief that transcended the practical obstacles in front of them.

Organizers spoke up, talking about the frustration of our predicament, the angst of workers, the tension of not knowing where we were headed. In the room we had the full range of spiritual practitioners—from devout Muslims, Christians, and Jews to atheists. As they talked, I sensed them gathering up their courage to leave the room, head to the airport or into the community, and engage our supporters in the day's work—putting one foot in front of the other, not sure where we would be at the end of the week but at least purposeful about our next steps. I turned the meeting over to our senior staff and left the room to tackle the second problem, which was just as pressing and a bit more daunting and complex: the campaign's main funder, a local SEIU leader, was panicking and had resolved, unilaterally, to redirect strategy, undermining the foundation of the entire effort.

UNTIL THIS MOMENT, the Sea-Tac campaign had represented a broad coalition, a coming together of unions, faith communities, and civic groups. The campaign was a confluence of different organizational and social cultures, bound together by the powerful idea that we would transform a community by lifting up airport jobs. Central to this vision was the recognition that the campaign was about building power in the workplace and the community, and the vital role that airport workers needed to play in their own liberation. Proposition 1 was not an end, but rather a demonstration of how we could build a powerful workers movement.

While the campaign was funded exclusively by unions—and largely by my union, SEIU—we invited broad participation in strategy development and planning from community and faith allies. The willingness of unions to move beyond their familiar operating zones—most notably, by uniting with the Muslim community to defend the workplace right to pray, and also by embracing the organizing ideas of Christian faith leaders—had built a level of trust in the community that would be vital to carrying us to electoral victory. But now this trust was in jeopardy, and its unraveling would have dire consequences for us.

At the epicenter of this behind-the-scenes drama was the president of SEIU 775, David Rolf. As head of the home-care and nursing-home workers union in Washington State, Rolf was willing to invest significant resources in bold campaigns when other union leaders shrank from commitment. Built from a tiny membership beginning in 2002, SEIU 775 had reached forty thousand members within a decade—caregivers in private homes and in long-term nursing facilities. Under Rolf's leadership SEIU 775 became a powerhouse, winning state-funded raises for the lowest-paid health-care workers and contributing significant dollars and shoe leather to political campaigns. It was just one of the five SEIU locals in the state—SEIU having established different local unions for the different industries in which it represented workers—but SEIU 775 had the highest public profile of the five.

Rolf had grown up in Cincinnati, gone to college on the East Coast, and plunged directly into union politics after school in 1991. While he lacked experience as a union member, Rolf went to work as an SEIU staff organizer in Georgia, and a few years later SEIU's national leadership sent him to Los Angeles to lead the campaign to organize seventy-four thousand home-care workers. An expert in the art of the political deal, Rolf negotiated a grand bargain with the Los Angeles County Board of Supervisors: home-care union recognition in exchange for giving up the right of workers to strike.[1] In 2001 Rolf moved to Seattle with direction from SEIU national leaders to build a Washington State home-care-workers union.

One of Rolf's first stops when he arrived in Seattle in 2001 was the headquarters of Seattle Union Now, the AFL-CIO's multiunion project I was directing at the time. I sublet Rolf a spare office so he could establish a base of operations as he laid the foundation for home-care organizing. What struck me as refreshing about Rolf, as I observed him in his first decade in Seattle, sometimes working directly with him, at other times watching from a different perch in the labor movement, was his creativity and ambition. We needed more big thinkers in the labor movement. But I also saw Rolf quickly become a polarizing figure in the Seattle labor community, disdainful of other unions and prone to making sweeping statements about the obsolescence of strikes and proclamations about "the death of collective bargaining."[2] For the union of the future, Rolf seemed to draw more inspiration from Silicon Valley entrepreneurs than from contemporary labor struggles. He approvingly quoted Intel CEO Andrew Grove's advice to him to focus on outcomes above all "and treat everything else—laws, strategies, structures—as secondary."[3] As I observed Rolf, workers, community allies, and collective decision making also fell into that secondary category. I saw the political campaigns that he led driven by strategies developed by top leaders, presented to the members with little discussion, and implemented with agility by a disciplined professional union staff. The primary role of members was to be mobilized for actions. Worker grievances, rather than dealt with through collective discussion and actions, were handled by a call center—union staff answering members' questions and providing services and advice. It was a robust, modern form of business unionism.

Rolf's perspective on the union doubtless was colored by his experience working with public sector workers in Georgia, where the union, lacking full collective bargaining rights under state law, focused on maneuvering politically to improve working conditions. The Los Angeles home-care organizing had been grounded in a political compromise, pushed forward by public rallies but forged behind closed doors with county leaders. In Washington State Rolf proceeded to build a large union membership, one whose power was based on his political strategy and savvy, much less so on collective worker decision making, leadership, and action. He expertly rolled out a political street operation that was unmatched in the labor movement. But it was a mobilizing operation that relied heavily on union staff, who were assigned quotas of workers to recruit for particular activities. In this scheme, it seemed to me, workers were pieces to be moved about on a chessboard, deployed in public actions, legislative hearing rooms, and at press conferences, given scripts of what to say in these public forums, but not encouraged to be the authors of their own emancipation. I saw his work as a political operation—a very competent one—but lacking in authentic worker power.

In 2011, when SEIU launched the Fight for a Fair Economy, Rolf was one of the primary boosters. Even though his local, SEIU 775, stood to gain no members from the airport campaign, he committed hundreds of thousands of dollars and many of his best staff to the effort. It was an exemplary gesture, the sort of measure that I wished more unions made.

Rolf spent little time in SeaTac—I consulted more closely with his deputies—but as 2013 unfolded he took a keener interest in the campaign, imagining how the SeaTac initiative could serve as the springboard for more $15 wage fights in the region and beyond. We all could see the larger potential, and it was exciting. Now, as the summer of 2013 turned to fall, there was just one problem with that vision: we might not even have a vote in SeaTac. Rolf was shocked. Overnight, he dove headlong into the campaign.

Immediately prior to the wrenching post–Labor Day campaign staff meeting, I had met with three of Rolf's top deputies. They informed me that Rolf intended to shift the staff organizers assigned to the airport, along with the community organizers, into a get-out-the-vote push. Earlier, campaign leaders from all of the key unions in the coalition—SEIU 775; SEIU Local 6; the Teamsters; UNITE HERE; and UFCW, the United Food and Commercial Workers International Union—had agreed to move some staff to door knocking, while keeping enough in the airport to continue to organize workers for the initiative campaign. These leaders recognized that Sea-Tac was fundamentally an organizing campaign: workers had to play a central role in the initiative drive because their collective action would be essential in the ballot campaign and beyond. Rolf saw it differently, as his deputies now explained: to him, this was a political campaign, and what mattered was mobilizing a successful vote. In Rolf's scheme, staff would leave the airport workers, the mosque and church leaders, and the community partners, and focus on a tightly disciplined, professional get-out-the-vote operation.

I protested, pointing out that Rolf hadn't consulted with any of the other union or community leaders. I worried that this move would undermine the nature of the movement we had built in SeaTac, damage relations with unions and community allies that were critical to our credibility in the city, and destroy the trust of airport workers. We might—assuming we got back on the ballot—still manage to win the SeaTac initiative with Rolf's political operation, but we would burn bridges in the process and lose any possibility of building a strong worker and community organization. At best the campaign would stand as yet another illustration of a labor movement that can fight for wages but fails to build working-class power; a ballot success, but a union-building failure.

But at this point, it was becoming clear to me, my opinion and protests were of little concern to Rolf. And, because SEIU 775 staff led the airport field organizing team, they were going to take orders from their president, not me. End of discussion.

So David Rolf's actions provoked internal upheaval, in the midst of a dangerous legal assault from Alaska Airlines, at the moment when the Sea-Tac unions and community allies most needed to stand together, when airport workers and campaign staff needed the confidence that comes with unified, present leadership. I was not going to abide his unilateralism, but neither was I going to fight the matter on my own. The Sea-Tac campaign was a coalition effort, and the other organizations needed to weigh in.

Immediately after stepping out of the campaign team meeting, I called leaders from the other unions, along with key community leaders, to inform them of Rolf's decision. They were the organizational presidents, directors, and other senior staff who had worked closely with me since 2011 in building the Sea-Tac campaign. I had worked with many of them as far back as twenty years in the Seattle labor movement—organizing, picketing, plotting protest, going

to jail together. Collectively, we had had healthy debates, some dis-
agreements, but on the whole formed a productive strategic group
that recognized the power of coalition and understood that the labor
movement needed to build something different. To them SeaTac was
a place to see what a new labor movement could look like. These
other union leaders all knew Rolf well. They were not surprised
when I told them Rolf had unilaterally decided to move staff out of
the airport. We began discussing how to respond.

Inside the airport, as the week progressed, with the organizers now
removed, a strange inertia settled in among airport workers, along
with their questions and doubts. Was there going to be a $15 ballot
initiative or not? The organizers had suddenly disappeared—where
had they gone? Were we going to continue meeting? Would we stage
job actions? What was happening with the initiative, and what could
they do to help us get back on the ballot? Few answers were forthcom-
ing. Some workers drifted into cynicism. "The union has their own
agenda. It's not about us anymore," SEIU Local 6 organizer Yasmin
Aden recalled one worker bitterly telling her.

With the coalition roiling internally and our lawyers working
against the clock, organizers called me to ask what they should do.
They had new assignments from Rolf's staff to contact voters, but
felt it was wrong to abandon the airport workers. That was the right
instinct, I told them, but do what you've been told. Yes, there's an
internal dispute, but we're working matters out with SEIU 775 leadership. And in your spare time, call as many airport workers as you
can. Let them know we're going to see the organizing fight through
with them, I said.

Our lawyers, meanwhile, had secured a hearing before the state
court of appeals. It would be Friday afternoon, September 6—four
hours before the five o'clock ballot printing deadline. We shuffled
into the downtown Seattle courtroom after lunch—attorneys for
the campaign, the city, and Alaska Airlines, plus media, union staff,
and a handful of workers and community allies. The three judges
filed in and immediately got down to questions. In a state with a rich
tradition of citizen ballot initiatives, the judges seemed immediately
dubious about Judge Darvas's decision to knock the proposition off
the ballot.

The hearing ended briskly at two o'clock. I walked across the court-house plaza with our lead attorney, Dmitri Iglitzin, and we sat down on a bench. Iglitzin felt good about the hearing. The judges seemed skeptical of Alaska's arguments. But it was possible to infer too much from the questions. Were we being overly hopeful? We needed the right decision, and fast. We tried chatting about other things, but my mind kept returning to the community of SeaTac, the workers and allies who had struggled so hard, and the consequences for all of us that hung in the balance. It was possible in that moment to imagine everything come crashing down.

At two thirty, Iglitzin's phone beeped, announcing a court deci-sion. He opened the e-mail: a unanimous decision in our favor, over-turning Darvas and restoring Proposition 1 to the ballot. Iglitzin and I embraced. Problem number one was solved; problem number two, the internal power struggle, still awaited a resolution.

Days after the court of appeals decision, Tracey Thompson, the prin-cipal officer of Teamsters Local 117, whose union had joined hands with the Muslim community in 2011 over the Hertz worker suspensions, con-vened a meeting of the five core Sea-Tac unions: leaders from her local, SEIU 775; SEIU Local 6; the UFCW; and UNITE HERE. Rolf attended and brought his deputies. Aside from SEIU 775, each of the unions either stood to gain new union members from a successful Sea-Tac campaign, or boost work standards for current members. Beyond institutional in-terest, they also recognized the greater labor movement purpose of the Sea-Tac campaign. I stayed away from the meeting, on the advice of Thompson and the other leaders—they wanted to deal directly with Rolf. Thompson opened the meeting and turned it over to her orga-nizing director, Leonard Smith. "This is an organizing campaign and the workers need to be involved in the initiative work," Smith recalled telling the group. "We can't just leave the airport and come back later." Then, as Smith and other meeting participants later told me, the other union leaders spoke up in turn about the need to keep organizers en-gaged with airport workers and community allies, and to maintain the coalition that had gotten the campaign this far.

Rolf pushed back, arguing that moving staff was essential to win the initiative. The other leaders insisted that it wasn't a question of staffing the get-out-the-vote drive or airport worker organizing; both were essential to the campaign's success. Sea-Tac was about building long-term power, not just winning at the ballot box. For the coalition to work, they said, there had to be equality of decision making at the table, regardless of the resources that any one organization had invested. Even though much of the campaign staff came from SEIU 775, the other union leaders would not abide a unilateral shift away from the airport.

The union leadership showdown produced what the campaign needed: acceptance by Rolf to return a number of organizers to airport and community assignments, and Rolf's designation of his top political staff to run the get-out-the-vote campaign. I welcomed the addition of SEIU 775 talent; voter turnout was their strength.

Yet it was a cold détente. Outwardly, the coalition moved forward, the campaign's larger purpose intact. But the previous easy camaraderie inside the coalition had been broken. Among the non–SEIU 775 staff, there was indelible mistrust of "Rolf's people," and we had to repair frayed ties with airport workers and community allies.

In that awkward interlude when campaign strategy hung in the balance, I reflected on the people who had embraced the campaign. Sheikh Abduqadir Jama had thrown in with the campaign, overcoming his own deep skepticism about unions, after he saw non-Muslim union members and organizers rally to the cause of the Muslim Hertz workers. Wheelchair attendants Saba Belachew, Assadollah Valibeigi, and the other airport workers, in thousands of conversations, had lobbied their coworkers to overcome fear and sign union cards. Baggage handler Alex Hoopes knocked on hundreds of SeaTac doors, soliciting support for Proposition 1, seeking to reclaim the future that Alaska Airlines had ripped away from him and the other baggage handlers in 2005. Initially reluctant even to register herself to vote, Sarah Mohamoud organized her apartment neighbors to support the campaign, because in Proposition 1 she saw the possibility of reuniting her family. The Reverend Jan Bolerjack, troubled by meeting hungry airport workers at her church, envisioned the campaign as a way to bring the living Gospel into the community. SeaTac City Council member Mia Gregerson had stepped out as a vocal supporter, fully recognizing that it would place her directly in the crosshairs of the Tea Party's political gunsights.

These and other activists had been drawn to the Sea-Tac campaign because they saw something new, different, and welcoming in the movement. The $15 initiative, to be sure, was a unifying rally point, but their engagement was driven by a profound desire to gain a voice, to realign power in the community. They were engaged as coauthors in this movement, not merely support actors handed preassigned roles. The further one got from the day-to-day workings of the campaign, the more distant and insignificant these voices must have seemed. They didn't go out of their way to garner attention.

And yet, at least to me and other campaign leaders, these voices were essential, not just because they supplied credibility to the union-led campaign, but also because they were helping to fashion a new kind of union. Trained union organizers like me were adept at managing strategy, planning rallies and actions, organizing meetings, building worker committees, and running door-to-door canvass operations. The community leaders and the workers were expert at a host of other essential skills, from navigating the networks and customs of immigrant communities, to blending faith principles with organizing tactics, to integrating their personal experiences with poverty and abuse into a compelling campaign narrative that would resonate with the public. These contributions were as essential as the money and mechanics of running a get-out-the-vote drive.

Apart from Rolf, the other labor leaders recognized the necessity of the broader, more inclusive coalition and strategy. It was the path that had gotten us this far. For the Teamsters' Leonard Smith, maintaining the coalition was not simply a value-add but "about whether we succeed or fail." The Teamsters, in particular, had witnessed the importance of trust building with new allies around the Hertz battle. They recognized how the union-community relationship borne of that struggle had propelled the airport campaign forward. They also must have recognized that what seemed to Rolf as the safest choice—reining in the campaign under the full control of his professional union staff—was in fact the most perilous path because it would tear asunder the foundation of trust and inclusion that we would need for the ballot and beyond.

In SeaTac, turning away from the workers and community to run a focused get-out-the-vote drive would have put union leaders on familiar ground, but it also would have broadly confirmed what workers and community leaders worried about all along: that when push came to shove, unions would abandon community friends and broader justice issues to wage a narrow ballot battle. Fortunately, the internal forces for a broader solidarity prevailed. But the very fact that the internal struggle had to be waged in the first place underscored the fragility of the new labor movement that was struggling to emerge.

BRUISED INTERNALLY BUT INTACT, the Sea-Tac coalition moved forward. We had eight weeks to execute a voter identification and get-out-the-vote drive through door-to-door canvassing. The canvass operation faced two challenges: First, convincing white voters— working class but largely conservative by area standards, and a majority of the electorate—that the initiative was good for the economy and community. And second, the canvass had to convince immigrants that winning was even plausible. Dozens of union staff were joined by airport workers and community supporters in door-to-door retail organizing, knocking on the doors of just about every household in the city of twenty-five thousand. We aimed to register new voters, win their commitment to support Proposition 1, and then make sure they turned in their ballots in the all-mail election. Canvassers also put up hundreds of yard signs and recruited the most enthusiastic supporters to campaign events.

On the other side, the business interests that lined up to oppose Proposition 1—Alaska Airlines, the chamber of commerce, the hotel and restaurant associations, parking lot and rental car companies, the airline contractors and airport concessions companies—fielded a robust canvass as well. In the older, single-family-home neighborhoods, our clipboard-toting staff and volunteers, a racially and ethnically diverse lot, frequently crossed paths with opponents, largely young white activists cruising the streets with fancy electronic tablets.

We rented giant billboards in SeaTac that advertised Yes for SeaTac, while the other side, which went by the name Common Sense SeaTac, put up huge banners along Pacific Highway, the main thoroughfare, urging a No vote. Competing campaign yard signs—ours blue, theirs green—dotted front yards, store windows, and intersections in every part of the city. Reverend Bolerjack and other community supporters were featured in literature we mailed to homes—in English, Somali, and Spanish—and in cable TV advertisements, advocating fellow voters to "do the right thing and give our community an opportunity to succeed." Other literature extolled the advantages of paid employee sick leave for both workers and passengers, and noted the beneficial ripple effect of higher wages throughout the local economy.

Common Sense SeaTac matched with its own print and television ads. Against images of picket fences and neat lawns, the No campaign warned of mass layoffs and business failures should Proposition 1 be adopted. By evoking images of the city's tranquil, semirural past, the No campaign deftly played on white voter anxiety. The newcomers certainly didn't live behind those picket fences. "Prop 1 is a misguided missile aimed right at SeaTac's taxpayers, young people, and small businesses, and Common Sense SeaTac is going to make sure every voter understands that," declared Vote No leaders Mike West and Scott Ostrander.[4]

Conservative talk radio commentators amplified the message, telling listeners that airlines would leave Sea-Tac if they had to pay workers $15/hour. When you look at the package of wages, benefits, and rights in the proposed law, they said, it amounted to a "virtual union contract" imposed by "outside big unions" that would cost the tiny city millions of dollars a year to enforce.

Puget Sound Sage, the community organizing group, issued a study showing how passage of Proposition 1 would give a $54 million boost to the SeaTac economy.[5] The conservative Washington Policy Center countered with its own policy paper, noting that the scope of the initiative—with "union-style requirements dictating how employers hire employees and what hours they may work"—was much broader than any existing living wage law in the country. The center's report predicted widespread business closures and layoffs.[6] Business owners echoed the report's findings in local media. Roger McCracken, owner of MasterPark, vowed to automate his parking lots if the measure passed. City council member Terry Anderson, a Tea Party favorite, wrote that one thousand low-income people would lose their jobs. And, she maintained, enforcing the law would cost the city millions—money that would be diverted from sidewalk and park improvement and law enforcement.[7] The *Seattle Times* editorial board urged voters to reject the measure because "it imposes what amounts to a labor contract written by social activists."[8] I couldn't dispute the characterization.

On top of the saturated campaign activity, national and international news media descended on the ten-square-mile suburb—NBC, the *New York Times*, PBS, Fox News, the BBC, the *Christian Science Monitor*, and Al Jazeera, among others. A community that was accustomed to living in the shadows between two metropolitan areas, Seattle and Tacoma, found itself in the media limelight. Mobile television broadcast trucks with their telescoping satellite dishes became regular fixtures outside campaign offices, city hall, and the airport. Journalists sought out voters in coffee shops, supermarkets, in the airport, and on the street.

"Tiny SeaTac has suddenly become a battleground for one of the biggest issues confronting the US economy—income inequality, or the widening gap between the rich and poor, which has risen to its highest level since 1917," reported the BBC.[9] "Made up of fast-food restaurants and hotels that cater to the town's eponymous airport, it's mostly a stopover for people in transit, a throughway on the twenty-five-minute drive to Seattle. But even those passing through cannot miss the alternating blue and green signs that now dot almost every lawn, billboard, and shop window of this suburb."

The BBC followed wheelchair attendant Saba Belachew as she went door-to-door in the apartment buildings around the airport. PBS's *NewsHour* did the same with Hertz worker Abdirahman Abdullahi as he canvassed neighborhoods, and they interviewed Reverend Bolerjack at her church's food bank.

But aside from the limited worker and community leader vignettes, most of the reporting defaulted to the frame of institutional battle—unions on one side, big corporations on the other. The *Washington Post* focused on the statistic of more than $2 million spent by unions and corporations on the ballot initiative,[10] a gross understatement because it failed to account for Alaska's litigation costs, which were probably $1 million or more prior to the balloting.

"SeaTac is now center stage in a national push for a $15 minimum wage," NBC News reported, noting wryly that the two sides spent "enough money to hire every registered voter in the city for a day at $15 per hour."[11]

The reporting served our broader institutional interest of project-
ing the union power image nationally and in stamping the $15 fig-
ure in the national conscience, but it largely missed the unfolding
narrative at the street level. That is, a workforce largely made up of
immigrants, backed by unions and progressive community forces,
was organizing for dignity and power against the region's most entrenched business interests.

Much of the grassroots organizing happened outside of the formal
campaign structure. Union staff tend to see the campaign world as
solely their creation: they make the campaign plans, set goals, give
assignments to workers, and track reports on progress. Beyond the
SeaTac canvass, which certainly was staff driven, more spontaneous
forms of organizing were taking place: workers on their own would
knock on the doors of apartment neighbors, talk to acquaintances in
the stores, and seek out friends in the mosques and churches. Those
of us on the campaign staff often heard about these activities long
after they had occurred.

I asked our organizers to capture what the airport workers were
saying in these conversations. And, while the number 15 was surely on
everyone's lips, I heard workers time and again translate the dollar figure beyond the financials and into their aspirations for human dignity,
more time with their loved ones, and opportunities to live and grow.
"If SeaTac Proposition 1 passes, it would change my life and my family so I could only have one job and spend more quality time with my
family," said Sheryl Molina, a shuttle bus assistant. "I won't have to
work long hours every day, and more than one job just to pay all my
bills and save nothing for the future," said night-shift baggage handler
Bereket Elala. "I'll be able to spend more time on my education and
concentrate better on my studies. I can have days off to spend with
my family." Powerful sentiments indeed, and vital to overcome the
doubt that also occupied workers' minds about the idea of getting
voters to approve an unprecedented pay raise.

One of the ways that the doubt surfaced was in the reluctance
of many workers to vote. Prior to 2013 quite a number of SeaTac's
immigrants who had gained citizenship were not registered to vote.
Many, like Sarah Mohamoud, the fisherman's wife, had been raised
to be wary of any involvement with the government. In their home

countries, Western-style voting was not part of the cultural fabric. Elections, if they were held, were shams. Many didn't understand how secret ballots worked. In advance of the October 8 voter registration deadline, we assigned campaign canvassers to knock on the doors of unregistered voters in the apartment complexes populated by airport workers. It took more than simply putting a voter registration form in front of workers; organizers also had to demystify the voting process, and in some cases debunk notions that voting could get them in trouble.

The most effective voter registration canvassers were themselves immigrants—staff organizers, airport workers, volunteers, and students. Immigrant rights groups like OneAmerica and African Diaspora of Washington went to community centers to register voters. A group of high school seniors signed up their peers as first-time voters. Imams from SeaTac's mosques invited us to set up voter registration tables outside Friday prayers. All told, the campaign registered 917 new voters in the three months before the deadline—a 9 percent increase in SeaTac's voter rolls. It represented a seismic shift in SeaTac's voter population, equivalent to registering 387,000 new voters in New York City.[12] As it turned out, these new voters would provide the margin of victory in November.

Then there was the challenge of getting new voters to cast their ballots. In 2011 Washington State had moved to an all vote-by-mail election system. Voters received their ballots in the mail about three weeks before the official election day. Getting out the vote meant going door-to-door beginning in mid-October to encourage people to fill out and mail in their ballots. Voting at home represented an improvement over the mad dash of getting people to the polls on a single election day. Under the mail ballot system, voters had ample time to review their ballots and research the issues before casting their votes.

But for new voters with questions about how to complete a ballot properly, voting at home could be an isolating, confusing experience. The ballot was double-sided, and SeaTac Proposition 1 was near the end on the back side, right ahead of school district elections. Voters had to fill out the ballot, place it in a security envelope, and then place that in a mailing envelope. They needed to sign the outer envelope, affix a stamp, and mail it. There was no polling station volunteer to guide voters through the mechanics. The ballot instructions could flummox experienced voters, and the county and state voter guides that also came in the mail—some 140 pages and 75,000 words in English between the two of them—were overwhelming.

To counter these difficulties, Omar Mumin, the community activist and former airport worker, suggested we produce and distribute a DVD video in Somali that explained Proposition 1 and how to vote. We come from an oral society, Mumin explained to me. Many Somalis didn't—or couldn't—read the Somali-language campaign literature that we had produced. But they would watch something at home on their TVs. In fact, he said, a lot of Somalis got updates from their community leaders by watching the local Somali cable programs.

The leaders of the largest area mosque agreed to appear in the video and see that it got distributed. The main Somali cable TV channel agreed to run it as a paid advertisement. On the first Friday after ballots arrived in mailboxes, Mumin and several volunteers began distributing the videos, featuring the director of Abu Bakr Islamic Center and the leader of the area's Somali family association. "Our religion teaches us to help people," said Ahmed Nur, the Abu Bakr director, on the video. "By voting for Proposition 1 you're not only helping workers. You are providing a great benefit to the community." I joined Mumin outside Abu Bakr, handing out DVDs to the hundreds of men and women who streamed through the doors at the conclusion of prayers. Others crowded around the campaign tables we had set up outside the mosque doors. I saw a number of airport workers exiting the mosque, getting into the spirit of the afternoon, taking others by the arm to the campaign tables, and handing out the videos. The enthusiasm was infectious.

The staff-led canvass also ramped up during the three-week balloting period, executing a laborious door-to-door effort to reach every voter who had pledged support for Proposition 1. Union retirees supplemented the canvass work with phone banking to senior voters. We staged ballot parties in local restaurants and at the mosques, where first-time voters could get assistance in completing and sealing their ballots properly.

The mood among airport workers and allies was upbeat, but those of us in campaign leadership were quite nervous: this election was going to be a lot closer than our outward enthusiasm suggested. We knew that the other side, with a blizzard of ads and mailers to supplement its canvass, was getting the No vote out. A campaign tracking poll in late October—just after ballots landed in mailboxes—showed us favored by a slim margin, with 54 percent support for Proposition 1 among registered voters. But that support was shaky at best, especially because younger voters—more heavily inclined to vote Yes—were slow to turn in their ballots. The older, white, conservative voters reliably cast their ballots. And with such a small voter pool—just over twelve thousand voters now, with new registrants—percentages could swing quickly.

Few people outside of the campaign leadership knew just how big a risk we had taken in going the initiative route in SeaTac. When we filed the initiative in the spring, our internal polling showed less than 50 percent support among SeaTac voters, "below our viability threshold," as our pollster had warned. That was a big understatement. Conventional election wisdom held that you need to start an initiative with overwhelming support—60 percent at the absolute minimum—and then fight to retain as much of that support as possible in the face of the Vote No campaign that inevitably besieged voters. In SeaTac we had started with a losing number and an untested theory that we could eke out a win if we could expand the electorate, motivate new, immigrant voters to vote in unprecedented numbers, and hold our own with older white voters. We were about to see if this gambit was brilliance or folly.

ON ELECTION NIGHT, November 5, campaign staffers, airport workers, and community allies packed into the Bull Pen, a local downscale sports bar just south of the airport. Don Liberty, the Bull Pen's owner, had been an early and avid initiative supporter, persuaded to get involved by a visit from Alex Hoopes and community organizers. Liberty had appeared in campaign ads and authored an op-ed in the local business journal, holding fast even after Tea Party activists threatened to boycott his business. In response to the Tea Party coercion, union members and campaign supporters went out of their way to patronize the Bull Pen. Going to the Bull Pen to order the greasy food, play the pull tab and video machines, drink pints, and catch football games on television became an act of political solidarity. Now, as sunlight faded on November 5, TV trucks with their extended satellite dishes surrounded Liberty's bar. Print reporters shouldered their way through the doors while TV crews staked out broadcast turf outside. Don Liberty's humble sports bar was ground zero for one of the biggest national stories of this election night.

We knew the drama likely would not conclude that evening. Because Washington State elections are by mail, there's an extended vote-counting period. On election night, county election boards tally the votes they have received up to that point—typically, about half of the total votes in an election. Over the course of the following days, the ballots of late voters come in. These are added to the tally and announced each afternoon. Any tardy ballot gets counted, as long as the postmark is not later than Election Day. County boards don't certify the final results until three weeks after Election Day; some ballots take that long to trickle in. So at the Bull Pen on November 5, we expected to get preliminary results, but we knew that unless we had an overwhelming lead, we'd have to wait for a final victory declaration.

Shortly after eight o'clock, those first results flashed across our smartphones and the bar's TV screens—Proposition 1 led, 54 to 46 percent. The room exploded in cheers, embraces, and high-fives. "Everybody deserves a living wage, and that's what I'm happy about," said airport concessions clerk Roxan Sibel. SEIU 775 president David Rolf stood in front of the cameras to declare victory. "For the first time in many years, the people who put fuel in jets might just be able to buy a ticket on one," he said.

Across town, the leaders of Common Sense SeaTac were not ready to concede. "We're still cautiously optimistic," opposition spokesman Gary Smith said. "Nobody really knows how many votes are to be counted still; it's entirely possible that this will turn around."[13]

Indeed, 54 to 46 percent was a heartening result given our gambit in running the initiative in the first place. But I was nagged by the less-heartening reality of the actual numbers: 1,772 yes, and 1,511 no, a 261-vote margin with at least 3,000 more votes to count. Would the late votes trend our way and bolster those numbers? That was our hope. We believed younger and newly registered voters—more supportive of Proposition 1—would disproportionately cast their ballots toward the end.

The next day, King County Elections released new vote totals. To our surprise, our lead didn't expand. It dropped to 236; then the following day, to 179; by the end of the week, we held a razor-thin margin of 43 votes, with hundreds left to tally. Inside the airport and throughout the community, our supporters were on tenterhooks. Seventy-two hours after election night, everyone recognized that the victory declaration had been premature. Those with smartphones were hitting the refresh button on their browsers at 4:30 p.m. every day, when election officials released new results.

A week after the election, our lead had shrunk to nineteen votes, with more than five hundred additional ballots to be opened. It was sheer emotional agony. But the campaign didn't stand still. Indeed, the canvassers, after a brief respite, returned to door knocking two days after the election, seeking to rehabilitate rejected ballots. Election officials will reject ballots that don't have signatures on the outer envelope, or have signatures that don't match the one on file. Many new voters forget to sign the outer envelope. Voters have three weeks from Election Day to cure these defects by signing an affidavit affirming that they forgot to sign the envelope, or that their signature had changed. In the days that followed November 5, canvassers worked diligently to track down initiative supporters whose ballots had been rejected, visiting them at work, finding them at relatives' homes, and in one case, crashing a baby shower.

The work paid off: 119 rejected ballots got rehabilitated through affidavits. County officials opened the ballots and added them to the count. After reaching the nadir of plus-19 eight days after the election, the daily ballot results began to trend in our direction. The last few hundred votes broke our way, reversing the first week's trend. On November 26, election officials released the final results: 3,040 in favor of the measure, 2,963 against. We had won by 77 votes, just over a 1 percent margin.

What made for the winning margin? With a race so close, you could credit any number of things: The meticulous and disciplined canvass, or the newly registered voters, or the rehabilitated ballots— each one of them, it could be argued, put us over the top.

A few weeks after the final tally became official, we held a gathering for 40 East African community leaders and airport workers at a local restaurant. Many were people we had first met after they saw unions stand up for Muslim prayer rights. I commended everyone on our 77-vote victory. The leaders in the room, in my experience, were preternaturally gracious and humble, averse to claiming credit. But Abdirahman Mohamed, a leader from Abu Bakr Islamic Center, broke custom and said, matter-of-factly, "We did it." Pointing in turn at each person seated around the room, he declared, "We made the difference." Mohamed's words of pride hung briefly in the air. Heads nodded in assent and people grinned broadly.

Then, just as abruptly, the moment of self-congratulation passed, the fleeting glow of immodesty vanishing as suddenly as it had appeared, and we got back to the business of the meeting.

NINE

BEYOND THE BALLOT BOX

THE SEATAC BATTLE didn't end with the ballot count. Alaska Airlines mounted an extensive series of court appeals aimed at nullifying the popular vote. Immediately following the election, Alaska gained a powerful ally: the Port of Seattle. Until now, the Port of Seattle commissioners—the five elected leaders of the port, which oversaw operation of the airport—had remained studiously neutral on Proposition 1. The initiative had placed port leaders in a tricky position. Every four years, commissioners stood for election before county voters. The port commission was a stepping-stone to higher elected office. To boost their electability, most commissioners worked assiduously to position themselves as defenders of working people, even while catering to the needs of port businesses. Port commissioners built close ties with the seaport's established longshore and metal trades unions and won over building trades unions by requiring union contracts on major construction projects. But they also cultivated ties with shipping and cruise lines, trucking companies, expeditors, tourist outfits, airlines, and airport concessions businesses, all of whom gave generously at election time. Commissioners found they could straddle these two worlds by encouraging employers to cooperate with existing port unions while doling out probusiness lease agreements and regulations and investing heavily in projects that furthered corporate interests—swanky new terminals, modern cargo and cruise ship facilities, and wide-ranging tourist marketing programs. The port-union bond represented the sort of rapprochement that epitomized the apex of labor-management relations, as imagined by many labor leaders post–World War II: unions accepted the primacy of the profit system, and in return were assured good jobs—for a portion of the working class.

The Proposition 1 result disrupted this détente and forced the commissioners out of neutrality. Just after the election, the five port commissioners—three Democrats, two Republicans—announced they would join Alaska in challenging the legality of Proposition 1.

In early December, lawyers for Alaska Airlines and the Port of Seattle told Judge Darvas that the city lacked any legal say-so over airport working conditions. The port's intervention carried a bitter irony: here was the public commission—itself created by a 1911 popular vote that loosened the iron grip of railroad trusts over the city's commerce—going to court to argue against democratic rule. The port and Alaska claimed that even though the airport resided within the city of SeaTac, voters had no legal authority over the port's domain. Going further, Alaska argued that the entire initiative was invalid, both inside and outside the airport, because of several other state and federal laws.

The voter-approved law was scheduled to take effect on New Year's Day—January 1, 2014. Judge Darvas took until December 27, just four days before implementation, to issue her decision. It was not a surprise: she ruled that the initiative was valid outside the airport, but that the city had no authority to legislate within the airport boundaries. Alaska and port commissioners celebrated; hotel, restaurant, and parking lot owners outside the airport groused, then scrambled to adjust their payrolls. Inside the airport and throughout the community, workers reacted with a mixture of resignation and anger.

For wheelchair attendant Habiba Jama Ali, the latest Darvas ruling was another low point in the long emotional roller coaster of Sea-Tac. It seemed especially cruel to her now to witness major corporations, government leaders from both major political parties, and the judicial system colluding to deny workers their due. And yet the workers continued their fight.

Soon after arriving from Somalia in 2010, Ali had been hired by Bags Inc. as a wheelchair attendant, transporting disabled and elderly

Sea-Tac passengers to their flights. For Ali, aiding passengers to navigate the bustling airport reminded her of what she so desperately wanted and didn't have her first night in America: directions and a helping hand. Lost in the maze of New York's JFK Airport and unsure about how to get assistance, she missed her connecting flight to Seattle and wandered through the terminals, napping on benches, until she located the gate where another plane transported Ali to her new home twenty-four hours later. Once settled in SeaTac and familiar with the airport's concourses and terminals, Ali found that caring for vulnerable people at the airport, reassuring them, and getting them safely to their flights gave her a personal satisfaction that her minimum-wage paycheck did not.

When she started at Bags, Ali and other wheelchair attendants had full-time work, even overtime if they wanted it. But when Ali was a couple of years into the job, Bags management cut shifts from eight to four hours and began requiring workers to scour the airport for spare wheelchairs before clocking in. Workers came in an hour ahead of their scheduled start time in order to find unused chairs. Ali complained to a coworker, Kadra Osman, a part-time attendant who also happened to be a staff organizer for Working Washington. "This is not right," Osman told her. She informed Ali that other Bags workers were beginning to organize a union. Ali got involved and became a leader in the union drive.

In March 2014, three months after Darvas barred Proposition 1 inside the airport, Ali led a delegation representing Alaska's 260 contracted wheelchair attendants and skycaps—largely Somali, Ethiopian, and Filipina women—to the Bags Inc. management offices to announce they'd formed a union. The manager refused to open the door. At the National Labor Relations Board hearing on the union election petition, the company was joined by Alaska's top lawyer in arguing that the workers weren't entitled to a local vote because they were covered by the Railway Labor Act, not the National Labor Relations Act. The labor board dismissed the objections and directed a secret ballot election. In the weeks leading up to the vote, Bags managers ordered workers to attend multiple rounds of antiunion meetings, spied on and threatened union supporters, and promised raises if workers voted against the union. Wheelchair attendant Mulat B.

Ayalew, a union activist who worked multiple airport jobs, recalled how a Bags supervisor trailed him as he escorted a passenger from a remote gate, through the terminal, and into the airport parking lot, probably close to half a mile of shadowing. After he dropped off the passenger, Ayalew headed back into the terminal with the empty wheelchair, stopping briefly to chat with other union supporters. The Bags supervisor produced a camera and started photographing him. On July 16 Ali, Ayalew, and their Bags coworkers soundly rejected management's campaign and voted to join SEIU Local 6. It was the biggest private sector union organizing win at the airport in a generation.

The Bags workers joined other Sea-Tac workers—taxi operators, shuttle drivers, rental car workers, and janitors—who, together totaling more than one thousand workers, had organized successfully into unions since the launch of the Sea-Tac campaign.

OUTSIDE THE AIRPORT PERIMETER, where $15 now was the law, the sky didn't fall. The owner of MasterPark had contributed more than $30,000 to the Vote No campaign in the fall, warning of layoffs should voters approve the initiative. By early 2014 he had dismissed any talk of layoffs as "foolish" and had installed a huge banner outside his main lot advertising $15/hour wages. He and other Sea-Tac parking lot operators reported a huge uptick in job applicants.[1] Scott Ostrander, the Cedarbrook Lodge manager who had tearfully warned of worker layoffs if the initiative passed, unveiled a $16 million hotel expansion plan—sixty-three more hotel rooms and a new spa, requiring twenty-five more employees to staff the growing facility.[2]

The litigation over SeaTac Proposition 1 advanced quickly to the state's highest court. In June 2014, Habiba Ali, Mulat Ayalew, Alex Hoopes, Saba Belachew, Samatar Abdullahi, and more than one hundred other airport workers and allies jammed into the hearing room of the Washington State Supreme Court to watch oral arguments.

Our expectations were high, but it took fourteen months for the court to rule. Finally, in August 2015, the Supreme Court issued its decision: the initiative was valid in its entirety. Workers and community members rejoiced, but another six months elapsed before Alaska exhausted long-shot appeals and Proposition 1 became settled law.

In March 2016 I met wheelchair attendant Assadollah Valibeigi one morning at a Starbucks near his apartment. Gleefully he showed me two consecutive pay stubs: one was for $9.47 an hour; the next for $15.24, the new inflation-adjusted minimum at Sea-Tac. In one fell swoop, Valibeigi's biweekly take-home pay had increased by several hundred dollars.

And since the High Court ruled that the initiative was valid, retroactive to January 2014, Sea-Tac workers began receiving significant back pay awards. In the spring of 2016 Habiba Ali went to the Bags manager with other workers to claim her missing wages. A part-time worker, she got a check for $6,300 after taxes. Some full-time workers got as much as $28,000. "All the people were yelling when we got the money. We were so happy," Ali recalled. "I never believed until they gave me the check."

For Ayalew, the raise and back pay—$24,000 owed him by three different airport contractors—meant that he could cut back from brutal eighty-hour workweeks to spend more time with his wife and toddler son. A hospital pharmacist in his native Ethiopia, Ayalew had dreamed of going back to school to get a degree in pharmacy or nursing. Now that could happen.

The awards didn't make Valibeigi, Ali, Ayalew, and their colleagues rich, but it gave them opportunities that were unimaginable before Proposition 1: they could work less, go back to school, live in simple comfort, send money to needy relatives, not worry month to month about making rent, and even consider a down payment on a modest home.

Though a union stalwart, Ali harbored doubts for the two years that Proposition 1 languished in court limbo. Maybe, after all, workers were doomed to fail, she thought. But, now, she said, "I believe we can do anything."

Likewise, Mohamed Sheikh Hassan, the Orcas Mosque leader, saw the Sea-Tac campaign not just in economic terms; it was about raising people's expectations and cementing their roles as civic activists in a new land. In particular, Hassan had seen Muslim women, normally consigned to behind-the-scenes roles in the patriarchal community, stepping forward. In decades to come, Hassan predicted, "It's going to be a lesson that once upon a time there were immigrant refugees from East Africa who started fighting for this fifteen dollars. They were there among the others, and women were there fighting too. We will teach our grandchildren."

JUDGE DARVAS'S POSTELECTION ruling notwithstanding, the 2013 SeaTac ballot win radiated outward, surging on the crest of the growing national discourse on income inequality. The first community to benefit directly from the SeaTac momentum was the city of Seattle. A month after the SeaTac vote, one hundred workers, activists, and organizers marched fourteen miles from Sea-Tac Airport to join up with fast-food workers outside Seattle City Hall, a poignant symbol of the next step in the fight for $15.

It was not surprising that Seattle became the next city where the battle would touch down. Indeed, even before the SeaTac ballots were counted, Seattle's stage was being set by two developments.

The first development centered on Socialist Alternative (SA), a national political organization with a few dozen active members in Seattle. In 2013 SA members decided to run a candidate against Richard Conlin, a sixteen-year incumbent on Seattle's city council. Conlin owned a liberal reputation but had alienated Seattleites by casting the sole vote on city council against a popular paid sick leave ordinance. To take on Conlin, SA tapped a community college economics professor, a union member and Indian immigrant who had played a leading role in the 2011 Occupy movement: Kshama Sawant.

Two weeks before her own Seattle primary election, Sawant came to SeaTac to support the airport workers. In Occupy and now as a political candidate, Sawant had earned a reputation as a fiery speaker, unreservedly calling workers to unite in class struggle against Boeing, Microsoft, and the other big corporations that dominated the regional economy.

Speaking at the packed, contentious July 2013 hearing inside SeaTac City Hall, Sawant brushed aside our campaign's admonition that speakers refrain from harsh, polarizing rhetoric. She rendered a blistering critique of Alaska Airlines and "corporate politicians" from both major parties. After the hearing, I debriefed the evening with a group of workers and union staff. What was the highlight? I asked them. The size of the crowd? Our clergy who spoke? The community members? The answers were immediate and forthright: none of the above. "We liked that Indian lady from Seattle!" a worker exclaimed. "Yes—she was the best," another said. Heads nodded and everyone seemed to agree: Sawant's lashing assault on corporate greed had stirred their passions and provided a level of moral clarity that our polished talking points lacked.

Sawant went on to score 35 percent of the vote in a three-way August 2013 primary, earning the right to face Conlin in the general election. Sawant and her party ran on a demand to raise Seattle's minimum wage to $15. Socialist Alternative members and supporters—many recruited out of the Occupy movement—staged rallies for $15, were a constant presence at union and community social justice actions, and door-belled aggressively. Conventional electoral wisdom says a progressive candidate has to appeal to moderate voters in order to win a general election, but Sawant's literature and stump speeches contained no such restraint. Sawant issued unabashed calls for worker justice, rent control, and a tax on millionaires. Sawant's bright red $15 Now! yard signs sported the image of a shouting worker with a raised fist—hardly the stuff of moderation.

Fortuitously for Sawant, a synergy developed between her campaign and SeaTac's. The prolific coverage of SeaTac by Seattle's TV and radio stations, newspapers, and blogs raised the visibility of Sawant's own signature issue. In her speeches she frequently hailed the airport workers and their initiative.

Many of us in unions were glad to see Sawant's candidacy but were skeptical that she could win. Over the years Seattle has seen its share of radical candidates who occasionally rattled the political establishment but in the end fell well short of winning office. While moved by the reaction she elicited in SeaTac, I figured it would be the same this year. Most unions made the practical decision to endorse Conlin, assuming he would cruise to victory.

But in the weeks leading up to November's election, Sawant's yard signs started sprouting up in working-class neighborhoods throughout Seattle. Coming home from SeaTac late at night, I would drive along the residential streets in my south Seattle neighborhood and see Sawant's $15 Now! signs newly planted in front yards or taped to apartment building windows. As Election Day neared, it seemed that this year, with the synergy between the SeaTac initiative and the Seattle race, a socialist might actually win. Conlin campaign staffers likely reached the same conclusion at about the same time. In late October they started desperately calling around to unions for help. But their panic came too late: the unions that endorsed him wouldn't turn out for his last-minute get-out-the-vote push.

On Election Day Conlin held a narrow margin over his challenger, but as late votes were tallied in succeeding days, Sawant surged ahead. She won by 3,000 votes out of more than 180,000 cast. Under the banner of $15, Seattle had elected its first socialist in a century.

The second major development to set the Seattle stage focused on the mayor's race. Incumbent Mike McGinn, a former Sierra Club leader who was holding elective office for the first time, faced off against State Senator Ed Murray, a long-time politician and leader in the state's marriage equality fight. By the late summer, with the SeaTac initiative dominating political headlines, both mayoral candidates endorsed the principle of a $15 minimum wage for Seattle. Both candidates staged events with fast-food and other workers protesting low wages. Murray, seeking to consolidate his business support, said he would support bringing labor and management together "to adopt a $15 wage standard . . . in a way that does not hurt small businesses." He proposed phasing in pay raises and exempting some companies.[3]

Between these two liberal candidates, Murray was more moderate on economics. He secured the endorsement of the chamber of commerce and the restaurant association—two employer groups we were fighting in SeaTac. The two big SEIU local unions, including Rolf's SEIU 775, also endorsed Murray, not because his position on $15 was stronger than McGinn's, but because union leaders believed there was a better chance that Murray could deliver a wage agreement. SEIU 775 president David Rolf committed hefty staff resources to get out the vote. On November 5 his bet paid off when Ed Murray was elected mayor.

The work of 2013 gave Seattle progressives an unprecedented political environment as the New Year arrived: a $15 minimum-wage initiative just adopted to the south of the city, ongoing high-profile fast-food worker protests in Seattle that echoed the national scene, a firebrand socialist elected to city council on a $15 platform, and a mayor who said publicly, "We know it's not a matter of if we will get to $15 per hour, but when and how we get there."[4] A poll in early 2014 showed that 68 percent of Seattle voters supported a $15 minimum wage.[5] It seemed to me that Seattle's $15 minimum wage was inevitable; the only question up for grabs was the pathway. Two widely divergent approaches quickly emerged.

Sawant called for a mass movement, building on SeaTac and her electoral victory. In early January 2014 nearly one thousand people jammed into city hall for the inauguration of the newly elected city leaders. Most were there for Sawant, not the mayor.

"Join with us in building a mass movement for economic and social justice, for democratic socialist change," Sawant declared, "whereby the resources of society can be harnessed, not for the greed of a small minority, but for the benefit of all people."[6] The crowd went wild with applause. Well, most of the crowd. Scattered through the assembly I could see small clusters of the more establishment politicos—elected officials, city hall staff, mainstream activists—wearing expressionless faces, perhaps just now coming to recognize that what had transpired in the election was not a fluke, but a harbinger of the dramatically shifting political terrain. Sawant and her Socialist Alternative party announced the formation of 15 Now, a grassroots organization that would lead the fight for $15 in Seattle and beyond.

With equal determination, the new mayor was committed to take the fight away from the burgeoning mass movement. He wanted a mannerly negotiation process, not the messiness of chanting socialists and their allies besieging city hall. Keenly aware that a labor-business wage battle in Seattle would make the SeaTac initiative fight look like child's play, Murray assembled an Income Inequality Advisory Committee (IIAC). Murray's committee was twenty-four handpicked business, political, community, and labor leaders. There were no minimum-wage workers on the panel, though the mayor wisely named Sawant to the committee, along with other city council members. Murray charged the IIAC with developing a wage proposal in four months. To chair the panel, he tapped SEIU's Rolf and Howard S. Wright, scion of one of Seattle's richest families and part owner of Seattle's iconic Space Needle.

Media coverage marveled at how the mayor's co-chairs were "men on opposite sides of the debate,"[7] but that description overlooked the more salient truth that the two cochairs, along with the mayor, were committed from the outset to cut a deal behind closed doors. Wright, being a practical businessman, understood that $15 wages were coming to Seattle and it was his responsibility to deliver an agreement that mitigated damage to business. If $15 was to be the minimum wage in Seattle, then business wanted it phased in over as long a period of time as possible. Wright also hoped that the negotiations would provide businesses an opportunity to win something they had not been able to achieve legislatively in Washington State: the ability to count tips or benefits as part of worker wages, in effect establishing a subminimum wage for many workers.

Rolf wanted to reap the harvest of the 2013 grassroots organizing. Having pushed Murray to embrace $15, Rolf also was now obliged to demonstrate to the mayor that he could deliver unions to sit down and reach a deal peacefully with business. For his part, Mayor Murray recognized that if he didn't steer a $15 negotiation process from city hall, Sawant's movement would lead it from the streets. Murray would have to manage his business and labor constituencies closely to make sure things didn't blow up. The payoff for a successful deal would be his coronation as a "big tent" mayor.

The IIAC set to work in early 2014 with public forums, two commissioned academic studies, a slew of media appearances, and a weekday symposium with national speakers. Unions mobilized rallies of fast-food and other low-income workers and turned out for the forums.

Six days after Sawant's inauguration, the new city council member and a leader of the Transit Riders Union led the founding meeting of 15 Now in the Seattle Labor Temple. It was held on a Sunday afternoon, scheduled to cater to workers. Hundreds of workers, students, retirees, and community and union activists filled the main meeting hall. The room was sweltering. Speakers celebrated the momentum for $15, but also voiced wariness of the mayor's IIAC and the loopholes and exemptions that already were being bandied about in the blogosphere—long implementation terms, exemptions or tax breaks for many businesses, a lower minimum wage for tipped employees;

perhaps not even $15. To push back against these concessions, Sawant and the other 15 Now leaders recognized they needed leverage, well beyond mobilizing demonstrations.

They found that leverage by taking a page out of the Sea-Tac playbook. 15 Now leaders declared that if the IIAC did not produce an acceptable deal, they would begin gathering signatures in April to qualify for a November ballot initiative. Were people in the hall ready to collect the signatures needed? Sawant asked. The crowd roared its approval.

A citywide initiative was the ugliest imaginable scenario for the mayor and the IIAC's two cochairs. It would pit the new mayor's labor and business constituencies against one another. Each would doubtless spend millions in the run up to a vote. A ballot fight would shred the city's cordial political culture and make it much more difficult if not impossible for Murray to advance his other policy priorities. The mayor and his cochairs certainly recognized that 15 Now was not issuing an idle threat. In January Socialist Alternative began to lay the groundwork by establishing 15 Now committees in working-class neighborhoods.

In addition to the organizing, Sawant and the 15 Now activists asked the larger Seattle unions to help fund initiative signature gathering. But Rolf's SEIU 775 and most other unions balked, placing their faith in the IIAC process. "It would be unwise for any group to assume future significant SEIU financial support for an initiative as long as there's a viable path to achieving a new minimum wage policy through the council," Rolf told reporters in early March.[8]

This was, I thought, a terrible mistake, a failure to recognize what produces bargaining concessions in the first place. In my experience bargaining union contracts and negotiating with politicians, I found that labor negotiators—both paid union staff and also union members—nearly always overestimate the importance of what happens at the bargaining table. The process of negotiating can become all-consuming. In that environment it becomes natural for participants to overvalue factors like the strength of the spokespeople, the authority of facts and data, the logic of the argument, or your relationship with your management counterpart. You begin to believe that the bargaining room is the center of the struggle. But it's not.

It's just the place where workers reap the rewards of the pressure that they've been able to impose on an adversary through collective workplace or street action, economic or political leverage, and media coverage. And the bargaining rewards will be in direct relationship to the amount of power that workers have been able to exert away from the table.

Working people had forced political leaders and the business establishment into a discussion of how to establish a $15 minimum wage. It took demonstrations of worker power to get to the point where the incoming mayor felt obliged to lead on raising wages. But the IIAC bargaining table would yield the best results for workers only if, once the committee was formed, that outside pressure were escalated. It was the wrong moment to ease up on the pressure of mass action.

Some Seattle union colleagues explained to me that they were comfortable focusing on the IIAC for the time being; if that failed, they reasoned, unions could pivot to the initiative route. They were anxious about the potential cost of an initiative, and a few were concerned that if unions showed too keen an interest in 15 Now's initiative during the IIAC discussions, then they wouldn't gain the trust of business and political committee members, talks would fail, and the mayor would blame them. They were committed to the inside game.

By mid-March, discussions inside and outside of the IIAC began to look at how the city could offset the business cost of wage increases, especially for small firms. Mayor Murray publicly talked about a multiyear wage phase-in, a popular idea especially if applied to small businesses. Union leaders suggested tax breaks. Business leaders said they wanted to be able to count tips and the cost of health benefits toward a $15 "total compensation" figure.

On March 15 Sawant announced to a rally of more than six hundred supporters that she would support a three-year phase-in of the new wage for small businesses.[9] Some of the IIAC leaders expressed surprise at Sawant's proposal. Perhaps they expected—or even hoped for—only unyielding demands from the socialist firebrand; inflexibility from Sawant would be easier for the political establishment to brush aside. But in announcing the phase-in plan, Sawant was demonstrating political agility and signaling her movement's readiness to draft an initiative that had a credible chance of getting voter approval.

And Sawant warned rally goers that they should be worried about the trajectory of talks inside the IIAC. "Right now, the debate is moving in the direction of total compensation and tip credit," she said. "That is a bad direction."[10]

"Tip credit"—or more accurately, tip penalty, since it penalizes tipped workers—was an issue that Washington State unions had kept at bay for years. Repeated drives by the restaurant and big business lobby to pass subminimum-wage legislation for tipped workers were defeated by huge union mobilizations in the state capital. Unions noted that tip penalty was "a direct grab into the pockets of some of our state's lowest paid workers."[11] Tips are not something workers can depend upon. "Whether or not I make a living shouldn't be up to what's basically a gift from customers. That's what my job should be paying me," a Seattle restaurant worker told the community group Puget Sound Sage, reflecting a common sentiment.[12]

But now in liberal Seattle, of all places, the tip penalty zombie was coming back to life. Thousands of restaurant and hospitality workers, baristas, hairdressers, cosmetologists, and tourism industry workers stood to lose the most with this subminimum wage for tipped workers. UNITE HERE had members at six downtown Seattle hotels, but their union lacked a seat on the IIAC. And labor's cochair on the committee had already shown his cards on the issue. "I don't care what's in the deal as long as there's a 'fifteen' in it," I heard Rolf tell his union staff. More publicly, Rolf explained why unions thought tip penalty was a bad idea, but in failing to label it as a deal breaker, he signaled to business that it could end up in the final package.

On April 14, 15 Now activists made good on their promise to advance a ballot initiative, submitting to the city clerk their proposal for a $15 minimum wage, with a three-year phase-in for small businesses and nonprofit organizations. The paperwork was a necessary step before signature gathering, which the organization said would begin at the end of the month—the same time that the mayor set for the IIAC's recommendations. On April 26 some five hundred people—mostly rank-and-file union members and political and community activists—mustered in a local high school gymnasium for a 15 Now conference to debate the elements of the proposed initiative and plan the signature-gathering drive.

The 15 Now initiative filing and mobilizing increased urgency behind the IIAC's closed doors, where substantive discussions had distilled down to the mayor and three labor and three business representatives. "Staving off an initiative battle was, in fact, the driving force behind Murray's commitment to getting a deal," observed reporter Josh Feit.[13]

On the morning of May 1, as thousands of people were getting ready for Seattle's annual May Day March, Mayor Murray convened a press conference to announce that the IIAC negotiators had reached a deal. With cochairs Rolf and Wright standing behind him, Murray stepped to the podium and declared, "Seattle workers are getting a raise." He unveiled the terms: not $15 now or anytime soon, but rather a three- to seven-year phase-in of a $15 minimum wage for all workers in the city, with subsequent minimum wages tied to cost-of-living increases. Some one hundred thousand workers would benefit. The length of phase-in varied based on the size of the business and whether it offered health benefits. Most workers—70 percent—would have to wait five to seven years before the $15 minimum wage kicked in.[14] And the tip penalty was included: tipped workers in businesses with under five hundred workers would make less than their non-tipped counterparts—as much as $3/hour less—over the next decade, until 2025, when the penalty would sunset. It was not a clean-cut deal. To describe the arrangement required a four-column chart showing the different minimum-wage levels for distinct groups of workers over the next ten years.

The deal, Murray explained, met his two objectives: getting low-wage workers to $15/hour while staving off an initiative fight. Wright called the agreement "the best outcome given the political environment," noting that it accomplished business's need for an extended phase-in period and for allowing health benefits and tips to count against wages. Rolf proclaimed that "with this announcement today, Seattle is leading the way toward a better economy and more robustly shared prosperity."

The deal indeed marked a watershed, allowing Seattle to claim the mantle of being the first major US city to establish a $15 minimum wage. But it did so without forcing businesses actually to provide $15 wages for several years. That afternoon, as I walked in the May

Day parade, the bright spring sunshine beaming down on marchers, I heard workers, community activists, and union staff trading opinions about the deal. The palpable pride of having achieved the historic agreement, of having struggled and forced the business and political establishment to concede something they wouldn't do on their own, was tempered by the disappointment of a long phase-in period and the health-care and tip offsets. The IIAC deal had yielded significant concessions to business in exchange for the right to say Seattle had won $15. One colleague who was close to the negotiations lamented, "We left money on the table."

Beyond the specific terms of the agreement and the nationally broadcast sound bites, the mayor had achieved a political masterstroke. Murray got to claim credit for leading a wage fight that he didn't create, and in securing the deal he won the allegiance of union and business leaders in opposing any contentious voter initiative.

Sawant and 15 Now were savvy enough to recognize that the voters wouldn't adopt a better deal than what the political establishment had bestowed. They suspended the initiative drive. The socialist council member railed against the insider agreement. Sawant noted that during the long phase-in period the rising cost of living would erode actual gains, and she warned of the precedent-setting danger of redefining wages to include tips and health-care benefits. But she recognized the overall historic achievement, as well as the reality that $15 was forced upon the political establishment. "Today's first major victory for fifteen will inspire people all over the nation," she said. But, she cautioned, "We need to recognize what happened here in Seattle that led us to this point. Fifteen was not won at the bargaining table as the so-called 'sensible compromise' between workers and business," but rather was "a reflection of what workers won on the street over this last year."

Yet there was something essential missing in the victory. Largely lost in the exuberance was the painful reality that unions had allowed the IIAC process to relegate worker power building. The Seattle fight for $15 had sprung from the Sea-Tac campaign, which in turn owed its roots to SEIU's 2011 Fight for a Fair Economy campaign. FFE had elevated the need to launch large-scale union organizing campaigns alongside the fight against income inequality. It properly recognized the necessity of building worker power, not just to fight for economic redistribution, but to rebuild the US labor movement. The initial call from New York City fast-food workers in late 2012 was for "$15 and a union." Sea-Tac workers had continued organizing for union recognition, before and after the ballot initiative drive, which itself was a power-building struggle. But in Seattle, SEIU leaders pointedly dropped the "and a union" portion of the rally cry for the prize of a closed-door wage deal. They preferred to cast their lot with a Democratic mayor rather than with a party of upstart socialists. In relegating the goal of building worker power, they missed an opportunity to build a new kind of labor movement.

PARALLEL TO SEATTLE, a $15 minimum debate was unfolding seven hundred miles to the south in San Francisco. But a different approach by San Francisco unions produced an equally distinct result.

As 2013 ended the two West Coast cities shared similar political attributes—active labor movements, with about 16 percent union density in each city; liberal mayors and city councils eager to raise wages; and a rising economic tide that was lifting worker expectations for better pay. As Seattle's mayor was calling for higher wages, San Francisco Mayor Ed Lee also announced his support for a minimum-wage hike. Lee, too, wanting to head off the growing street movement, promised to assemble a labor and business committee to hash out a solution. "We'll do this the Ed Lee way," his spokeswoman said. "Get everyone in the room."[15]

But unions didn't trust the mayor to get to $15 on his own. In April 2014 SEIU Local 1021, the largest city union, along with community allies, filed an initiative to bring the city's minimum wage to $15 in two years. Business leaders fumed. The union-led initiative "flies in the face of collaboration and partnership," complained chamber of commerce CEO Bob Linscheid. "This initiative is nothing more than a thinly veiled attempt to influence the outcome of the consensus-building process that will begin this week under the leadership of Mayor Ed Lee."[16]

But labor's leverage worked. Two months after the San Francisco initiative filing, the mayor's panel announced agreement on a ballot measure to increase wages to $15 within three years, surpassing the Seattle timeline. "All San Francisco employers will be paying $15 an hour by 2018," declared San Francisco supervisor Jane Kim, who brokered the deal. And, pointedly contrasting her city's agreement to Seattle's, she noted, "There will be no tip credit, no health care credit. These are pure wages workers will be bringing home to their families."[17] The San Francisco Chamber of Commerce, recognizing that the union-drafted alternative was worse for business, got behind the agreement. In November San Francisco voters approved the measure with a resounding 77 percent yes vote.

Goodwill hadn't driven the San Francisco agreement to a more successful conclusion than Seattle. Nor was the Bay Area political alignment more hospitable. Labor simply pursued a strategy grounded in a recognition that power from the outside produces better results at the bargaining table.

Just as San Francisco voters set a new standard in wage laws, voters across the bay in Oakland overwhelmingly approved a single-step leap in the city's minimum wage from $9/hour to $12.25/hour, plus five paid sick days per year. A month later, in December 2014, two months in advance of his mayoral reelection, Chicago Mayor Rahm Emanuel rushed a phased-in $13/hour minimum wage through city council. In May 2015 the Los Angeles City Council voted to raise the city minimum wage in stages to $15/hour by 2021. The same month the city of Emeryville, California, a small city tucked between Oakland and Berkeley, set a new standard—a $16/hour minimum wage, to be instituted in stages by 2019. Tellingly, none of these wage laws included Seattle's concessions on tips or health-care benefits.

In the four years following the 2011 Fight for a Fair Economy launch, seventeen states, from Massachusetts, Vermont, and Connecticut, to Nebraska, South Dakota, and Arkansas, to Alaska and Hawaii, adopted higher minimum-wage laws. Things moved fast. In the spring of 2015, New York governor Andrew Cuomo proposed a $10.50 minimum wage, assailing a $15/hour floor as too high. But within a year he had recanted his lowball offer, approved a $15 minimum wage for fast-food workers, and secured agreement with state legislators on phasing in a $15 minimum for all workers.[18] Within hours of the New York bill signing, California governor Jerry Brown put his signature on a similar phased-in $15 minimum-wage bill.[19]

Corporations and their political patrons were on the defensive, trying to limit the size and speed of the raises. Thirty miles south of
Seattle, Tacoma businesses headed off a $15 minimum-wage initiative
by offering a $12/hour ballot measure to compete against it. "There
are two ways to be at the table—sitting around it, or on the menu,"
the local chamber president explained. The $12/hour business mea-
sure won out.[20]

Where politically feasible, such as in Missouri, North Carolina, and
Alabama, business executives killed local movements by getting legislatures to adopt state laws preempting local wage laws. But business
was playing catch-up to the unfolding national narrative. In the three
and a half years since the November 2012 New York fast-food worker
call for $15/hour and union recognition, some seventeen million
workers won pay raises through voter initiatives, legislative action,
administrative rule making, or because individual companies raised
base wages.[21]

None of this happened out of political benevolence or enlight-
ened business attitudes. Across the country, emboldened fast-food,
child-care, home-care, airport, and other low-wage workers were
moving the political dial with job actions, walkouts, civil disobedience
protests, and shareholder meeting rallies. National days of action,
managed closely by SEIU and its FFE affiliates, garnered widespread
TV coverage in dozens of media markets. Courageous workers spoke
out, shining a light on grinding poverty—seventy-nine-hour work-
weeks, abusive supervisors, the misery of living in one's car, chronic
hunger, and mounting debt.

The wage fight also aligned with other struggles. The Black Lives
Matter movement joined with the fight for $15, Walmart workers, and
allies to link the fights against police brutality and economic inequality. The Reverend William J. Barber II, the North Carolina pastor and
founder of the Moral Monday movement, marched with McDonald's
workers and spoke to a fast-food workers' convention about the moral
imperative to raise wages. Day laborers—mostly undocumented
workers in the informal economy who wouldn't benefit directly from
statutory pay increases—added the demand for immigration reform
and became some of the most reliable attendees at wage protests.

As with Sea-Tac, these budding alliances showed early glimmers of a new kind of labor movement that fused the range of contemporary social and economic fights into a single struggle.

Yet even as the workers and unions tallied up wage victories and supporters celebrated, there was a set of figures that told a different story: in the four years since SEIU leaders declared a dire emergency and launched the Fight for a Fair Economy, private sector union density continued to decline. The "7 percent problem" that SEIU leaders talked about with such urgency in the winter of 2011 had become, by 2015, a 6.7 percent problem. What began as a bold vision to organize private sector workers and rebuild worker power had largely tapered into an exciting—yet limiting—campaign around wages. SEIU's Fight for a Fair Economy certainly had changed the national discourse about low pay, but had not reversed the overall downward slide of unions.

And then, as if to put an exclamation mark on matters, came the 2016 elections. The campaign and its aftermath, from Bernie Sanders's remarkable insurgency to Donald Trump's brutal and ugly win, laid bare the deep alienation and pain felt by broad swaths of working people and exposed the full scope of the union movement's existential crisis. The problem facing America was, indeed, much more profound than an imbalance of income, and uncomfortable questions about the purpose and survival of unions could no longer wait for a more convenient season.

TEN

BEYOND $15

The Social Movement Union

BEGINNING IN 2011 SEA-TAC was a local organizing experiment, testing the idea that a broad alliance could take on and defeat entrenched corporate powers, and in doing so would serve as a model for a new social justice movement. Sea-Tac blended traditional union organizing with deep community relationships that reached across faith, cultural, and language boundaries. Under the campaign's banner slogan, Make Every Airport Job a Good Job, the movement embraced a range of demands—from the right to pray to the right to live free of economic privation. It drew both from faith traditions and political ideology to articulate a call for worker and community power. It called on all who were immersed in it—campaign staff, workers, and community allies—to ignore convention, circumvent broken law, and tap the creativity of ordinary people. It organized workers into traditional bargaining units, as well as into nontraditional forms of collective action.

Outside of Sea-Tac the campaign gained national prominence as the first-in-the-nation $15 initiative. But at its core, Sea-Tac was about much more than a dollar figure.

By the summer of 2014 it was clear to me that the Sea-Tac experiment—at least in the eyes of the SEIU leaders who controlled the major purse strings—had run its course. Staff from the organizations that constituted the Sea-Tac coalition were deployed to new campaigns. A handful of local SEIU and Teamsters staff remained to continue the airport worker organizing, building on the momentum of the July 2014 wheelchair attendants' union election win.

Sea-Tac and its progeny seemed to offer both a glimpse into the potential of a new labor movement as well as a cautionary tale about the extraordinary difficulty of transforming existing unions and maintaining a focus on building power. The prospect of economic gain was alluring for many union leaders, and as $15/hour wage fights fanned out nationally, it was clear that in many cities the wage win came at the expense of attention to the much more arduous but vital union-building task. The Fight for a Fair Economy goal of building durable worker power, so clearly and urgently articulated to us by national SEIU leaders in 2011, had been subordinated to the easier economic prize.

Certainly the wage fights represented vast improvement over the business union model that has dominated the US union movement. And surely the wage victories eased the crushing poverty that millions of workers faced, while building worker confidence in struggle. But wage fights alone are not nearly enough to turn the tide of corporate greed that has produced vast inequality in all facets of American life—jobs, housing, health, educational opportunity, and basic human rights. The labor movement—the collective power of workers—must claim a much higher ambition than tweaking the level of economic inequality in society. The idea of a union—the power of workers uniting in action to fight for the things they need—remains today the most potent and effective foundation in the fight for a just society. But the hard truth is that the union movement as it currently exists isn't capable of building and sustaining the kind of power needed in today's economic and political reality. It is failing, for four interlocking reasons.

First, the ebbing numerical strength of unions translates into diminished political and economic clout. Just as growing corporate control creates a positive feedback loop that leads to greater power concentration, shrinking union power creates its own vicious cycle. The mainstream media, always quick to report on the latest union setback, reinforce a sense of powerlessness and futility among working people.

Second, most unions are constrained internally by limited vision and an outmoded structure. Unions struggling for basic survival are ill resourced and ill equipped to imagine and create a broad, vibrant social justice movement. Imprinted with the 1950s business unionism model, they are caught in defensive issue fights, responding to the needs of their members, an ever-diminishing fraction of the US workforce. Many union members, in turn, come to see their organization as an insurance policy against misfortune, not a vehicle for achieving hopes and dreams.

Third, most unions operate today with a worker representation and collective bargaining model that fails to meet the interests and needs of a large and growing proportion of today's workforce. Contingent and contracted workers, independent contractors, workers who regularly move from one low-paying job to another, and workers in the informal economy—for these people traditional collective bargaining won't address their needs.

And fourth, unions have failed to tap the full potential of working people. Most union leaders limit their concerns to members' workplace issues, giving short shrift to the reality that workers have hopes, worries, talents, and passions outside of employment. Likewise, workers don't see unions as places to address the myriad issues they confront in life.

These hurdles add up to a movement of limited vision and capacity. To be sure, today's leading union contract battles and campaigns against economic inequality are valiant, necessary fights that deserve broad support. But on their own they will be insufficient to overcome the societal problems created by power inequality. We may end up slowing the downward slide, but the balance of power will remain unaltered.

Nor will we be rescued by clever policy fixes emerging from academic quarters and think tanks that seek to mitigate the worst aspects of contingent work and precarious employment. Portable benefit schemes, greater regulation of precarious work, and the like may appreciably lessen the pain for many. Yet as with wage fights that only seek to raise minimums, plans that fail to challenge the business motives of control and profit that lie at the center of these new employment arrangements will fall short of what workers need.

We need to build a new labor movement—one that is unafraid to talk about power and class, embraces all, and whose scope of engagement spans the broader struggles for social justice, civil rights, and democracy along with economic rights. This may seem to be a daunting challenge, but the solutions are not distant; indeed, we are surrounded by them.

In the 1965 film *Flight of the Phoenix*, a cargo plane crash-lands in the Sahara Desert. The survivors stumble out of the plane onto sand dunes more than one hundred miles from any civilization. They have limited food and water. They survey the plane and immediately see that it is too damaged to ever fly again. After a couple of days waiting in the shade of the wreckage, they realize that there will be no rescue. They grow despondent until one of them, an aircraft designer, announces, "We have all the parts we need to build a new airplane." They hack apart the old plane and cobble together a new one from the salvaged pieces. On the brink of starvation, they complete the improvised plane, manage to take off, and fly away to safety.

Today's union movement, in spite of the best of intentions and yeoman efforts, is grounded and will not fly again. You need look no further than the inexorable downward trend of overall union density—from a post–World War II high of one union member for every three workers to less than one in eight workers today. And there will be no rescue from outside—no political savior, no legislative bombshell, no single dramatic blow that turns things around.

The sooner we collectively recognize this, the sooner we can get on with building a powerful new movement. And, just as in *Flight of the Phoenix*, the elements for building this new movement can be found within the present debris, in the lessons we glean from Sea-Tac and other contemporary struggles—innovative power-building strategies, deep alliances, new organizations that emerge to span workplace and community life. We have to find the right parts and put them together. But it will require a radical restructuring and reordering, and a much bolder vision; indeed, we need a different conception of workplace unions and their role within a broader labor movement.

IN THE LAST EIGHTY YEARS, the most prominent labor organizations in the United States can be described as either economic unions or political unions.[1] Economic unions focus largely on improving the circumstances of their members within society's existing industrial relations and political structures. The unions that dominated the post–World War II formation of the AFL-CIO represent this type: "bread-and-butter" unions, they are keen to bargain good contracts for dues-paying members and endorse mainstream party politicians, focusing on their members' immediate economic interests; society's broader problems are of secondary, and perhaps only cursory, interest. Historically in the United States, most unions are economic. Some have a proud record of strikes and shop-floor power struggles against management. But most of them have been organized with the post–World War II culture of business unionism, in which members pay their dues and come to expect their grievances and bargaining to be handled by professional staff.

Political unions, in addition to bargaining for their dues payers, reach beyond workplaces to advocate in the political arena for the interests of society as a whole. Unions advocating for Obamacare and SEIU's Fight for $15 campaign are two contemporary examples of political unions advocating for interests beyond those of their own members. Political unions may cultivate a muscular public profile and a social justice orientation, but like economic unions, they don't challenge the existing economic or political order. They endorse mainstream political candidates and are leery of alternative or insurgent political parties. Their struggles focus within the confines of the existing political system. Some do a better job than others at engaging members in the broader political struggles, but most still practice the business unionism model of servicing their members, fostering the image of the union as an intermediary between workers and employers or workers and political leaders.

Both economic and political unions focus largely on economic redistribution. Neither contests the primacy of the profit system, preferring to manage—not challenge—the problems that capital imposes on workers and communities. So while political unions promote higher area minimum wages, big business races ahead with new forms of worker exploitation that escape the reach of the new wage laws and other legally prescribed job protections and benefits.[2]

Indeed, by containing their arena of struggle within existing industrial relations laws and political structures, by steering clear of basic questions of power and the purpose of an economy, economic and political unions serve to reinforce the social stability of the capitalist system. So as welcome as political unions are compared to their more narrowly focused economic union cousins, they fail to provide the direction and leadership to tackle power inequality.

We have to look beyond national borders to find any union formation of significant scale that approximates what is needed to rebuild worker power in US society today. In developing countries, workers have long been forced to struggle against the twin tyrannies of imposed neoliberalism and severe political repression. Particularly in the global south, workers recognized that workplace issues were intimately related to broader economic and political fights and struggles for basic human rights. Workplace-based organizations built broad alliances with like-minded community movements to take on the full range of injustice doled out by those in control. Black industrial and mining workers, under the banner of the Congress of South African Trade Unions (COSATU), extended the concept of the workplace strike to society at large, helping to bring down apartheid. Filipino workers waged community-wide "strikes of the people" to protest everything from rising fuel prices to the Marcos dictatorship. Young Brazilian workers in emerging privatized industries have formed unions that blend workplace and community struggles seamlessly, elevating issues like the rights of sexual minorities and working-class cultural expression along with better wages and other working conditions.[3]

What's common to these union movements is an expansive definition of "the union," a commitment to build broad alliances, and a readiness to challenge the assumptions of capitalism and advance an alternative vision of society. These formations are commonly labeled social movement unions.

The Filipino Alliance of Progressive Labor describes a social movement union as one that "recognizes the broadness of workers' interests and the diversity and complexity of work arrangements. As such, it is geared toward the struggle for workers' rights in all aspects—economic, political and socio-cultural—and at all levels—local, national, global." In short, the alliance concludes, "the strategic objective of social movement unionism is nothing less than social transformation."[4]

What would it take to create a powerful new labor movement in the United States that embraces the core elements of a social movement union? I believe there are three bedrock principles to guide justice activists: aim higher, reach wider, build deeper.

Aim higher: articulate a bolder vision of a just society that stands as a stark counterpoint to capitalism. This vision starts with a sharp critique of the capitalist system—not just what has happened to wealth distribution in this country, but identifying how the economic and political system has by design produced such immense inequality. The disruption in the US airline industry beginning in 1978 is but one example of how big business seized control over a sector of the economy and repurposed it to meet the interests of private profit. The plummeting living standards that befell Alex Hoopes and hundreds of thousands of other airline industry workers had nothing to do with individual moral failings, lack of training or education, worker overreach, or amorphous "market forces." Rather, it was an intentional design by people in control of the levers of power. You could look at any number of other sectors of the economy and see identical developments.

Big business and finance have their clear vision of a future economy; workers must develop their own. The Occupy movement was on the right track in 2011, tapping widespread popular anger at Wall Street to spark a national conversation about capitalism's failure to meet the needs of the 99 percent. Occupy opened up an important space to imagine a new social order. But unions missed an opportunity by failing to build upon Occupy's critique, instead diverting energy into pragmatic battles—like Obama's 2012 reelection campaign—that raised the justice banner but steered clear of any serious discussion about what an economy built to fulfill human needs, not profit, might look like. Worthy as they were for engaging a new generation of activists, most of the leading post-Occupy struggles cut short a vital national discussion, one that urgently needs revival.

Beyond pointing out the failures of capitalism, a new labor movement must define a bold, unapologetic vision of society and economy, one that inspires millions of workers to engage and take action. In its own hyperlocal way Sea-Tac provided a stage for such a transformational conversation, raising basic questions about why good airport jobs had gone bad and how workers and the community needed to fight back. The hearty reception that greeted Kshama Sawant in SeaTac and then Seattle, replicated nationally in 2016 on a much grander scale by Bernie Sanders's presidential run, shows that working people engaged in struggle are eager to take up the idea of democratic socialism.

Yet another lesson of Sea-Tac is that this potent, sustained movement must rest on more than economic and political principles. A movement should draw upon the values that emanate from our deepest human emotions and desires for justice and community. The call for spiritual morality, whether advanced by organized religion or secular humanist yearnings, has played a decisive role in leading struggles throughout history. The civil rights movement of the 1950s and '60s and the abolitionist movement of a century earlier are but two examples of struggles that were propelled forward by powerful calls for spiritual morality. Today, the Moral Mondays movement, born in North Carolina and fusing direct action with a spiritually based call for justice, offers similar promise.

The vital role of a moral framework crystallized for me at the 2013 Alaska Airlines shareholders meeting. When the Reverend John Helmiere and his fellow clergy stood up to issue their prayer for worker justice, they were connecting material demands to spiritual values, deftly shifting the terrain from dollars and cents to values and justice. Convened for their annual showcase of economic success, the Alaska executives dared not challenge the clergy.

This foundation of spiritual morality is widely underappreciated or downplayed in most quarters of today's union movement. Entire campaigns are conceived and launched with little consideration for the role of surrounding faith communities or how faith and moral perspectives can propel organizing. Spiritual leaders routinely are contacted by union organizers only when campaign leaders decide they need a respected community leader to validate the struggle, or when the campaign is in dire crisis and needs a rescuer. Yet the moral call for a social order that places human needs above private profit, woven into the fabric of a campaign from the start, is vital to the movement's future success.

Reach wider: redefine who constitutes "the labor movement" to include all workers. To realize the full collective power of workers, a new labor movement has to reject the historic definition of the movement as comprising only workers who are members of unions, and instead embrace the full spectrum of the working class and working-class-based organizations. My organizing colleague Abdinasir Mohamed noted that from the perspective of East Africans, defining the union solely as a workplace-based organization makes little sense because workers "belong to the community, they have places of worship, they have community centers, and there is no way we can separate the community from working people.

"If we selectively define who is in the labor movement, then we are cutting off people who are struggling with housing issues, people who are not working in the airport but maybe have their own small businesses in the community. Those people are also part of the labor movement, and we should not limit our fight," he said.

Today, antiforeclosure groups, tenant rights organizations, advocates for ending homelessness, worker centers, immigrant rights organizations, parents standing up for public education, groups fighting police brutality, civil rights groups, health-care advocacy organizations, faith institutions—all of these and more, along with workplace unions, are organized expressions of the interests and desires of working people. They are essential building blocks of a powerful labor movement. Unions need to embrace these groups not as allies to be invited in only after strategy has been set, but as unions in the community—part of the core of the labor movement.

This wide embrace is rarely practiced today. Leading union campaigns reflexively distinguish one part of the labor movement from the working class overall. Union organizers routinely ask allies to turn out to support workers in bargaining, on strike, or lobbying for legislation—but as supporters, not co-architects. This limits the creativity and power of the movement. As British academic Richard Hyman has noted, "The boundaries of union inclusion are also frontiers of exclusion. . . . In compartmentalising workers, unions traditionally have compartmentalised solidarity."[5]

Fault here lies with US unions' establishment of artificial boundaries defining who was "inside" or "outside" of labor. In the aftermath of World War II, most unions funneled attention into the collective bargaining model of industrial relations, which advanced pay and rights for many but created a separation between dues-paying union members and the broader labor movement of all working people. Workers outside of any collective bargaining structure came to be called—and to call themselves—"nonunion," and many saw their basic economic interests as distinct from dues-paying union members. Over time, this notion of differentness among workers has become embedded not just in the procorporate media but also in US working-class culture, weakening all workers—both "union" and "nonunion." This cultural failure to unite along class interests created political openings for union-busters like Wisconsin governor Scott Walker, but perhaps just as insidiously it's spawned the sort of thinking that produces workers like SeaTac Tea Party members Vicki Lockwood and Kathleen Brave, solidly working-class members who come to believe that unions are narrow, self-interested groups.

Probably no one recognized this historic union weakness more acutely than the late Tyree Scott, a Seattle electrical workers union member and militant activist. An African American electrician trained in the marines, Scott had to muscle his way into the exclusionary building trades unions in the 1970s. Along with other black construction trades workers, he led fights to open up job opportunities to workers of color—shutting down job sites through direct action, often butting heads with union leaders in the process. Twenty years later he'd often raise the question Whose labor movement is it anyway? and would answer simply: It belongs to all of us. The problem, he maintained, was that "one sector of our movement has appropriated the voice of all of us."[6]

Building a broad labor movement will require a vastly different approach to alliance building. Plenty of union campaigns today engage what organizers label "coalitions." But a coalition on paper is not necessarily a true working partnership, a relationship that incorporates the strategic ideas and talent of participants. Often unions invite faith groups and community allies to help out, but the scope of engagement is confined within the boundaries of the campaign's existing goals and decision-making structure. The campaign welcomes a group that commits to turn out a certain number of people for a rally, a clergy member to stand before cameras at a press conference, or a community leader to deliver a predetermined message to elected officials. But the ally's particular assets—moral authority in the community, language or cultural skills to reach out to a sector of the workforce, research savvy, or political connections—are employed strictly in a utilitarian manner. These are fundamentally transactional relationships, failing to tap the full potential of a true partnership.

Transformational relationships, on the other hand, embrace not just the ally's talents but also create space for the ally to participate in the decision-making process and influence the campaign's goals and culture. A true partnership recognizes that the most potent campaign is produced by sorting through the ideas of all participants and groups. Implicit in a true partnership relationship is that all parties—including the workplace union—need to be ready to embrace new perspectives and to change themselves.

This cultural makeover in alliance building is going to be enormously difficult. Today's expectation among most union leaders, accepted by all too many community allies, is that the organization providing the most dollars and staff gets to call the shots. But community allies bring other assets, like relationships, credibility, or cultural competence, which can't be measured monetarily but are just as vital.

This point came home to me early in the Sea-Tac campaign as we struggled to engage the East African community. Following the union stand to support the Muslim Hertz workers' right to pray, what impressed Sheikh Abduqadir Jama—until then, a union skeptic—was that "you came down to us" and sought their expertise. He became a key community advocate for the campaign, opening up his mosque to union gatherings, encouraging Muslims to get involved, and advocating alongside workers and other clergy in a private meeting with Alaska Airlines CEO Brad Tilden.

Likewise, in the run up to Alaska's 2013 shareholders meeting, clergy, community activists, and workers designed the specific meeting interventions—the prayer, the chanting, skit, singing, and questions. The complicated hodgepodge of activities that unfolded turned out to be a beautiful synergy of moral framing and righteous indignation, far from what an individual campaign operative would have developed.

Neither Sheikh Jama nor the community activists brought money or staff into the campaign. But their credibility and creativity added value beyond any traditional campaign measurement.

Build deeper: cultivate the ideas and leadership of workers. It's not enough to have big ideas and a broad group of stakeholders. A powerful new labor movement must embrace the principle and practice of authentic worker engagement and leadership. In US unions today, this is far too rare. Most union leaders and professional union organizers are trained to regard workers as people to be influenced, persuaded, moved into action—instruments to be activated for the benefit of a greater institutional goal that the workers themselves may have only vaguely bought into. Union staff are trained that it's their responsibility to "move workers" and to "organize workers." Most of what passes for worker involvement today just touches the surface of tapping true worker intelligence and leadership. Union democracy—not just voting rights but the genuine engagement of worker ideas—is given lip service.

This union staff perspective of worker-as-instrument has it exactly backward. The idea of a union is, at its essence, workers uniting to fight for the things they need. The union staff organizer's job is to be the instrument of that group: to help cultivate worker aspirations, draw out their ideas, introduce skills, and bring forward the lessons of previous organizing struggles so that workers can learn from the past and embrace a coherent campaign plan. To be sure, a union staff organizer is responsible for bringing personal and institutional expertise to bear in a campaign, but these ideas must not smother worker innovation and creativity. The history of union organizing reminds us that workers will take extraordinary risks and endure tremendous sacrifice—as long as they have ownership over the campaign.

Community organizer Claudia Paras told me the biggest lesson she took from working on the Sea-Tac campaign was simply that "the solutions are found within those who are most experiencing the problems, if they're given time and resources to work on them."

In Sea-Tac we practiced this approach with the best of intentions. Sometimes we succeeded; often we fell short. The cabin cleaner Samatar Abdullahi persevered in late 2012 in conveying his conviction to me that the campaign needed to focus on forming unions at the airport. His intervention helped me and others gain clarity over a major strategic question in the campaign. That clarity proved pivotal: it kept the campaign focus on building worker power, even as we moved into the political arena with the $15/hour initiative. Similarly, Christian faith activists planned the tactics, prayers, and speeches for the 2012 International Human Rights Day march inside the airport, the one that moved wheelchair attendant Saba Belachew to recognize the power of the moral voice in the airport workers' struggle. Yet at numerous other times, campaign exigencies led to inadequate worker consultation and input. The temptation to cut corners was always present, and the campaign often suffered when organizers—myself included—yielded to those impulses.

One challenge, especially for trained staff organizers, is in discerning worker wisdom. It usually doesn't come in clearly labeled packages. Cesar Chavez, the founder of the United Farm Workers, noted that "we should not expect them to come and say, 'Mr. Organizer, what we want is a program,' and then draw a little picture for us and color it in with detail. They will not do that. We must pay very close attention to the people; because in their own action, in their very breath, they are telling us what they want all the time."[7]

A different way to think about worker engagement and leadership is to view union organizing through the lens of "accompaniment," a term introduced half a century ago by liberation theology priests working with rural campesinos in Latin America. In carrying forth their ministry of "a preferential option for the poor," they positioned themselves not as church authorities coming to aid the impoverished, but as equal partners with farmers in a struggle for social transformation. Liberation theology and its method of accompaniment spread through Latin America, sparking land reform movements, strikes, and even revolutions in Nicaragua, Mexico, Peru, Brazil, and elsewhere. El Salvador's archbishop Oscar Romero was an outspoken proponent of accompaniment before he was assassinated by that country's military in 1980.

A few years ago labor activist Staughton Lynd wrote that the US labor movement could benefit greatly by applying the concept to unions. The union organizer brings technical, legal, and campaign knowledge, but the worker's life experiences are equally valuable. Both bring essential ingredients to the organizing enterprise. With accompaniment, Lynd noted, "no longer do we have one kind of person helping a person of another kind. Instead we have two persons exploring the way forward."[8]

I won't, of course, romanticize accompaniment. Workers can come up with foolish ideas as easily as union leaders and staff organizers can. But in Sea-Tac, as in other union campaigns, I also saw how authentic engagement with workers and community allies—as cocreators, not simply as people to be mobilized—stimulated creativity and opened up windows to greater possibilities. The other staff organizers and I had extensive experience to contribute to the Sea-Tac strategy. But so did the airport workers: many had advanced educations, had escaped wars, been homeless, gone hungry, and learned to deal with oppressive bosses and horrible working conditions. They had known economic privation beyond what most union leaders could imagine. Those experiences taught them unity, courage, creativity, and adaptability—all valuable tools to inform the organizing campaign.

What would it take to develop accompaniment in union organizing? The challenge is largely battling the prejudices in our own minds and organizational cultures: staff organizers often have low expectations of workers, and many workers hold back because they don't believe their experiences are revealing or their ideas are valuable simply because that's what they've been taught throughout life. Charles Payne, writing about civil rights movement organizers Ella Baker and Septima Clark, practitioners of accompaniment, noted that their understated legacy was "a faith that ordinary people who learn to believe in themselves are capable of extraordinary acts, or better, of acts that seem extraordinary to us precisely because we have such an impoverished sense of the capabilities of ordinary people."[9]

Viewed in that light, the success of union leaders and staff organizers depends less on their loquaciousness and technical skill and more on their ability to get people to believe in themselves and each other. This requires a basic respect for workers. That's an innate quality, not something you can train union leaders or organizers to do. Nor can you overestimate its value. Respect bridges cultural, language, and other chasms. It represents the germinating seed of a powerful new movement, one that unleashes the full creativity and collective organizing potential of workers.

THESE THREE BEDROCK PRINCIPLES—aim higher, reach wider, build deeper—are entirely within the control of union leaders and members. The principles don't depend at all on acquiescence or agreement by any outside forces. They don't require a change in laws or an improvement in the political climate. They don't rely upon an agreement with business interests. We can start toward them today.

Advocates for social movement unions certainly can look to other societies for templates, but in doing so we shouldn't idealize them. The principles of social movement unionism are transferable, but movement strategies and histories are subject to the specific circumstances of their own times and places. Scanning other experiences, we see both inspiring models and cautionary tales. In South Africa, for instance, COSATU played an exemplary role as a social movement union in helping to overthrow apartheid. But after COSATU joined the new African National Congress–led government, the union federation allowed itself to fall into the compromising position of supporting privatization and other neoliberal policies.

Nor will a new labor movement appear on the scene in a thunderbolt. It won't be planned like some grand scheme from inside a union headquarters or self-appointed innovation center, unveiled with a dramatic rollout of vision and resources, and executed with discipline through a central command-and-control operation. Rather, it will take shape as experiments—some inside the existing union movement, more outside—play out, bear fruit, adapt, and join up with one another; experiments whose successes inspire more daring and ambitious ventures. These will be movements committed to disrupt convention, surprise opponents, invent new forms of struggle, and circumvent the dead-end routes that political and business elites—and many union leaders—hold up as legitimate reform pathways.

It needn't start big. Tyree Scott and his fellow construction workers built a movement by shutting down segregated job sites through direct action. They began with a dozen protesters. A few dozen socialist activists upset the political order of a major US city by electing one of their own and forcing the establishment to endorse a $15 minimum wage. Those are but two examples of groups that worked outside of labor unions to create powerful local working-class movements. In both instances, indeed, union leaders initially opposed the movements and only came around once it became clear that the insurgents had popular momentum and staying power.

In contrast, Sea-Tac exemplifies social movement union experimentation done within existing union structures. When unions diagnosed that they lacked the ability on their own to beat Alaska Airlines, they united with the wider community and in doing so embraced a social conception of a union. When business obstructed the established legal pathway of addressing the movement's demands—union recognition and collective bargaining—the workers pursued an innovative ballot box strategy to achieve power and economic improvement. With boisterous demonstrations, protesters broke established rules at the airport, inside the Alaska Airlines shareholders meeting, and at company headquarters. We disrupted past behavioral expectations and convention. We broke the rules because the rules for airport workers, as with workers throughout the economy, are rigged to make workers lose.

The transformational nature of experimentation and disruption also showed up at the individual level: Omar Mumin overcame his disbelief with the idea of a $15 minimum wage and developed an informational video that became a vital part of the East African community's get-out-the-vote effort. The Reverend John Helmiere discovered that you can violate no-trespass laws at the headquarters of a major corporation with impunity if you have enough people with you. Alex Hoopes, Saba Belachew, Habiba Ali, and their peers learned that airport baggage handlers, wheelchair attendants, and other minimum-wage workers could spur a national, and even international, conversation about inequality with a bold idea and an unyielding determination to persevere.

These basic accomplishments—raising people's expectations about their capabilities and collective power, and founding a new type of union within the union movement—bear learning from and replicating. Yet Sea-Tac also showed the distinct limitations of incubating a social movement union within existing institutional structures. Most Sea-Tac union leaders recognized the value of creating a new type of workplace and community union in order to build power for airport workers. But to the principal local campaign funder, SEIU 775's David Rolf, Sea-Tac's goal was to win a ballot battle. Those conflicting goals were manageable internally—until Judge Darvas tossed Proposition 1 from the ballot and provoked a crisis that nearly destroyed the Sea-Tac experiment from within.

It's because of experiences like this that many justice activists and observers are rightfully skeptical about how much change can spring from existing union institutions. As Mark and Paul Engler have noted, "While bureaucratic institutions may have positives, they also bring constraints. Because organizations have to worry about self-preservation, they become adverse to risk-taking. Because they enjoy some access to formal avenues of power, they tend to overestimate what they can accomplish from inside the system. As a result, they forget the disruptive energy that propelled them to power to begin with, and so they often end up playing a counter-productive role."[10]

But this is a tension to wrestle with, not avoid. Unions have resources—millions of members, organizing talent, and the capacity to mobilize on a mass scale. They have a key role to play in labor's transformation, in two ways: First, unions must defend what workers have achieved in the workplace and society, by investing in new organizing campaigns, waging contract battles to secure and improve working conditions, and leading fights in the political arena to maintain and expand rights for all workers. That's not enough, of course; focusing alone on that work has gotten the union movement into its current predicament. Unions also must support—financially and politically— the experimentation that is vital to building a true labor movement that embraces all workers. That includes welcoming the uncomfortable, disruptive energy that accompanies such movement building.

I've no illusions about how difficult this will be. The continuing assault on unions leaves most organizations and leaders in defensive postures, scrambling to survive by clinging to narrow strategies based on outdated assumptions about labor-management relations or fanciful expectations of what the political establishment wants to or can deliver to workers. Existing unions have deeply entrenched cultures centered on a workplace-based collective bargaining model that meets the needs of a decreasing proportion of the working class. Most unions seem unwilling or unable to embrace the sea change that is necessary; unreformed, those unions will continue to wither. Desperate times are killing fields for risk taking, especially for organizations struggling to retain their ebbing power. And yet, creativity, risk taking, and disruption on a broad basis are precisely what is needed.

Yes, the institutional hurdles are enormous. Yet I've no doubt that a new labor movement, founded on social movement union principles, is possible. The elements of this movement, like pieces of the broken airplane strewn across the desert in *Flight of the Phoenix*, are everywhere all around us, embedded in the daily struggles of working people.

Undocumented workers struggling to survive in the cash economy form worker centers, win area wage standards, and forge self-defense alliances against wage theft and deportation. Walmart workers experiment with a fusion of social media and industrial action, linking up with Black Lives Matter and other emerging community struggles to take on the retail behemoth. Uber and other rideshare drivers organize strikes and demand new laws protecting their right to organize. Renters and homeowners mobilize sit-ins and direct actions against evictions and bank foreclosures. School teachers strike to defend the social principle of quality public education for all, and in doing so unite with parents to push back against the corporatization of our schools. Southern US workers, taking on the international auto manufacturers, blend faith-infused workplace organizing that recalls the civil rights movement along with outreach to autoworkers around the world.

What unites workers in these varied efforts is the common belief that the fight doesn't stop at the workplace and that, through unity and struggle, a better world is possible. None of these examples represents a full-fledged social movement union. But each contains at least a rudimentary recognition that the fight is about power, each offers a critique of modern-day capitalism, and each contains bold strategies and new relationships that we can employ in building a formidable new labor movement.

The other truth about these struggles, as with Sea-Tac, is that progress is never linear. We have to proceed with confidence about our bold vision of a just society, even in the absence of validating markers. Desperate for something to stop the onslaught that capitalism inflicts upon the 99 percent, we may yearn for quick results and grand gestures to illuminate a clear path forward. We seek shortcuts, or hope for luck—some miraculous turn of events, or the election of a political leader who will lead us into the promised land. But there will be no rescue, no miracles, no shortcuts. Big change won't come from the brilliance of individual leaders or a political masterstroke, but rather by combining the thousands of acts of simple courage and grace that on their own may seem inconsequential, but together make for wholesale transformation. From these daily lessons, from the wreckage of our present circumstances, we can create a new labor movement, win back power for working people, and build a just society.

ACKNOWLEDGMENTS

MY LONG JOURNEY OF BOOK WRITING began not voluntarily but with a gentle if insistent push helpfully administered by Hedrick Smith one afternoon following a long day spent together interviewing Sea-Tac workers and community activists. When someone of Smith's Pulitzer Prize–winning stature says, "You need to write a book," it's advice to be taken seriously. Smith went on to provide invaluable feedback on early drafts of the book outline. Likewise, two other acclaimed writers far out of my league, David Kusnet and Paul Loeb, offered vital publishing advice and direction early on. Many conversations with my fellow labor-movement troublemaker, Jane McAlevey, further shaped the book idea and purpose. McAlevey, herself a published author, connected me with literary agent Diana Finch, who supplied expert and tireless guidance far beyond what I imagined an author would get.

I am greatly indebted to my coworkers at the Hillman City Collaboratory, my neighborhood social justice center, where I did a lot of the writing. They lent support and feedback when I sought it, coffee and distractions as needed, and the space to focus quietly when I was on deadline.

Some dear colleagues volunteered many hours reading my manuscript and providing critical feedback. Aiko Schaefer helped me think through how to write about the concept of power. Karen Rosenberg and Hilary Stern offered great advice on chapter structure, flow, and the art of the narrative. Thanks also to Mike Annee for volunteering his time and talent to produce the author's photograph, and to Jonathan Lawson for the cover picture.

Numerous academic leaders provided valuable opportunities to hone my ideas at workshops and conferences: Elaine Bernard at the Harvard Trade Union Program; Ken Jacobs and Karen Orlando at the University of California, Berkeley; Alastair Woods and the Canadian Federation of Students-Ontario; and Mike McCann, Larry Kushney, George Lovell, and Andrew Hedden at the University of Washington's Harry Bridges Center for Labor Studies.

In writing the book, I was fortunate to have been accompanied by others who sought to preserve the voices of many of the original Fight for $15 grassroots activists. Professor McCann and labor archivist Conor Casey, along with a team of UW students, have assembled an amazing treasure trove of material in an archive collection, the SeaTac/Seattle Minimum Wage Project. More than fifty digitized interviews and hundreds of documents from the SeaTac and Seattle $15 campaigns are available at http://content.lib.washington.edu/projects/sea15/index.html.

Trevor Griffey, formerly of the University of Washington and now at California State University, Long Beach, generously took the time to help me think through some of Seattle's formative social movements that laid the foundation for what happened in SeaTac, in particular the fight to desegregate the building trades unions in the 1970s and the 1999 World Trade Organization protests. The staff at the University of Washington Libraries' Special Collections were tremendously helpful in my historical research of the Seattle labor movement, from the 1919 General Strike to contemporary events. Lawrence Mishel of the Economic Policy Institute offered excellent resources on how to think about the $15 wage fights in the context of overall economic trends.

Jeff Johnson and Lynne Dodson, two stellar leaders at the Washington State Labor Council, AFL-CIO, offered me their convention platform to discuss and shape my ideas with hundreds of union members and community activists throughout the state.

Richard Bensinger and the Reverend Mike Roberts connected me with clergy in Mississippi, who contributed vital lessons about how faith and justice issues are being applied in contemporary Southern autoworker organizing. Bill Fletcher, a veteran of labor struggles and a film buff to boot, introduced me, a cultural troglodyte by comparison, to the movie *Flight of the Phoenix*, which I reference in the book as a metaphor for thinking about a new labor movement.

Several of my articles in recent years served as early chapter drafts or as analytical content that I employed in *Beyond $15*. I'm indebted to the many magazine and journal editors who published my work, including Rabbi Michael Lerner and Alana Price at *Tikkun*, Dr. Paula Finn at *New Labor Forum*, Al Bradbury at *Labor Notes*, Susan Gleason and James Trimarco at *Yes! Magazine*, Don Hazen at *Alternet*, Micah Uetricht at *In These Times*, and Daniel Blackburn at *International Union Rights*.

What can one say about a publishing house that takes a gamble on a first-time book author and puts an entire team at your disposal? My manuscript found a welcome home at Beacon Press, where senior editor Joanna Green offered excellent advice on restructuring and sharpening the story. Also pitching in hugely to this project were Ayla Zuraw-Friedland, Nicholas DiSabatino, Tom Hallock, Alyssa Hassan, Marcy Barnes, Pam MacColl, Christian Coleman, and Susan Lumenello. Abby Collier did superb copyediting.

Most of all, I'm indebted to the many workers, faith activists, community leaders, and organizers who came together, took on an improbable battle against corporate and political giants, and, in making history, challenged all of us to think about what a powerful labor movement can and must become. I sincerely hope this book captures our collective experiences and lessons; any shortcomings are my responsibility alone. And while there are far more airport workers, community activists, organizers, and other colleagues than space allows me to name, I want to note in particular those who took the time to be interviewed or to offer especially vital information for this book: airport workers Abdirahman Abdullahi, Samatar Abdullahi, Yusur Aden, Nimo Ahmed, Habiba Jama Ali, Mulat B. Ayalew, Saba Belachew, Socrates Bravo, Alex Hoopes, Mohammed Kadhim, Pascasie Mukaruziga, Alex Popescu, Assadollah Valibeigi, and Hosea Wilcox; faith leaders the Reverend Paul Benz, the Reverend Jan Bolerjack, the Reverend Lauren Cannon, the Reverend Mike Denton, the Reverend Edward Donalson III, Michael Douglas, the Reverend Dick Gillett, Carol Harris, Mohamed Sheikh Hassan, the Reverend John Helmiere, Sheikh Mohamed Ileye, Sheikh Abduqadir Jama, the Reverend Josh

Liljenstople, Anita Manuel, the Reverend Horace McMillon, Father Jack Mosbrucker, Kaeley Pruitt-Hamm, and Michael Ramos; community and workplace activists Mohamed Aden Ali, Laura Davenport, Luis Escamilla, Sahra Farah, Jim Freese, Yemane Gebremicael, Mark Glover, Abdullahi Jama, John Kohlsaat, Violet Lavatai, Sarah Mohamoud, Kathi Oglesby, and Johannes Teklemariam; union and community organizers Yasmin Aden, Genevieve Aguilar, Ahmed Ali, Robert Hickey, Abdinasir Mohamed, Omar Mumin, Elsa Ogbe, Claudia Paras, Leonard Smith, Brianna Thomas, and Cetris Tucker; the Casa Latina worker leadership team of Felis Barrera, Freddy Dubón, Beatriz Guaillas Carangui, Marta Guevarra, Araceli Hernandez, Estuardo Mejía, Jose Oblitas, and Hilary Stern; and political leaders Mia Su-Ling Gregerson and Kshama Sawant.

Finally, this book would not have been possible without the unyielding patience and love of my wife, Carolyn McConnell, and our daughters, Natalya McConnell and Tamar Rosenblum. Together, their unconditional support, offered in countless ways, carried me through the most difficult periods of this project. And I am forever grateful to the people who brought me into this world and began to shape the person I became: my mom, Rachel Rosenblum—a union and political activist in her own right—and my dad, Myron Rosenblum, who unfortunately passed away a year before this book reached publication. May his memory be a blessing and an inspiration.

AUTHOR INTERVIEWS

MORE THAN FIFTY INDIVIDUALS gave their time to be interviewed for this book. Whether or not directly quoted, each one of them provided valuable insights and observations that informed my writing. All interviews were conducted in person in the Seattle area unless otherwise noted.

Abdirahman Abdullahi	September 26, 2014
Samatar Abdullahi	October 3, 2014
Yasmin Aden	April 25, 2015
Yusur Aden	October 4, 2015
Nimo Ahmed	October 4, 2015
Mohamed Adan Ali	November 16, 2014
Ahmed Ali	January 23, 2015
Habiba Jama Ali	July 22, 2016
Mulat B. Ayalew	July 28, 2016
Saba Belachew	April 24, 2015
Rev. Paul Benz	September 16, 2014
Rev. Jan Bolerjack	July 31, 2014; September 24, 2015
Socrates Bravo	May 4, 2015
Rev. Lauren Cannon	September 5, 2014
Sahra Farah	March 19, 2015
Jim Freese	November 21, 2015 (phone)
Yemane Gebremicael	September 16, 2014
Rev. Dick Gillett	September 16, 2014
Mia Su-Ling Gregerson	September 26, 2014; February 6, 2015 (phone); December 11, 2015
Trevor Griffey	November 23, 2015 (phone)
Carol Harris	October 3, 2014

Mohamed Sheikh Hassan	September 12, 2014
Rev. John Helmiere	September 10, 2014
Robert Hickey	May 13, 2015 (phone)
Alex Hoopes	February 2, 2014
Sheikh Mohamed Ileye	September 30, 2014
Sheikh Abduqadir Jama	September 30, 2014
Mohammed Kadhim	April 14, 2015
John Kohlsaat	January 7, 2015
Violet Lavatai	October 12, 2015
Rev. Horace McMillon	December 2, 2015 (phone)
Lawrence Mishel	October 31, 2014 (phone)
Abdinasir Mohamed	January 6, 2015; November 5, 2015
Sarah Mohamoud	November 18, 2014
Pascasie Mukaruziga	February 4, 2015
Omar Mumin	September 6, 2014
Kathi Oglesby	April 23, 2015
Claudia Paras	November 4, 2015
Kaeley Pruitt-Hamm	June 3, 2015 (phone)
Michael Ramos	October 31, 2014
Kshama Sawant	October 14, 2014
Leonard Smith	January 28, 2015
Johannes Teklemariam	January 27, 2015
Brianna Thomas	December 9, 2014
Cetris Tucker	January 28, 2015
Assadollah Valibeigi	June 2, 2015
Casa Latina worker leadership team: Felis Barrera, Freddy Dubón, Beatriz Guaillas Carangui, Marta Guevarra, Araceli Hernandez, Estuardo Mejía, Jose Oblitas, Hilary Stern	March 18, 2015

NOTES

PREFACE: LESSONS IN POWER

1. Jeremy Brecher, *Strike!* (Boston: South End Press, 1972), 222–23.
2. Rachel Burstein, "The Fight over John Q: How Labor Won and Lost the Public in Postwar America, 1947–1959" (PhD diss., City University of New York, 2014), 86n46, http://academicworks.cuny.edu/gc_etds/179/.
3. BAC Local 7, "AFL-CIO History," accessed January 21, 2016, http://www.baclocal7.org/history.aspx?zone=History&pID=1631.

CHAPTER 1: AN INTRODUCTION TO POWER INEQUALITY

1. Steven Greenhouse, "With Day of Protests, Fast-Food Workers Seek More Pay," *New York Times*, November 30, 2012, http://www.nytimes.com/2012/11/30/nyregion/fast-food-workers-in-new-york-city-rally-for-higher-wages.html.
2. Ibid.; Emily Jane Fox, "McDonald's, KFC, Burger King Workers Protest in NYC," November 29, 2012, http://money.cnn.com/2012/11/29/smallbusiness/fast-food-strike-mcdonalds/index.html; and Yum! Brands, "Staying the Course: China and a Whole Lot More," http://www.yum.com/investors/annualreport/12annualreport/2012yumAnnReport.pdf, 1.
3. Steven Greenhouse, "Wage Strikes Planned at Fast-Food Outlets," *New York Times*, December 1, 2013, http://www.nytimes.com/2013/12/02/business/economy/wage-strikes-planned-at-fast-food-outlets-in-100-cities.html.
4. Tom Kertscher, "Just How Wealthy Is the Wal-Mart Walton Family?" *Politifact* Wisconsin, December 8, 2013, http://www.politifact.com/wisconsin/statements/2013/dec/08/one-wisconsin-now/just-how-wealthy-wal-mart-walton-family; Josh Bivens, "Inequality, Exhibit A: Walmart and the Wealth of American Families," *Working Economics Blog*, Economics Policy Institute, July 17, 2012, http://www.epi.org/blog/inequality-exhibit-wal-mart-wealth-american.
5. Luisa Kroll, "Inside the 2015 Forbes 400: Facts and Figures About America's Wealthiest," September 29, 2015, http://www.forbes.com/forbes-400/#tab:overall_page:10.
6. Katie Johnson, "For Those Juggling Multiple Jobs, the Workweek Never Ends," *Boston Globe*, December 5, 2014, https://www.bostonglobe.com/business/2014/12/04/juggling-three-jobs-wears-down-dunkin-donuts-worker/6CrnRhle1

Og5eyzqFw2tQK/story.html; Laura Clawson, "Hundreds of New York City Fast Food Workers Strike," *Daily Kos*, November 29, 2012, http://www.dailykos.com /story/2012/11/29/1165629/-Hundreds-of-New-York-City-fast-food-workers -strike; Valarie Long, "Why the Movement to Boost Fast-Food Wages Matters to the Black Community," BlackAmericaWeb.com, September 5, 2013, http:// blackamericaweb.com/2013/09/05/why-the-movement-to-boost-fast-food-wages -matters-to-the-black-community.

7. Rebecca Kaplan, "Obama: Income Inequality 'The Defining Challenge of Our Time,'" CBS News, December 4, 2013, http://www.cbsnews.com/news/obama -income-inequality-the-defining-challenge-of-our-time. Even the business media recognized the power of the personal story: "US Labour: High Stakes on Low Pay," *Nicosia Business Review Worldwide*, April 14, 2015, http://nicosiamoneynews .com/2015/04/14/us-labour-high-stakes-on-low-pay.

8. "S&P 500 CEOs Make 354 Times More Than Their Average Workers: AFL-CIO," *Huffington Post*, April 15, 2013, http://www.huffingtonpost.com/2013/04/15/sp -500-ceos_n_3085601.html.

9. Jake Miller, "Poll: Strong Support for Minimum Wage Hike," January 8, 2014, http://www.cbsnews.com/news/poll-strong-support-for-minimum-wage-hike; John Nichols, "An 87 Percent Vote for a $15-an-Hour Wage," *Nation*, March 19, 2014, http://www.thenation.com/blog/178928/87-percent-vote-15-hour-wage; National Employment Law Project, "New Poll Shows Overwhelming Support for Major Minimum Wage Increase," January 15, 2015, http://www.nelp.org/content /uploads/2015/03/PR-Federal-Minimum-Wage-Poll-Jan-2015.pdf.

10. Noam Scheiber, "Democrats Are Rallying Around $12 Minimum Wage," *New York Times*, April 22, 2015, http://www.nytimes.com/2015/04/23/business /economy/democrats-are-rallying-around-12-wage-floor.html.

11. Economic Policy Institute, "Raising the Federal Minimum Wage to $10.10 Would Give Working Families, and the Overall Economy, a Much-Needed Boost," March 13, 2013, http://www.epi.org/publication/bp357-federal-minimum-wage -increase.

12. Pew Research Center, "An Uneven Recovery, 2009–2011: A Rise in Wealth for the Wealthy; Declines for the Lower 93%," April 23, 2013, http://www.pewsocial trends.org/2013/04/23/a-rise-in-wealth-for-the-wealthydeclines-for-the-lower-93.

13. When examining inequality in society, wealth disparity is a more relevant measurement than income disparity. See the Century Foundation, *A Tale of Two Recoveries: Wealth Inequality After the Great Recession*, August 28, 2013, p. 3, http:// tcf.org/work/workers_economic_inequality/detail/a-tale-of-two-recoveries.

14. See, for instance, the estimate in David Rolf, *The Fight for $15: The Right Wage for a Working America* (New York: New Press, 2016), 179.

15. The annual cost is roughly $8–$12 billion, using data from Sally Banjo to calculate Walmart's cost to raise minimum pay to $15/hour: "Pay at Wal-Mart: Low at the Checkout, But High in the Manager's Office," *Wall Street Journal*, July 23 2014, http://blogs.wsj.com/corporate-intelligence/2014/07/23/pay-at-wal-mart-low -at-the-checkout-but-high-in-the-managers-office.

16. Frances Fox Piven and Richard A. Cloward, *Poor People's Movements: Why They Succeed, How They Fail* (New York: Vintage Books, 1979), 1.

CHAPTER 2: POWER SHIFT

1. "Biography," Rep. Adam Smith's webpage, accessed June 15, 2015, http://adam smith.house.gov/about/biography; Alicia Mundy, "Can Raging Moderate Make Any Difference?" *Seattle Times*, May 27, 2007, http://www.seattletimes.com /seattle-news/can-raging-moderate-make-any-difference; "Adam Smith," Ancestry.com, accessed June 15, 2015, http://freepages.genealogy.rootsweb .ancestry.com/ffibattle/reps/smithadam.htm.

2. Puget Sound Sage, "Below the Radar: How Sea-Tac Airport's Substandard Working Conditions Hurt Our Region and How Other Major Airports Changed Course Toward Growth and Prosperity," March 2013, http://pugetsoundsage .org/downloads/Below_the_Radar.pdf.

3. "Rep. Adam Smith (D-Wash.)," Roll Call, accessed June 15, 2015, http://media.cq .com/members/520?rc=1.

4. Barbara Peck, "30 Years After Airline Deregulation: Who is the Big Winner?" *Ohio State University Law School Magazine*, Winter 2009, http://moritzlaw.osu .edu/all-rise/2009/01/30-years-after-airline-deregulation.

5. Jill D'Onfro, "Marc Andreessen: Carl Icahn Killed an Entire Airline," *Business Insider*, March 18, 2014, http://www.businessinsider.com/marc-andreessen-carl -icahn-killed-an-entire-airline-2014-3.

6. Eric Weiner, "Lorenzo, Head of Continental Air, Quits Industry in $30 Million Deal," *New York Times*, August 10, 1990, http://www.nytimes.com/1990/08/10 /business/lorenzo-head-of-continental-air-quits-industry-in-30-million-deal .html?pagewanted=all.

7. Hobart Rowen, "Airline Deregulation Isn't Working," Philly.com, July 24, 1987, http://articles.philly.com/1987-07-24/news/26197032_1_airline-deregulation-paul -stephen-dempsey-airline-oligopoly.

8. "Delta is Ready for Job Cuts," CBS News, September 26, 2001, http://www.cbsnews .com/news/delta-is-ready-for-job-cuts.

9. Kate Snow, Dana Bash, and Ted Barrett, "Congress Approves $15 Billion Airline Bailout," CNN, September 22, 2001, http://edition.cnn.com/2001/US/09/21 /rec.congress.airline.deal.

10. Rodney Ward, "September 11 and the Restructuring of the Airline Industry," *Dollars & Sense*, 2002, http://www.dollarsandsense.org/archives/2002 /0502ward.html.

11. Ibid.

12. *Washington Post* column reprinted by Sluggo, David Montgomery, "The New Take on Flight Attendants: Thank You for Flying with Us," October 1, 2001, http://slu2ggo.org/flightattendants.html.

13. Associated Press, "US Airways Files for Bankruptcy," Fox News, September 13, 2004, http://www.foxnews.com/story/2004/09/13/us-airways-files-for -bankruptcy.

14. Associated Press, "United Airlines Finally Flies out of Bankruptcy," NBC News, February 2, 2006, http://www.nbcnews.com/id/11126203/ns/business-us _business/t/united-airlines-finally-flies-out-bankruptcy/#.VOS8mE03NMs.

15. Associated Press, "UAL CEO Gets $39.7M Compensation in 1st Year out of Bank-ruptcy," *USA Today*, March 27, 2007, http://usatoday30.usatoday.com/travel /flights/2007-03-27-united-ceo-compensation_N.htm.

16. Mark Skertic, "Tilton's Prize: $15 Million," *Chicago Tribune*, January 12, 2006, http://articles.chicagotribune.com/2006-01-12/business/0601120227_1_towers-perrin-united-airlines-bankruptcy.

17. Chris Isidore, "Delta Air Lines Files for Bankruptcy," CNN, September 15, 2005, http://money.cnn.com/2005/09/14/news/fortune500/delta; Gina Pace, "Delta Pilots OK Concessions, Pay Cut," CBS News, May 31, 2006, http://www.cbsnews.com/news/delta-pilots-ok-concessions-pay-cut.

18. Jeremy W. Peters, "Losses at Northwest and Delta, but JetBlue Reports a Profit," *New York Times*, April 22, 2005, http://www.nytimes.com/2005/04/22/business/businessspecial3/losses-at-northwest-and-delta-but-jetblue-reports-a-profit.html; Micheline Maynard, "Delta Asks Pilots' Union for Second Round of Cuts in Wages and Benefits," September 13, 2005, http://www.nytimes.com/2005/09/13/business/13northwest.html.

19. Maynard, "Delta Asks Pilots' Union."

20. "Union Votes to Take Cuts at Northwest," *New York Times*, June 10, 2006, http://www.nytimes.com/2006/06/10/business/10air.html?adxnnl=1&adxnnlx=1430323240-P7zZiEtf+OZonjNhEZIIjg; Michael Kuchta, "Machinists Reach Reluctant Agreement with Northwest," *Twin Cities Daily Planet*, May 20, 2006, http://www.tcdailyplanet.net/news/2006/05/20/machinists-reach-reluctant-agreement-northwest.

21. Associated Press, "Northwest Paid Counsel Before Chapter 11 Filing," NBC News, June 16, 2006, http://www.nbcnews.com/id/13372250/ns/business-us_business/t/northwest-paid-counsel-chapter-filing/#.VOvGMko3PIU.

22. Barry T. Hirsch and David A. Macpherson, "Earnings, Rents, and Competition in the Airline Labor Market," *Journal of Labor Economics* 18, no. 1 (2000): 136, http://www.academicroom.com/article/earnings-rents-and-competition-airline-labor-market; Barry T. Hirsch and David A. Macpherson, "Union Membership and Coverage Database from the Current Population Survey: Note," *Industrial and Labor Relations Review* 56, no. 2 (January 2003): 352.

23. Janet Wild, "Airlines Turn to Outsourcing to Keep a Lid on Costs," *Financial Times*, April 25, 2014. Reprinted in Gulf News Aviation, http://gulfnews.com/business/aviation/airlines-turn-to-outsourcing-to-keep-lid-on-costs-1.1324115; "Extreme Airline Management: An Interview with David Siegel, CEO, US Airways," *Ascend: A Magazine for Airline Executives*, October 2003, http://issuu.com/sabreholdings/docs/ascend_2003_issue2b.

24. "John Menzies plc Full Year 2013 Results Presentation," slide 26, Menzies Aviation, March 4, 2014, accessed February 25, 2015, http://www.menziesaviation.com/item/list/p/30/ref/Latest-Presentations.

25. Lawrence H. Wexler, chief counsel, DAL Global Services, LLC, to Sergio Salinas, president, SEIU Local 6, March 28, 2013; in author's possession.

26. "Who We Are," Delta Global Staffing, accessed January 22, 2016, http://deltaglobalstaffing.com/aboutus.php.

27. "Swissport at a Glance," Swissport International Ltd., http://www.swissport.com/fileadmin/downloads/presentation/111114_Swissport_Factsheeet_2014_RZ_EN_low.pdf, accessed February 25, 2015.

28. Megha Bahree, "Up from Ground Zero," *Forbes*, May 9, 2008, http://www.forbes.com/global/2008/0519/066.html.

29. "Frank Argenbright Jr.," SecurAmerica, http://www.securamericallc.com
/about-us/executive-biographies/frank-argenbright.php; "Where We Are,"
Air Serv, accessed March 2, 2015, http://www.airservcorp.com/where_we
_are.php.

30. Ruchika Tulshyan, "Argenbright: SecurAmerica Aims for a Billion," *Atlanta Business Chronicle*, April 25, 2013, http://www.bizjournals.com/atlanta/print-edition
/2013/04/19/argenbright-securamerica-aims-for-a.html?s=print.

31. Ibid.

32. "John Menzies plc"; "Network," Menzies Aviation, accessed March 2, 2015,
http://www.menziesaviation.com/network/list/p/16/ref/Network.

33. Air Carriers' Outsourcing of Aircraft Maintenance," Federal Aviation Administration Report Number: AV-2008-090, September 30, 2008, p. iii, accessed February 19, 2015, https://www.oig.dot.gov/library-item/29183.

34. "Third-World Mechanics Paid $2 Per Hour for Boeing, Airbus Jet Repairs,"
KIRO-TV, July 27, 2011, accessed September 19, 2016, https://www.youtube
.com/watch?v=lTPW4wDfz8o.

35. US Department of Transportation, Office of Inspector General, "Air Carriers'
Outsourcing of Aircraft Maintenance," September 30, 2008, https://www.oig
.dot.gov/sites/default/files/WEB_FILE_Review_of_Air_Carriers_Outsourced
_Maintenance_AV2008090.pdf.

36. Jim Douglas, "American Airlines to Outsource Aircraft Maintenance to China,"
AvStop.com, September 16, 2012, http://avstop.com/september_2012
/american_airlines_to_outsource_aircraft_maintenance_to_china.htm.

37. David Parker Brown, "Alaska Airlines Now Flies Bombardier CRJ-700 Regional
Jets via SkyWest," *Airline Reporter*, May 20, 2011, http://www.airlinereporter
.com/2011/05/alaska-airlines-starts-to-fly-crj-700s-via-skywest; "Alaska Airlines
Expands Partnership with SkyWest, Adds New Routes," Alaska Airlines,
http://splash.alaskasworld.com/Newsroom/ASNews/ASstories/AS_20141125
_045610.asp; Robert J. Boser, "SkyWest Airlines: Non-Union Success Story,"
AirlineSafety.com, September 2005, http://airlinesafety.com/unions/Skywest
NonUnionAirline.htm.

38. Dominic Gates, "Financial Turbulence Rocks Alaska," *Seattle Times*, October 17,
2004, http://old.seattletimes.com/html/businesstechnology/2002065360
_alaska17.html.

39. Gene Johnson, "Judge Declines to Order Alaska Airlines to Rehire Ramp Workers," *USA Today*, June 3, 2005, http://usatoday30.usatoday.com/travel/news
/2005-06-03-alaska-jobs_x.htm.

40. "Alaska Airlines Baggage Handlers Reject Offer," Aero-News Network, May 9,
2005, http://www.aero-news.net/index.cfm?do=main.textpost&id=deb7of2f
-5d57-4253-86b4-33d873a42ad7.

41. Melissa Allison, "Alaska Airlines Outsources 472 Baggage-Handling Jobs," *Seattle Times*, May 14, 2005, http://community.seattletimes.nwsource.com/archive
/?date=20050514&slug=alaska14.

42. See, for example, "A Thousand People in the Street - Musicians' Strike 1997
(Seattle)," YouTube video, 11:46, posted by "Local76493AFM," April 11, 2013,
https://www.youtube.com/watch?v=bnHgLvnXB8I.

43. "Alaska Airlines Contracts with Menzies Aviation for Seattle Ramp Services," Alaska Airlines, May 13, 2005, http://splash.alaskasworld.com/Newsroom /ASNews/ASstories/AS_20050513_031258.asp. Note time of press release: 3:15 a.m.

44. "Boeing Sees AMR Bankruptcy as Positive Long-Term," *Smart Business*, November 30, 2011, http://www.sbnonline.com/boeing-sees-amr-bankruptcy -as-positive-long-term.

45. Jacqueline Palank, "AMR's American Eagle Hires Bain to Review Labor Costs," *Wall Street Journal*, January 1, 2012, http://blogs.wsj.com/bankruptcy/2012/01 /10/amr%e2%80%99s-american-eagle-hires-bain-to-review-labor-costs.

CHAPTER 3: GAME CHANGER

1. "Worth a Million? Many are in King County," *Seattle Post-Intelligencer*, May 1, 2007, http://www.seattlepi.com/business/article/Worth-a-million-Many-are-in -King-County-1235980.php.

2. "SeaTac, Washington (WA) Income Map, Earnings Map, and Wages Data," City-Data.com, accessed October 19, 2015, http://www.city-data.com/income /income-SeaTac-Washington.html; "Seattle, Washington," City-Data.com, accessed October 19, 2015, http://www.city-data.com/city/Seattle-Washington .html.

3. "Seatac, Washington: Census 2010 and 2000 Interactive Map, Demographics, Statistics, Quick Facts," CensusViewer, accessed October 19, 2015, http:// censusviewer.com/city/WA/SeaTac.

4. "About Us," Global to Local, accessed September 19, 2016, http://www.global tolocal.org/about-us-1; Dan Dixon, "Global to Local Initiative in SeaTac and Tukwila, WA" (presentation to SEIU Healthcare 1199NW, May 17, 2011), in the author's possession; Seattle and King County Public Health Department, "King County City Health Profile SeaTac/Tukwila," December 2012, accessed October 23, 2015, http://www.kingcounty.gov/healthservices/health/data/CityProfiles .aspx; "Child Nutrition," State of Washington, Office of Superintendent of Public Inspection, accessed October 7, 2015, http://www.k12.wa.us/ChildNutrition /Reports.aspx; US Census Bureau, "Selected Housing Characteristics" and "Selected Economic Characteristics," accessed October 7, 2015, http://factfinder .census.gov/faces/nav/jsf/pages/community_facts.xhtml.

5. Drew DeSilver, "Killinger Got $25M in WaMu's Final Year," *Seattle Times*, April 12, 2010, http://www.seattletimes.com/business/killinger-got-25m-in-wamus -final-year.

6. "Home Foreclosure Statistics," Statistic Brain, accessed October 10, 2015, http:// www.statisticbrain.com/home-foreclosure-statistics; "Bankruptcy Statistics: How Many People File Bankruptcy Each Year?" BCSAlliance.com, accessed October 10, 2015, http://www.bcsalliance.com/bankruptcy_statestats.html; Center on Budget and Policy Priorities, "Chart Book: The Legacy of the Great Recession," accessed October 7, 2015, http://www.cbpp.org/research/economy/chart-book -the-legacy-of-the-great-recession.

7. US Department of Labor, Bureau of Labor Statistics, "Union Members Summary," October 23, 2015, http://www.bls.gov/news.release/union2.nro.htm; Mayer, "Union Membership Trends."

8. Andy Stern, *A Country That Works: Getting America Back on Track* (New York: Free Press, 2006), 70–71, 105.

9. Ben Smith, "New Labor Plan: Nationwide Protests," *Politico*, April 21, 2011, http://www.politico.com/story/2011/04/new-labor-plan-nationwide-protests-053547.

10. Ibid.

11. SEIU, "The Fight for a Fair Economy Review" (report published internally, January 2013).

12. Barry T. Hirsch and David A. Macpherson, "Union Membership and Coverage Database from the CPS," http://www.unionstats.com/, see 2010 spreadsheet in "Union Membership, Coverage, Density, and Employment by State and Sector, 1983–2014" and "U.S. Historical Tables: Union Membership, Coverage, Density and Employment, 1973-2014."

13. "Airport Statistics," Port of Seattle, http://www.portseattle.org/About /Publications/Statistics/Airport-Statistics/Pages/default.aspx, see 2008–2012 Activity Reports.

14. "Minimum Wage in 2011—Updated," *Employee Rights Blog*, EmployeeRights.com, January 1, 2011, http://employeeissues.com/blog/minimum-wage-2011; Alliance for a Just Society, "2011 Job Gap Report: Searching for Work That Pays," January 2011, http://allianceforajustsociety.org/wp-content/uploads/2012/11/2011-Job -Gap-Report.pdf.

15. Tiffany Ran, "Airport Workers Fight for Better Wages—Part 1 of 2: International Worker's Rally Draws Attention to Conditions for Airport Workers," *Northwest Asian Weekly*, June 7, 2012.

16. Working Washington, "SeaTac Airport Workers Announce Federal Lawsuit Against Sound Transit," April 5, 2012, accessed February 13, 2016, http://www .workingwa.org/blog/2012/04/05/seatac-airport-workers-announce-federal -lawsuit-against-sound-transit.

CHAPTER 4: BRIDGING THE TRUST GAP

1. Associated Press, "Hertz Suspends Muslim Workers for Praying on Job," CBS News, October 7, 2011, http://www.cbsnews.com/news/hertz-suspends-muslim -workers-for-praying-on-job.

2. "Jay Gould Quotes," Quotes Museum, accessed January 24, 2016, http://www .quotes museum.com/author/Jay_Gould.

CHAPTER 5: A MORAL MOVEMENT

1. Tay Yoshitani, e-mail message to Port of Seattle Commissioners, June 8, 2012, in the author's possession.

2. Alaska Air Group, "Annual Meeting," digital recording, May 15, 2012, in the author's possession.

CHAPTER 7: SPEAKING TRUTH IN THE HALLS OF POWER

1. Alaska Air Group, "Annual Meeting," digital recording, May 21, 2013, in the author's possession.

2. Working Washington, "Soaring Profits, Failing Communities: How Alaska Airlines Has Let Down Workers and Our Communities—and What Its Leaders Can Do to Fix the Problem," May 2013.

3. Frank Finneran, Holiday Inn general manager, e-mail message to SeaTac City Council, May 10, 2013, in the author's possession.
4. Win/Win Network, "SeaTac Voter Profile Report," 2012, in the author's possession.
5. Ibid.
6. City of SeaTac, "SeaTac City Council Meeting," video recording, July 23, 2013, in the author's possession.

CHAPTER 8: UNION TROUBLES, COMMUNITY WIN

1. Tyrone Beason, "David Rolf: The Man Who Would Make Unions Matter Again," *Seattle Times Pacific Northwest Magazine*, March 22, 2013, http://www.seattletimes.com/pacific-nw-magazine/david-rolf-the-man-who-would-make-unions-matter-again.
2. Harold Meyerson, "The Seeds of a New Labor Movement," *American Prospect*, October 30, 2014, http://prospect.org/article/labor-crossroads-seeds-new-movement.
3. Ibid.
4. "Common Sense SeaTac Leaders Point to Initiative's Harm to City, Residents of SeaTac," *Highline Times*, October 21, 2013, http://www.highlinetimes.com/2013/10/21/opinion/common-sense-seatac-leaders-point-initiative%E2%80%99s.
5. Amy Martinez, "Study Says SeaTac's Prop 1 Would Boost Economy by $54M," *Seattle Times*, September 25, 2013, http://www.seattletimes.com/business/study-says-seatacrsquos-prop-1-would-boost-economy-by-54m.
6. Washington Policy Center, "Summary of Proposition 1, to Enact Mandated Worker Benefits in SeaTac," October 2013, http://www.washingtonpolicy.org/sites/default/files/Proposition%201%20-%20Shannon.pdf.
7. Terry Jarvis Anderson, "Vote No on SeaTac Proposition 1," *Seattle Times*, October 28, 2013, http://www.seattletimes.com/opinion/guest-pro-con-seatac-prop-1-for-a-15-minimum-wage.
8. "Editorial: No on SeaTac Prop. 1 for a $15 Minimum Wage," *Seattle Times*, October 16, 2013, http://www.seattletimes.com/opinion/editorial-no-on-seatac-prop-1-for-a-15-minimum-wage.
9. Kim Gittleson, "One US Town's Battle over the Minimum Wage," BBC News, November 5, 2013, http://www.bbc.com/news/business-24811045.
10. Reid Wilson, "In Tiny Washington Town, Millions Spent on Minimum Wage Bill," *Washington Post*, November 6, 2013, http://www.washingtonpost.com/blogs/govbeat/wp/2013/11/06/in-tiny-washington-town-millions-spent-on-minimum-wage-bill.
11. "SeaTac $15 Minimum Wage Vote May Set National Tone," NBC News, November 5, 2013, http://www.nbcnews.com/business/seatac-15-minimum-wage-vote-may-set-national-tone-8C11535650.
12. Sam Roberts, "New York: Voter Turnout Appears to Be Record Low," *New York Times*, November 6, 2013, http://www.nytimes.com/news/election-2013/2013/11/06/new-york-turnout-appears-headed-for-record-low.
13. Linzi Sheldon, "SeaTac $15 Minimum Wage Supporters Declaring Victory," KIRO-TV, November 6, 2013, http://www.kirotv.com/news/news/seatac-15-minimum-wage-supporters-declaring-victor/nbjW7.

CHAPTER 9: BEYOND THE BALLOT BOX

1. Amy Martinez, "$15 Wage Floor Slowly Takes Hold in SeaTac," *Seattle Times*, February 13, 2014, http://www.seattletimes.com/seattle-news/15-wage-floor -slowly-takes-hold-in-seatac.

2. Marc Stiles, "The Nation's Best Airport Hotel Is in SeaTac, and It's Expanding," *Puget Sound Business Journal*, December 12, 2013, http://www.bizjournals.com /seattle/news/2013/12/11/the-nations-best-airport-hotel-is-in.html; Marc Stiles, "Once Controversial $15-an-Hour Minimum Wage Now a Shoulder Shrug in SeaTac," *Puget Sound Business Journal*, December 22, 2014, http://www .bizjournals.com/seattle/blog/2014/12/once-controversial-15-an-hour-minimum -wage-now-a.html; Danny Westneat, "Fancy SeaTac Hotel at Center of Wage Debate," *Seattle Times*, December 21, 2013, http://www.seattletimes.com/seattle -news/fancy-seatac-hotel-at-center-of-wage-debate.

3. Joel Connelly, "Ed Murray's Vision: Meat and Potatoes, No Greens," *Seattle Post-Intelligencer*, October 3, 2013, http://blog.seattlepi.com/seattlepolitics/2013 /10/03/ed-murrays-vision-meat-potatoes-no-greens.

4. Office of the Mayor of Seattle, "Mayor Murray: 'Together, We Will Get to $15 Per Hour, and We Will Get It Right,'" March 5, 2014, http://murray.seattle.gov /15minimumwagehearing/#sthash.IHohaacv.dpbs.

5. Afternoon Jolt, "Wednesday Jolt: Poll Shows Strong Support for $15 Minimum Wage," *Seattle Met*, February 12, 2014, http://www.seattlemet.com/articles/2014 /2/12/polling-shows-strong-support-for-15-minimum-wage-february-2014.

6. Council Connection, "Councilmember Sawant City Council Inauguration Speech," January 6, 2014, http://council.seattle.gov/2014/01/06/councilmember -sawant-city-council-inauguration-speech.

7. Karen Weise, "How Seattle Agreed to a $15 Minimum Wage Without a Fight," *Bloomberg Business*, May 8, 2014, http://www.bloomberg.com/bw/articles /2014-05-08/how-seattle-agreed-to-a-15-minimum-wage-without-a-fight.

8. Josh Feit, "Minimum Wage Task Force Co-Chair Says Discussions are 'On Track,'" *Seattle Met*, March 12, 2014, http://www.seattlemet.com/articles/2014 /3/12/minimum-wage-task-force-co-chair-says-discussions-are-on-track -march-2014.

9. Jesse Lessinger, "March for $15 on March 15th in Seattle: 750 People Rally to Raise the Minimum Wage," 15 Now!, March 17, 2014, http://15now.org/2014/03/marc h-for-15-on-march-15th-in-seattle-750-people-rally-to-raise-the-minimum-wage; Paul Bigman, "Seattle Marches to a $15 Beat," *Portside*, March 17, 2014, http:// portside.org/2014-03-18/seattle-marches-15-beat.

10. Dominic Holden, "News Shorts," *Stranger*, March 19, 2014, http://www .thestranger.com/seattle/news-shorts/Content?oid=19094706.

11. "Minimum Wage and Tip Credit," Washington State Labor Council's Legislative Position Papers, 2001 Session, in the author's possession.

12. Puget Sound Sage, "Policy Brief: Who are Seattle's Tipped Workers?" April 2014, http://pugetsoundsage.org/downloads/Tipped%20Workers%20in %20Seattle.pdf.

13. Josh Feit, "What Do We Want? $15! When Do We Want It? In a Little While!" *Seattle Met*, July 30, 2014, http://www.seattlemet.com/articles/2014/7/30/history -of-seattles-minimum-wage-law-august-2014.

14. Marieka M. Klawitter, Mark C. Long, and Robert D. Plotnick, "Who Would Be Affected by an Increase in Seattle's Minimum Wage?" University of Washington, March 21, 2014, p. 19, http://murray.seattle.gov/wp-content/uploads/2014/03/Evans-report-3_21_14-+-appdx.pdf.

15. John Coté, "Ed Lee Backs Significant Increase in Minimum Wage," *SFGate*, December 10, 2013, http://www.sfgate.com/default/article/Ed-Lee-backs-significant-increase-in-minimum-wage-5053183.php.

16. John Coté, "SEIU Files S.F. Ballot Plan for $15-an-Hour Minimum Wage," *SFGate*, April 8, 2014, http://www.sfgate.com/bayarea/article/SEIU-files-S-F-ballot-plan-for-15-an-hour-5384131.php.

17. Marisa Lagos, "S.F. to Put $15 Minimum Wage on Ballot," *SFGate*, June 11, 2014, http://www.sfgate.com/bayarea/article/S-F-to-put-15-minimum-wage-on-ballot-5542191.php.

18. Patrick McGeehan, "Cuomo Pivots Again as He Seeks a $15 Minimum Wage," *New York Times*, September 10, 2015, http://www.nytimes.com/2015/09/11/nyregion/cuomo-pivots-again-as-he-seeks-a-15-minimum-wage.html; New York Governor's Press Office, "Governor Cuomo Signs $15 Minimum Wage Plan and 12 Week Paid Family Leave Policy into Law," April 4, 2016, https://www.governor.ny.gov/news/governor-cuomo-signs-15-minimum-wage-plan-and-12-week-paid-family-leave-policy-law.

19. David Siders, "Jerry Brown Signs $15 Minimum Wage in California," *Sacramento Bee*, April 4, 2016, http://www.sacbee.com/news/politics-government/capitol-alert/article69842317.html.

20. Dave Jamieson, "Tacoma, Washington, Passes $12 Minimum Wage," *Huffington Post*, November 4, 2015, http://www.huffingtonpost.com/entry/tacoma-minimum-wage_563a87bee4b0b24aee48db44.

21. National Employment Law Project, "Fight for $15 Impact Report," April 12, 2016 http://nelp.org/publication/fight-for-15-impact-report-raises-for-17-million-workers-10-million-going-to-15.

22. US Department of Labor, Bureau of Labor Statistics, "Union Members Summary," January 28, 2016, http://www.bls.gov/news.release/union2.nro.htm.

CHAPTER 10: BEYOND $15

1. Terminologies differ; I've distilled definitions largely from Kim Scipes, "Understanding the New Labor Movements in the 'Third World': The Emergence of Social Movement Unionism, a New Type of Trade Unionism," *Critical Sociology*, 1992, http://labournet.de/diskussion/gewerkschaft/smu/The_New_Unions_Crit_Soc.htm; Michael Schiavone, "Social Movement Unions and Political Parties (in South Africa and the Philippines): A Win-Win Situation?" *African and Asian Studies 6* (2007): 373–75.

2. Noam Scheiber, "Growth in the 'Gig Economy' Fuels Work Force Anxieties," *New York Times*, July 12, 2015, http://www.nytimes.com/2015/07/13/business/rising-economic-insecurity-tied-to-decades-long-trend-in-employment-practices.html.

3. Schiavone, "Social Movement Unions," 378–82, 386–90; David Flores et al., "Social Movement Unionism and Neoliberalism in São Paolo, Brazil: Shifting Logics of Collective Action in Telemarketing Labor Unions," *Sociologists Without Borders* 6, no. 1 (2011): 87–96.

4. "Part Four: Social Movement Unionism," Alliance of Progressive Labor, p. 8, accessed November 30, 2015, http://www.apl.org.ph/APLPrimer/aplprimer _part4.pdf.

5. Richard Hyman, *Understanding European Trade Unionism: Between Market, Class & Society* (London: Sage Publications, 2001), 170.

6. Tyree Scott, "Whose Movement Is It Anyway?" unpublished essay, April 1997, in the author's possession.

7. Cesar Chavez, "A Union in the Community," ca. 1969, p. 7, Miller Archive, University of California-San Diego Library Farmworker Movement Documentation Project, libraries.ucsd.edu/farmworkermovement/essays/essays/MillerArchive /029%20A%20Union%20In%20The%20Community.pdf.

8. Staughton Lynd, *Accompanying: Pathways to Social Change* (Oakland, CA: PM Press, 2012), 4.

9. Charles M. Payne, *I've Got the Light of Freedom: The Organizing Tradition and the Mississippi Freedom Struggle* (Berkeley: University of California Press, 2007), 5.

10. Mark Engler and Paul Engler, "Can Frances Fox Piven's Theory of Disruptive Power Create the Next Occupy?" *Waging Nonviolence*, May 7, 2014, http:// wagingnonviolence.org/feature/can-frances-fox-pivens-theory-disruptive -power-create-next-occupy.